Dog Food Logic

Making Smart Decisions for Your Dog in an Age of Too Many Choices

Linda P. Case, MS

Dogwise™ Publishing

Wenatchee, Washington U.S.A.

Dog Food Logic
Making Smart Decisions for Your Dog in an Age of Too Many Choices
Linda P. Case, MS

Dogwise Publishing
A Division of Direct Book Service, Inc.
403 South Mission Street, Wenatchee, Washington 98801
1-509-663-9115, 1-800-776-2665
www.dogwisepublishing.com / info@dogwisepublishing.com

Library of Congress Cataloging-in-Publication Data
Case, Linda P.
  Dog food logic : making smart decisions for your dog in an age of too many choices / by Linda P. Case, MS.
      pages cm
  Includes bibliographical references and index.
  ISBN 978-1-61781-138-8
  1. Dogs--Nutrition. 2. Dogs--Food. I. Title.
  SF427.4.C37 2014
  636.7'0887--dc23
                                2013045528

ISBN: 978-1-61781-138-8

Printed in the U.S.A.

More praise for *Dog Food Logic*

Not often does one consider a book of this sort to be a "page turner." Sure...a book may be very readable and the material presented accurate and informative. But, in so many instances, reading page after page of scientific jargon can be a sure cure for insomnia. So..., a "page turner"...really??? That's exactly what I found when I picked up this book for the first time and read every single word in spite of a hectic schedule. Simply stated, this book was very difficult to put down, and it was with great displeasure that this happened to me on several occasions throughout the reviewing process.

Perhaps it was the writing style of the author—relaxed and sometimes emotional, yet at the same time scientific, credible, and understandable. Perhaps it was the examples used to illustrate major points—story-like, but with just the right content of scientific rigor and hard facts. Perhaps it was the balance of topics provided—from the emotional (e.g., Food is Love) to the highly scientific (e.g., What's So Special About a Dog's Nutritional Needs?). Whatever it was, I found this to be a very compelling presentation of topics related to pet animal nutrition and the pet food industry that provides the foods for these animals. Rarely, if ever, can one find the variety of topics presented in this text to be under one cover. The author clearly has done due diligence in investigating the 11 major topics covered in the book, then distilling and summarizing that information into an entertaining, factual, educational presentation that will benefit readers regardless of their expertise (or lack thereof) in this discipline. There is something in this book for everyone interested in pets and what they eat. And there is no question that a pet owner will come away with a great deal of awareness of the complexities associated with the seemingly easy task of choosing the proper food for his/her animal companion.

Dr. George C. Fahey, Jr., Professor Emeritus of Animal Sciences, University of Illinois at Urbana-Champaign

Dog Food Logic is an indispensable book for any pet owner who wants to make thoughtful, informed decisions about what to feed his or her canine companions. The dog food industry is a bewildering, ever-changing landscape of companies and brands, and dog owners are inundated with marketing masquerading as science, with rigid advice from self-declared experts, and with fads every bit as intense and short-lived as those in the human weight loss business. *Dog Food Logic* cuts through the noise and chaos and provides pet owners with a rational, science-based approach to evaluating their pets' dietary needs and their feeding choices.

Rather than simply telling dog owners what food to buy, *Dog Food Logic* provides a concise and comprehensible guide to the three main subjects we must understand in order to make sound feeding choices: the science of canine nutrition, the nature of the dog food industry, and the pitfalls in our own ways of thinking that make us susceptible to marketing hype and irrational decisions. Rather than trying to tell us what to feed, Ms. Case empowers dog owners to make choices consistent with the needs of our individual pets and our own values.

In *Dog Food Logic,* the author displays a deep understanding of not only the science of nutrition but of the human-animal bond. Feeding our pets is more than providing them with essential nutrients. It is an expression of love and one of the most enjoyable shared experiences between pet and owner. Ms. Case understands that the emotional nature of feeding our animal companions must be appreciated and nurtured, but that it can also make us vulnerable to manipulation. Advertising and advice about what to feed our pets often plays on our anxieties about their health and happiness and our desire to do everything possible to ensure a long and healthy life for our dogs. Ms. Case is able to help us see through such manipulative marketing and make sound feeding decisions based on science while still respecting the role of feeding in the deep bond between owners and our pets.

As a veterinarian, a scientist, and a dog owner, I have waited a long time for a book like *Dog Food Logic,* one which I can enthusiastically recommend to my clients and colleagues. After reading *Dog Food Logic,* you will of course have a deeper understanding of canine nutrition, the pet food industry, and how to make good choices about feeding your pet. But you will also have a greater understanding of yourself as a pet owner and a consumer. Understanding how we make choices, and how those choices can be influenced by the quirks of our own thought processes and by the manipulative power of marketing, enables us to make better decisions about all aspects of our pets' care. If we apply the same critical thinking and evidence-based approach to behavior and training, veterinary care, and all the other decisions we make as pet owners, we will better caretakers with happier, healthier pets.

Brennen McKenzie, MA, VMD, President, Evidence-Based Veterinary Medicine Association, author of SkeptVet Blog http://skeptvet.com/Blog/

To Mike, my best friend and life companion,
who read every single word of this book
and provided invaluable advice, insight, lots
of great conversation and laughter, and of
course, the occasional glass of wine.
You are simply the best.

And to our family of dogs—Cadie, Vinny, Chip
and Cooper, who bring endless joy, laughter
and fun to our lives, every single day.

Table of Contents

Acknowledgments

This book would not have been possible without the help of many long-time nutrition and dog training colleagues and friends. These folks have not only helped with this project in particular but have also been outstanding mentors, scientists, trainers, teachers and friends for many years. Thank you all for your willingness to chat with me about the many topics that this book involved and for the loads of expertise and dog-feeding experiences that you so generously shared. Most of all, thank you for your continued love for *"all things dog;"* the dogs of America are the better for your care and your passion. My sincere appreciation to Roger Abrantes, Greg Aldrich, Eric Altom, Patty Brewster, Jessica Buchholz, Marcie Campion, Dan Carey, Jill Cline, Gail Czarnecki, Steve Dale, Gary Davenport, Leighann Daristotle, Maria de Godoy, David Dzanis, George Fahey, Beth Flickinger, April Hammer, Diane Hirakawa, Russ Kelley, Jessica Lockhart, Pam Lowrey, Kim Matsko, Bruce MacAllister, Jackie Mertens, Sandy Myers, Melody Raasch, Dan Rode, Kate Shoveller, Greg Sunvold, Kelly Swanson, Mike Ward, Pam Wasson, Greg Watt and Lauren Zverina. And very special thanks to the great folks at Dogwise Publishing, who have been fabulous to work with from the very start of this project through to its fruition: Jon Luke, Lindsay Peternell, Charlene Woodward, Larry Woodward and all of the staff who have worked so hard to make the book a reality.

Introduction

At a recent dog training conference while presenting a talk about dog nutrition, I asked the audience what the most common question that they received from training students regarding nutrition and feeding practices for dogs. Without hesitation, five hands shot up. Four of the five attendees said that they were repeatedly asked some version of the question "What food should I feed to my dog?" The fifth said that she most often heard "What food do you feed to your dogs?" Everyone else in the room was nodding. This consensus led nicely into a discussion about the veritable explosion of dog food choices that confront all owners every time that they walk down the aisle of their local pet supply store. Today there are dog food brands and product lines for dogs of differing sizes, ages, activity levels, lifestyles and even breeds. And within each of these dog-related categories, we must then also choose among food types (cooked, raw, dehydrated, freeze-dried, extruded, canned), preferred ingredients (grains or no grains, chicken, bison, fish or partridge, potato or tapioca), and the inclusion of specific nutrients (omega-3 fatty acids, glucosamine, antioxidant vitamins). Added to all of this is the worry that has originated with concerns regarding food safety (has this brand been recalled lately? Is there a risk of salmonella or aflatoxin?). It is no wonder that many dog owners just throw up their hands in confusion and turn to their veterinarian, their dog trainer or Joe next door (who happens to know a lot about dogs) to recommend a dog food to them.

Even in the face of all of this frustration and confusion, dog owners and pet professionals tell us that they consider providing optimal nutrition to be an essential component for dog health and wellness. Additionally, our dogs' nutrition is an aspect of their lives over which we as owners exert almost total control. As a result, the responsibility of selecting the *best* food for our dog always weighs heavily upon our minds. And more so today than ever before (and for reasons that we explore in this book), dog folks seem to be seeking the holy grail of pet nutrition—that particular feeding philosophy, ingredient or nutrient that will guarantee their dogs' long-life, peak health and performance success. Yet, paradoxically, as we will see, having a plethora of dog food choices does not necessarily aid us in smart decision making for our dogs, and may even hinder the process. More is more, but is it necessarily better (or easier)?

In essence there are three basic components to good (smart) decision making for our dogs' nutritional health: *Dog Food Logic,* if you will. We need a strong emotional attachment to the idea of making the best choice for our dogs and an understanding of how that attachment affects our choices; we also need a grounding in the science of canine nutrition (an understanding of what we know to be true and proven versus what is mere speculation or conjecture); and we need a set of strong critical thinking skills to allow us to sort truth from marketing hype when evaluating dog food companies, brands and products. It is these three things that I am going to provide in the pages of *Dog Food Logic.*

We begin in the first section by examining the love—the emotional component to feeding dogs—and how the powerful emotions linked to the love that we have for our dogs influences our ability to make well-reasoned decisions (you may be surprised at how this actually works). An understanding of how the human brain makes decisions (many times beneath our conscious awareness) and how certain cognitive traps can affect us will set you squarely on the path toward becoming a skilled critical thinker. We then move on to an examination of science and its practice. Learning to recognize the difference between evidence-based information and anecdotal evidence (or hyperbole) is an important component of clear decision making. Then we will examine the explosion in marketplace choice and the resulting number of decisions that we are forced to make when simply attempting to pick a dog food—does this empower us or paralyze us, and how do we traverse the landscape of too many foods to choose from? The second section examines the nutritional science component of the puzzle. We explore the history of canine nutrition and its study, and the nutrient requirement differences among the dog's life stages and activity levels, as well as the variety of feeding approaches that can impact a dog's nutritional health and well-being. Note: you will *not* find directions for feeding or recommendations for foods within these chapters. Rather, an understanding of what is known about canine nutrition, what is theorized and what remains unproven (or is blatantly wrong) is information that will be added to your growing tool belt of critical thinking skills. The final section of the book delves into the present day world of the pet food industry, and it examines the companies that own, make and market your dog's food. The intent of these chapters is to provide you with the final piece of information that is needed to effectively distinguish among foods according to their ingredients, their form, their nutrient content and the claims that are made about them. The goal remains to help you to differentiate between those choices that are supported by evidence and those that reflect mere marketing hype and advertising ploys designed to sell more food.

Although there are no simple or single answer to the question "What should I feed to my dog?" we do have nutritional science and the evidence that its study has generated (and continues to generate) to guide us. We also have our critical thinking skills and the ability to avoid making errors in thinking, responding to anecdotes or falling for marketing ploys that are designed with a greater interest in selling products than nurturing dogs. Together, this knowledge and these skills can aid you in choosing critically and carefully for your dog, while still allowing that feeding our dogs is caretaking, it is nurturing and it is love—as much as it is science.

*In the text, key concepts are shown in bold type when first mentioned.

1

Food Is Love

The Case dogs have an evening dinner ritual. This ritual has not changed much in the last few years and deviates very little in its nightly performance. It begins, like clockwork, at 8:15 p.m. and is currently directed by Cadie, our senior Golden girl. Mike (my husband) typically feeds the dogs their evening meal, so is her usual target. As the self-appointed "dinner getter," Cadie takes her responsibilities very seriously. She is in charge of checking the time (apparently every 15 seconds after 7:00 p.m.), of carefully tracking potential human movement towards the utility room where the dog food resides, and of counting dogs to determine when everyone is in the house and ready to eat.

When all key factors are in place, Cadie declares "Game On!" and the ritual begins in earnest. First comes the *unrelenting stare:* laser-beam eyes capable of burning holes through flesh. Cadie's style is impressive; she sits rock solid still, barely breathing, eyes fixed on Mike's face. If the stares do not elicit the desired result (dinner), she gradually inches closer until she is perched on the couch, Snoopy vulture-style, her cute little snout hovering inches above Mike's face. If there is still no food-related movement, she adds the woofing: persistent little barks timed at two-second intervals for maximum annoyance. The paw on the arm is added last and occasionally Cadie feigns a dramatic hunger-induced swoon. (Okay, I made that last part up, but it really seems like something she would try.) Finally, if all else has failed and it looks like dinner may not be forthcoming, Cadie enlists her second-in-command, Vinny the Brittany, to help.

With two dogs hovering with pleading eyes, Mike finally gets to his feet and walks towards the utility room. An explosion of happiness erupts! It is time for a DOG PARTY!!! Four dogs, all running, spinning, barking, more spinning, joyous, joyous Dinner Time, Dinner Time—a time for celebration! As Mike measures food into bowls, he sings the Case Dinner Time song (♫ Who wants dinner? Who wants dinner? Everybody does! Everybody does! ♫). All four dogs crowd around for the measuring into bowls, Cadie keeping a keen eye on portions. Once the food is doled out, sitting is required prior to eating and all of the dogs adhere to the single hard and fast dinner rule—eat only from your own bowl. When everyone has finished their meal, the dogs are then allowed to play musical bowls, each thoroughly inspecting and licking every bowl. Finally, dinner complete, everyone goes outside for a potty break, knowing that tomorrow will be another day, complete with a new joyous opportunity for food and the celebratory dinner time ritual.

Do you have a dinner time ritual with your dog? Does your dog have very specific and endearing "dinner-getting" behaviors? Do you have a particular way of responding to these? And, tell the truth…do you have a dinner time song? When we think about our daily lives with our dogs, we consider many shared enjoyments. And with our dogs, just as with our human family and friends, dinner is not just about nutrition and food—it is also about joy and affection, and ritual. Indeed, there is perhaps no other aspect of our lives with dogs in which we show love more consistently than the decisions that we make about what, how and when we feed them.

How many meals?

Let's begin with an easy assumption: dog people love their dogs. I certainly adore my family of four. Each dog is an individual who brings me joy, laughter, contentment and a degree of life peace that I am thankful for each day. And if you are reading this book, I would bet the farm that you have at least one dog, possibly more, and that you too consider your dog to be a family member, best friend, dog sport partner, exercise pal, cuddle buddy, perhaps all of the above. I also submit that a substantial proportion of us spend a great deal of time (some may say an inordinate amount of time) training our dogs, grooming them, tending to (and worrying about) their health care and, of course, feeding them. Feeding is something that *all* dog folks spend time doing at least once daily, more typically twice per day. For many of us, selecting and providing food treats to use as positive reinforcers is also an integral part of our training philosophy.

Adding up all of this feeding over the lifetime of a single dog equates to scores of meals and countless treats. A simple calculation shows that an average dog owner will provide more than *10,000 meals* over the lifetime of a single dog (see Figure 1.1). These meals add up to a lot of pet feeding experience, experience that leads us to develop strongly held beliefs, opinions and daily rituals. Some of these beliefs and practices will be supported by scientific evidence and founded in nutritional fact, while others…well…perhaps not so much.

Average Dog's Lifespan: 14 Years

Fed: 2 Meals per Day

365 x 14 x 2 = 10,220 meals!

Figure 1.1 Average number of meals fed during a dog's life.

So, dog owners feed a lot, no doubt about that. In addition, there is a unique feature of dog feeding that does not typically apply to other food-related experiences, such as those that we have with our human family and friends. As dog owners we all exercise absolute and complete control over the type and the quantity of food that our dogs consume. With the exception of children, most of us do not dictate what other people in our lives eat each day. Our natural sense of an individual adult's right to make these choices for him or herself generally prevents us from intruding upon these decisions. The situation is very different with our dogs. Although we may occasionally joke about "who really is in control in the relationship" we all know that it is not our dogs who decide what they will eat or when they will eat it. We do. And, because of the ultimate power that we yield in our canine relationships, we can choose to do this well, we can choose to do it poorly, or sadly, we can choose to not do it at all. Witness all of the dogs who are left abandoned in homes or dumped at shelters each year, whose owners simply stopped caring about (and feeding) them. Providing food comprises the most very basic level of caretaking—dogs starve and die if they are not fed. Less dramatically, they do not thrive if they are fed poorly. If we love our dogs (we do), and desire long and healthy lives for them (without question), then we must feed them well. And to feed them well, we need to make healthful choices for them. And that, in a nutshell is what *Dog Food Logic* can help trainers, owners and all sorts of dog professionals to do.

Experiment—find your food

Let's conduct a little experiment. Envision a five-year-old Golden Retriever mix named Muffin. Her owner, Jack Spratt, would like to feed Muffin a dry food that is formulated for adult dogs who are at a normal weight and have a moderate level of activity. This category is referred to as "adult maintenance" foods in the pet food industry. Jack's neighbor Joe (who, by the way, knows a lot about dogs) has mentioned to him that that lamb is a good protein source for dogs. So, Jack decides to select a food that contains lamb as its primary protein source. This is his only selection criterion. Jack begins his search using the internet. He types "adult dry dog food with lamb" into the search engine. Instantly, more than 50 pages of results are returned—try it yourself, you will be amazed. Reading just the first ten pages of results, Jack finds *34 separate brands* of dry, adult maintenance dog food that contain lamb or lamb meal as the primary protein source. (These brand names are listed in Figure 1.2; keep in mind that this is not a complete list, just what was listed in the first portion of an online search!) But, you say, most people still do not shop for dog food on the internet; they go to their local pet supply store or grocery store for pet food. Surely, their choices are more limited there? Yes, they are…a bit. A walk through the aisle at Jack's local pet supply store found 17 different brands of food that met Jack's criteria. His local PetSmart provided more than that—21 separate lamb-based adult dog food brands. Yikes! How will Jack ever be able to choose a food for Muffin?

The number of pet food choices that are available to pet-owning consumers today is mind-boggling. It is no surprise that owners often become overwhelmed with the entire endeavor, and in frustration make their decisions either through habit (what their family has always fed their dogs), in accordance with their veterinarian's recommendation or simply by economy or convenience. Some owners (though we are all loath to admit that this could be us) make selections in response to celebrity endorsements, clever advertising claims or that cute dog on the bag that just looks just like our dog Muffin.

Brands of adult maintenance dry dog foods with lamb or lamb meal		
Acana	Iams Healthy Naturals	Professional
Avoderm	Innova	ProPac
Blue Buffalo	Kirkland	ProPlan
California Natura	Natural Choice	Purina One
Canidae	Nature's Logic	Sammy Snacks
Castor & Pollux	Nature's Recipe	Science Diet
Diamond Naturals	Nutrisca	Solid Gold
Dr. Foster & Smith	Nutri Source	Sportmix
Eagle Pack	Nutro Grain Free	Triumph
Eukanuba	Nutro Natural Choice	Wellness
Halo	One Beyond	
Iams	Premium Edge	

Figure 1.2 Selection of dry (extruded) dog foods containing lamb or lamb meal as a primary protein source.

What dinner time *feels* like

So, part of the struggle that we experience with feeding our dogs has to do with the overwhelming number of choices that are available in today's marketplace. Additionally, the role that our emotions play in the decision-making process also influences our ability to make healthful choices for our dogs. It is a fact that nutrition is a science that is governed by the same scientific principles and methods as all hard sciences such as biology, chemistry and physics. However, for most of us, applying the principles of sound nutrition to our dogs' daily lives generally does *not feel* like science. Rather, like our daily feeding rituals, nutrition feels more like love, and caretaking and nurturing. It is a caretaking responsibility that is steeped in emotion. And indeed, providing good nutritional care should feel good, and the deep love and commitment that we have for our pets is essential to caring for them well. Of course, how could we make good decisions for our dogs if we did not care about them? However, it is also possible that our emotions and the cognitive biases that go along with them may, on occasion, get in the way of good decision making.

When it comes to the role that emotions play in our brain's decision-making processes, there is good news and there is bad news. Let's start with the good news. Today, we know without question that our emotions are essential for effective decision making. This is true for all things that are important in our lives, including the healthcare choices that we make for our dogs. Until recent years however, the prevailing belief about human emotions was that they interfered with clear thinking and with our ability to make sound decisions when faced with important choices. Neuroscience and psychology historically divided human cognition into two distinct "types": rational thinking (reason) and the murky, touchy-feely thoughts that were associated with emotion. In school, we were taught that these two ways of thinking were frequently at odds with each other, often pulling us in opposite directions. We have probably all been admonished at some point in our lives to "Use your head, not your heart" when faced with an important decision. Popular culture has also glorified rational thought at the expense of emotion; consider Mr. Spock and Data from the Star Trek series. These characters purportedly made infallible decisions precisely *because* they were lacking emotions and were capable of using only their rational brains to make the correct (i.e., most logical) decision. It was assumed that allowing emotions to influence us interfered with deliberative thought and the ability to choose correctly. However, scientific discoveries about how the human brain processes information have shown that not only do we regularly rely upon our emotions when making decisions, but that our feelings are actually essential in this process.

The earliest evidence of a connection between the brain's decision-making functions and emotions came from Antonio Damasio, a neurologist who works with patients experiencing brain disorders and injuries. In the early 1980s Damasio met with a patient who had had a small, benign tumor removed from his brain. The tumor was located in an area of the brain called the orbito-frontal cortex, which is located just behind the eyes. The patient, identified as "Elliot," had achieved a full recovery from his surgery, both physically and intellectually. For all intents and purposes he should have been able to resume a normal life. However, in the months following his recovery, Elliot was fired from his job, his wife left him, he was scammed by a con man and he was forced to file for bankruptcy. His life completely fell apart. These events all transpired as a result of a single psychological problem that stemmed from his recent brain surgery; *Elliot had become incapable of making decisions.* This disability did not involve only those choices that needed consideration and deliberation; it pertained to everything from the momentous to the mundane. Most telling, routine daily tasks, such as which socks to put on or what to eat for breakfast caused Elliot to deliberate for hours, with every option weighed, analyzed and considered, leaving him still unable to choose. In his book *Descartes's Error* (1994) Damasio describes a scenario in which he attempted to schedule a future appointment with Elliot. For more than 30 minutes, Elliot agonized over the problem, considering numerous dates/times and listing multiple reasons for and against each potential selection. Reading this description is difficult enough; Damasio relates his frustration and temptation to simply scream at the poor man to stop as he sat through this mind-numbing scenario.

Subsequent psychological tests revealed that, in addition to his profound inability to make decisions, Elliot had also completely lost his ability to *experience emotions;* he showed no reaction whatsoever to events and scenes that would normally evoke strong emotions such as joy, fear, disgust or aggression in a normal person. Indeed, when Damasio interviewed Elliot's family and coworkers, they described him as having turned into an expressionless automaton, a person who was there physically but seemed to have disappeared emotionally. Damasio found this connection between Elliot's inability to make choices and his loss of feelings to be odd, given the belief of that time that we needed only the ability to reason to make decisions. In the ensuing years, Damasio went on to study other patients who had lost specific regions of the brain that control our basic emotions, either through traumatic injuries or because of organic disease such as cancer. Along with other researchers, Damasio began to map and study the regions of the brain that are responsible for generating emotions. They discovered that the limbic region and a small almond shaped structure within it called the amygdala are responsible for the basic emotions such as fear, joy, aggression and impulsiveness. The orbito-frontal cortex, the region of the brain that was damaged in Elliot, connects the regions of the brain that generate emotional responses to the areas thought to be responsible for weighing options and for making decisions—choosing.

Damasio explains the connection between emotions and decision making in terms of current stimuli coming into the brain, coupled with memories of past events. It works like this: His theory, called the **somatic marker theory,** postulates that the brain stores emotional memories of our past decisions along with the eventual outcomes of those decisions, both good and bad. Although our memories of past events and the decisions that we made often feel clear and detailed, in reality the way that we store memories is less precise. It is our emotional state when the event (or decision) occurred that is stored and is subsequently retrieved when we need to compare it to a present-day dilemma. Our brain subsequently "fills in" the details for us (this is one of the reasons that our memories are often quite faulty). Therefore, it is the *memory of emotions* that influence our current decisions, not the details of how we weighed options, analyzed cost-benefits and reasoned through a particular decision in the past. Indeed, Damasio states that our emotions appear to be most important for decisions that involve options that are difficult to differentiate among, or when making decisions that include a moral or ethical component. Examples include making choices that empathize with others and consider another person's or animal's welfare and decisions that go against our own self-interest. There is also evidence that, as our minds are presented with more and more options and have excessive amounts of information to process, the likelihood that we will rely more heavily upon our "emotional pathways" than upon our ability to reason increases.

And now for some of the bad news. While our emotions may be essential for decision making, we remain generally unaware of this connection and lack the ability to monitor or influence it. This is because most of the important information processing that the brain performs takes place subliminally, beneath the surface of our conscious awareness. Consider the enormous task of your brain. As you navigate through the day, all of your special senses—vision, hearing, smell, touch and taste—are sending your brain millions of small bits of sensory information, every second. All of this information must be processed, analyzed and sent back to various motor neurons and organs in a form that allows you to act on the incoming sensory information. The brain accomplishes this rapidly and efficiently by utilizing neural shortcuts that operate below the level of your conscious awareness. By comparison, although our conscious brains are highly capable, they are embarrassingly slow at these types of sensory processing tasks. And here is the interesting bit: regions of the brain that control emotions are intimately involved in this subconscious process and engage regularly and rapidly with the brain's sensory processing systems. Ultimately, the repackaged information that bubbles to the surface of your conscious awareness consists of a composite of perceptions that partially represent what you are seeing/hearing/smelling, but are also influenced by past experiences and emotions. What this means to us as we move through the world each day is that the emotional centers of our brain continually influence what we see, hear, feel *and think* in response to events taking place in our lives. This reactive (and largely subconscious) approach to processing sensory input is highly useful when faced with immediate danger (and so, it is speculated, was selected for during evolution) as well as for the hundreds of small and inconsequential decisions that we make every day. In these cases, the probability of error is typically very small while the benefits are great (efficiency, rapid reactions, staying alive). Alternatively, for decisions that we intend to deliberate upon, preferring to take some time to examine our options and weigh the pros and cons, this subconscious and automatic emotional input can lead to errors in judgment and unwelcome biases.

We have all had experiences in which we have reacted in the "heat of the moment" by saying or doing something that we regretted later. These situations can involve negative emotions such as anger (firing off that ill-conceived email to the boss) or more positive feelings such as love or infatuation (perhaps it wasn't such a good idea to get engaged after that wild weekend in Vegas). Common sense tells us to slow down, wait for the emotions to subside and deliberate before acting (at least until the next time). In these cases, we realize that fleeting and often intense emotions are directly influencing our choices, and we are quite aware of the outcome (good or bad though it may be). However, as we have discussed, emotions that have long-subsided but that influenced us in the past can resurface to influence present-day actions. This should not be surprising, of course. However, the problem once again lies in the fact that we are not consciously aware of these influences.

Dan Ariely, a neuroeconomist, has studied this effect and writes about it in his book *The Upside of Irrationality*. Ariely and several colleagues wanted to find out if emotions that are associated with a particular experience or event in the past will influence decisions that are made when a similar pattern of experience is encountered in the future. Remember, many of our important memories are stored as "emotional packages," which leads to a resurfacing of these emotions whenever we retrieve the memory. If past emotions led to impulsive or ill-conceived decisions, would they continue to influence us? In other words, are we subconsciously doomed to repeat our past mistakes? Ariely set up a series of experiments in which he induced human subjects to be in either an annoyed or a happy frame of mind. Immediately following this "mood-setting treatment," subjects participated in a game called the Ultimatum Game, a classic research technique that is used to test a person's degree of fairness and inclination to either reward or punish another individual. Not surprisingly, they found that people who were in a foul mood were significantly less fair (and more punitive) toward their partners, while those who had been induced to feel happy and content treated their playing partners with greater fairness. These results are neither surprising nor earth shattering. We have all experienced this type of effect—having a fight at home may lead to a foul mood at work and snapping at a colleague.

The interesting and remarkable part of the experiment came later. The researchers speculated that the pairing of a particular emotion (in this case, emotions that were completely manipulated and irrelevant to the experience) with an event would become part of a person's "blueprint" or pattern of experiences, stored in memory to inform future behavior and decisions. Sure enough, the experiment supported this theory. They sent the study participants away and asked them to return later in the day, when presumably the induced emotional states (irritation or happiness) had completely dissipated. The subjects then repeated the Ultimatum Game and their behavior and decisions were measured. Indeed, the researchers found that the subjects who had been irritated earlier in the day continued to be more unfair and punishing than did those

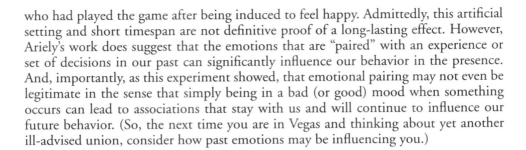

who had played the game after being induced to feel happy. Admittedly, this artificial setting and short timespan are not definitive proof of a long-lasting effect. However, Ariely's work does suggest that the emotions that are "paired" with an experience or set of decisions in our past can significantly influence our behavior in the presence. And, importantly, as this experiment showed, that emotional pairing may not even be legitimate in the sense that simply being in a bad (or good) mood when something occurs can lead to associations that stay with us and will continue to influence our future behavior. (So, the next time you are in Vegas and thinking about yet another ill-advised union, consider how past emotions may be influencing you.)

Dog day decisions

How might this new knowledge about emotions and the brain's decision-making processes relate to the decisions that we make for our dogs? First, whether we are aware of it (or like it) or not, our emotions are intimately involved with our decision-making mind. And, our emotional mind apparently kicks in most dramatically in situations in which we are faced with too many choices, we are experiencing information overload, or when we are passionately invested in the decision that must be made. And, to boot, emotionally laden decisions of our past, regardless of how accurate they were, can subconsciously inform our present-day behavior and choices. All of these components are in play when we are making health and nutrition choices for the dogs we love:

- **Information overload.** The number of food choices before us is enormous and many of these appear identical, making it difficult to differentiate among brands.

- **Empathy.** We care deeply for our dogs and consider ourselves to be completely responsible for their health through the decisions that we make. Without question, our emotions play a role in our nutrition decisions, with or without our conscious consent.

- **Past experiences.** Our past decisions with other dogs, especially those that were highly emotional, will affect how we interpret present-day information and provide a template for new decisions.

While we all like to believe that we are "cool calculators," capable of making well-reasoned choices, evidence shows that our emotions are sitting next to us in the cockpit acting as co-pilot. And, when decision making is at its most difficult, our emotions may actually be flying the plane. Because feeding our dogs is a form of caretaking that many of us are heavily invested in, our emotions will have a very strong influence on the choices that we make for our dogs' nutritional health. This effect also has its advantages. For example, Damasio emphasizes that good decision making should not ignore emotions (as we have been traditionally taught) because this can discount valuable information and may underestimate the importance of past experience. Rather, we must learn to recognize and temper the emotional brain in constructive and positive ways. Our emotions can also lead us astray. For example, how we *feel* about a food, a company, an approach to feeding, may interfere with our ability to collect information, weigh it carefully and make well-supported decisions. One way to view this relationship is that while it is impossible to make good decisions about things that we do not care about, it is equally risky to allow our emotions to completely govern our opinions without seeking factual information. We can perhaps say that our emotions bring the "caring" part to the decision-making party. Our rational mind, on the other hand, provides us with the capacity to collect information and facts, and to weigh the merit and degree of importance of different sets of information; it brings **science** and **logic** to the party.

Loving our dogs and wanting the best for them (emotional mind) and gathering factual information (rational mind) can work together to help us to make wise choices for our dogs. While it is important to recognize that our caring and emotions inform our decision making, it is equally important to recognize (and avoid) the cognitive biases that emotions can lead to. In Chapter 2, we examine several of these **cognitive errors** (also called **logical fallacies**) and provide some specific examples of their influence on pet nutrition and feeding practices. But before we do this, let's look at how "loving our dogs too much" can bias our rational decisions, leading to one of the most common and serious health risks in dogs today.

Food as love run amok

In American culture, feeding trends for dogs tend to closely follow similar practices that have become popular in human nutrition. This is true for new practices and foods that may be beneficial or have been shown to be either neutral or pose a health risk. We will examine many of these examples throughout the book, but I would like to begin with a trend that is both prevalent and risky, and of interest because of its close association to human behavior and health. This is the fact that the epidemic of overweight conditions among the American people is now mirrored in the *waistlines of our pets*. In 2012, the Centers for Disease Control (CDC) reported that more than 66% of American adults are currently overweight or obese. And our dogs are following closely behind. Results from the Association of Pet Obesity Prevention's (APOP) annual survey in 2012 reported that 53% of dogs are classified by their veterinarians as being either overweight or obese. As we have become more portly and less active, so too have our dogs.

In the APOP survey, both veterinarians and dog owners assessed dogs' weight and body condition. While the veterinarians found more than 50% of the dogs and cats that they examined to be overweight, less than half this number of dog owners (22%) identified their own dog as being overweight. Another recent survey of dog owners found that owner underestimation of a dog's body condition was nearly 20 times more common in dogs who were overweight than in normal or underweight dogs. APOP founder Dr. Ernie Ward refers to this cognitive disconnect as the "fat pet gap." He suggests that Americans' perceptions of what is normal in dogs has been gradually distorted, leading to a view of the overweight body type as ideal. In other words, fat dogs have become the "new normal." This led Ward to comment, "Pet obesity is plainly a people problem, not a pet problem. The most important decision pet owners make each day regarding their pet's health is what they choose to feed."

Clearly, a number of owners are making bad choices and are not feeding well. And even worse, we are often not aware of these bad decisions and how they are affecting our dogs' body condition and weight. The health risks of being obese for dogs are well documented. Overweight pets are more likely to develop problems with mobility, joint arthritis and heart disease. When undergoing even low-risk surgical procedures, their chance of dying from complications is higher, and overall life expectancy, just as with humans, is shorter for overweight animals. An overweight dog's quality of life is also affected—fat dogs have a more difficult time handling hot weather, become fatigued more easily, and are less active and playful. Although many dogs certainly enjoy the large meals and added treats, being overweight limits their ability to play, go walking and to spend quality time with their human family members.

Of course, the reasons that we overfeed pets (just like the reasons that we overfeed ourselves) are multiple and complex. Two of the most important influencing factors are reduced exercise and simply *feeding too much food* (more about this later). Another component, and one that is difficult to measure, is the feeling that we are doing something good for our pets, that we are expressing love when we feed them. Any owner who experiences a dog jumping with joy at the sight of her dinner bowl or enjoys the daily dinner dance of a family of dogs knows that feeding our pets is a highly gratifying experience. Just as most of our cultural celebrations involve a gathering of family and friends for a meal, so too do our celebrations of love with our pets. Like me, if you have a dinner ritual with your dog, you too are doing more than just providing proper nutrition each day when you feed. You are expressing the deep emotions of love and nurturing and joy that go along with feeding our dogs and that inform our daily decisions about how best to care for them.

Many of us also use food as a potent and highly effective primary reinforcer when training. While the shift from force-based training to practices based upon positive reinforcement has benefited millions of dogs (and trainers), it has also led to multiple feeding opportunities for dogs each day. And the issue is not simply the amount of food that is provided. Good trainers are highly capable of subtracting food treats used in training from a dog's daily ration and carefully monitoring body weight and condition. When we train using positive methods, we build stronger and more loving bonds with our animals—still a positive and good thing. However, we cannot and should not ignore the fact that these daily training periods further strengthen the association between food and love and continue to inform our choices. Here is an example: One of the trainers who works for me at my dog training center uses a smelly (horrendously stinky, actually) fish-based soft treat as a high-value treat for dogs who are not food-motivated or in situations that warrant something really, really yummy for the dog. The fact that these treats work like a charm with the most difficult-to-motivate dogs definitely influences our opinion about and use of them. However, they are also not well balanced nutritionally and cause diarrhea in some dogs because of their high fat content. In this case, our emotions (dog loves these, training goes well, happy day!) will influence our decisions about using the smelly and highly desirable treats. This does not mean that we should stop using them—simply that we must be aware of the emotional influences on our rational brain as we make decisions regarding the healthfulness of the training treats that we select for our dogs.

So, what is the solution? Shall we become cold calculating owners who view the provision of food and healthy nutrition as simple chemistry? Of course not! Food as love is a good thing…provided we are aware of our actions and monitor our choices while keeping a discerning eye upon our tendency to "love too much." For example, when treats are given as a show of affection, these should be carefully subtracted from the dog's daily ration. Similarly, training treats must always be accounted for. In fact, there is a growing trend to supply all of a pet's daily ration either during training or in combination with some type of enjoyable food delivery toy. This can work, if the total quantity of food is carefully measured. Because it is much easier to prevent obesity than to treat it, raising dogs with a careful eye on their waistlines is essential. And finally, owners must build habits that utilize *other* outlets for love and affection. The majority of dogs love to go walking, especially when the daily route is varied and when they have the opportunity to sniff, greet a few neighbors or play ball in the park. And trainers know that regular training sessions are great for a dog's mind and for his body, and serve to further strengthen the loving bond between owner and dog. Let's change up the paradigm a bit—food is love *and* good nutritional science. Let's now examine why we need the science half of the equation to make smart choices for our dogs.

2

Why We Need Science

"Science is a long history of learning how not to fool ourselves."

Richard Feynman (1918 - 1988)

Two years ago, my friend Pam's six year old Akita, Bruino, was diagnosed with bone cancer. Bruino had had his share of health issues during his short life; he was a rescue puppy born to a severely malnourished and neglected mother, he developed several skeletal disorders before he was a year old, and he later required surgery to repair the cruciate ligament in his left knee. Still, throughout all of this, Bruino remained an easy-going and friendly fellow, getting along well with people and dogs and never quite seeming to realize that he greatly outweighed his owner and the majority of his canine friends. When Bruino started to limp during a walk one day, Pam assumed that either the surgical repair to his knee had failed or that he was developing arthritis in that knee. Unfortunately, x-rays revealed the problem to be something much worse: a bone tumor located in his femur.

We are fortunate that we live in a university town with a veterinary college and an excellent cancer care clinic. Bruino was examined the next day by a team of board-certified veterinary oncologists. Information was presented to Pam about the disease, its prognosis and several options for Bruino's care. Although amputation is frequently the treatment of choice with osteosarcoma, Bruino's large size coupled with his mobility problems made him a poor candidate for this option. After consulting with the veterinary oncologists, the orthopedist who had performed Bruino's knee surgery, her own veterinarian and her training friends, Pam opted to provide Bruino with several palliative rounds of chemotherapy and also to enroll him in a clinical research trial that was testing the effects of a bone-salvaging drug for dogs with osteosarcoma. Pam and I also discussed Bruino's diet and she made some changes that were designed to support his body condition, reduce inflammation and possibly slow tumor growth.

Bruino responded well to treatment. His pain and swelling were reduced and his quality of life continued to be very good. During this time, Pam was in contact via email with a number of dog folks who she knew from being involved with Akita rescue. One acquaintance, we will call her "Jane," took it upon herself to inform Pam via email that feeding Bruino a commercial diet during his young life had almost certainly led to his cancer. Further, this woman proclaimed, if Pam would just start to feed Bruino the homemade diet that she recommended plus a concoction of nutritional supplements that she would provide, this would slow progression and could even *cure his cancer.* Like most of us, Pam would do anything possible to help her beloved dog. She considered changing Bruino's food and purchasing the packets of supplements. Pam trusted that this person was sincere in her claims. This was a known dog enthusiast who clearly believed in her own words and in the results that her prescribed diet and supplements could bring. (I would add that I like to think she never intended to be the source of the emotional pain that her words caused to Pam). After more thought, more discussion with me and with Bruino's team of veterinarians, Pam decided to stay with her planned course and to not use the diet that Jane was promoting. During our last discussion about this, Pam commented, "Well, if her diet works so well, wouldn't there be studies showing that it worked, and wouldn't more people be using it?"

Yes indeed, that is certainly the right question to be asking.

Mistakes were made…but not intentionally

The woman foisting unsolicited food advice upon Pam was probably sincere (though arguably insensitive). She believed that feeding her homemade dog food and providing a nutrient supplement could prevent cancer from developing in healthy dogs and cure disease in diagnosed dogs. Most readers will agree that this is a pretty extravagant claim. Yet, she insisted with conviction, and Pam, in a state of emotional turmoil, considered giving it a try. We all hear and read such claims in popular press, on the internet or when talking to Joe next door (who happens to know a lot about dogs). Why is it that we, as supposedly the most intelligent species on the planet, are so susceptible to believe such claims and often make decisions in response to assertions that are accompanied by little or no supporting evidence? Why do we sometimes make choices that seem to be a good idea (i.e., they *feel* right) but in reality the option that we choose has no actual evidence supporting its benefit or superiority?

We learned in the previous chapter that our emotions, important and essential as they are, not only influence our behavior but frequently do so without our conscious awareness. Additionally, our brains efficiently process information using a set of mental shortcuts called **heuristics** that enable us to rapidly observe a scene, extract meaning from it and react in what is (usually) an appropriate manner. And, as with the emotional input, all of this mental work takes place beneath the surface of our consciousness. It is only the *result* of processing the incoming information (the action or reaction) that we are consciously aware of. It does not feel this way because we are also masters at "back-reasoning." If asked why we made a particular decision or choice, we can immediately explain why. However, at the time that the choice is made, functional MRI (fMRI) studies have shown that the processing is much too rapid to have allowed us to work through the series of logical steps to reach the choice—at least not consciously. Again, the benefits of this subconscious system are its processing speed and efficiency.

However, with every benefit there comes a cost. The price that we pay for rapid-fire analysis is that our brains miss details—details that may be essential in certain situations for reliable decision making. And, just as with emotionally influenced choices, we are unaware of these missed details. Before reaching the conscious level of "Act now, do this!" our brains fill in a set of details for us, using our unique set of beliefs, experiences and expectations. For most processing and decision making, this system works well because past patterns often accurately predict current patterns. However, the system is also biased by our opinions and beliefs, and so can make mistakes. As a set, these mistakes are referred to as **cognitive biases**, predictable patterns of thought and behavior that lead us to draw incorrect conclusions. A similar set of errors are called **logical fallacies**. These refer to faulty arguments that lead to errors in logic—again, without our awareness—usually because we are highly invested in supporting a particular answer or solution.

Happily for us, psychologists, neuroscientists and behaviorists have been studying these biases and fallacies for many years. Although we cannot completely prevent them (that subconscious mind thing again), we can be aware of the existence of these traps and their potential to lead us astray when making choices. Just as many of us are talented dog trainers, we can also become effective "mind trainers," teaching ourselves to avoid or correct for these traps when making decisions for our dogs' health (and for other important things in life). Let's take a look at some specific types of cognitive biases and logical fallacies that may unduly influence us as we try to select foods, choose the best feeding approach and make decisions for our dog's nutritional well-being.

Confirmation bias
Confirmation bias is the tendency to seek out and remember information that matches what we already believe, and to ignore or discount information that is not in agreement with our preformed views. This tendency is so strong that when we find information that supports our position, we judge that source as impeccable and the information to be solid and well founded. And, when we are forced to address evidence that does *not* support our position, we quickly decide that the source is unreliable or that the information is biased or flawed. (More insidiously, however, we often avoid being confronted with such evidence in the first place.) Psychologists explain that confirmation bias is almost impossible to completely avoid because as humans, we…well…hate to be wrong. Being forced to confront and explain information that is in direct contradiction to our cherished beliefs puts us into an uncomfortable psychological state called **cognitive dissonance**. Being "in dissonance" is threatening to our sense of self, and so it is generally something that we avoid like the plague. What's more, the more emotionally invested we are in a particular belief or opinion, the more susceptible we are to falling prey to confirmation bias.

A well-cited study performed at Stanford University in 1979 demonstrated confirmation bias in action. A group of 48 undergraduate students who either favored or opposed the death penalty were asked to read and evaluate two academic and well-documented articles about whether or not capital punishment reduces violent crime in society. One of the papers concluded that it was a deterrent while the second concluded that it did *not* provide a deterrent. Each provided data and well-reasoned arguments that supported their conclusions. After reading both studies, the group of students who were strongly opposed to capital punishment assessed the paper that was aligned with their position as well-researched and as having strong and convincing arguments. Conversely, they rated the paper that supported capital punishment as poorly researched and having multiple methodological errors. Similarly, the group that held the opposite opinion and supported capital punishment evaluated the paper that agreed with their views highly and the paper in opposition as significantly flawed.

Interestingly, rather than learning from reading multiple sides of the issue and considering other opinions, the researchers found that participants' initial views were *stronger* at the end of the study, leading to increased polarization of opinions!

We all reinforce confirmation biases when we seek out companions who hold the same beliefs that we do and spend time conversing with them, doing a lot of nodding and gushing emphatically "Yes, I agree!! I know, isn't that the truth!" Again, this is human nature; it *feels* good when we are around like-minded friends. And, of course, it is practical. For example, if you love to train and show in agility competitions and have Border Collies, then you have a lot in common with others who do the same, and probably enjoy their company, learn from their training approaches, etc. It would actually be rather odd for you to hang out with conformation handlers who raise and show Afghan Hounds. Still, spending all of our time with others who hold similar views feeds our biases and cements our beliefs. We are all well served to be aware of this tendency and the biases it supports and to keep confirmation bias in check for an important reason. In his book *Why People Believe Weird Things,* science writer Michael Shermer explains that many of our stereotypes and prejudices are continually reinforced by confirmation bias. For example, he describes a study in which a group of adults were asked to view a video of a child completing a verbal test. Half of the adults were informed that the child was from a high socioeconomic class and the other half were informed that the child was from a low socioeconomic class. After viewing the video, the subjects assessed the child's intelligence and academic ability using a set of numerical rating scales. Although they all viewed the same video, participants who believed the child was from a well-to-do home rated the child's ability significantly higher and above her grade level while participants who believed the child was from a less privileged upbringing rated the child's performance as poor and below her grade level. Simply having a preconceived (and completely artificial) belief about the child led people to confirm this belief when they evaluated her intelligence.

Similar forms of confirmation bias can occur with dog folks and professionals. For example, if you are a trainer, do you hold strong opinions about the temperament and trainability of certain breeds? When you meet an individual of one of these breeds (or a mix containing that breed) do your beliefs about the breed's behavior influence how you react to and train the individual dog? Keep in mind, stereotypes are heuristics (mental shortcuts) that our brains naturally develop to allow us to categorize the world and recognize patterns. They are highly efficient and often very effective. But these shortcuts come with risks, with confirmation bias at the very top of the list. When you work with dogs, does an unconscious need to confirm your beliefs affect your training or teaching?

Confirmation bias is also at work in health care when we become convinced that a dog's itchy skin is caused by the chicken meal in her diet and then attend to only those signs that confirm this belief (itchy skin, commercial food containing chicken meal) and ignore signs that her problem skin may have other causes (seasonal allergies, parasites, flea allergy dermatitis). As with our emotional mind and decision making, confirmation bias is so much part of our brain's way of doing business that we can never be completely free of it. However, being aware of our tendency to seek out data that support closely held beliefs can help us to open our minds, seek alternate explanations and weigh information carefully and objectively. We will explore specific techniques and approaches to doing this in Chapter 3.

Post-hoc fallacy

Post-hoc fallacy, formally called *post hoc, ergo propter hoc*, translates to "after this, therefore because of this." This common logical fallacy is the cause of many superstitions and false beliefs. We commit a post-hoc error whenever we assume that because two events occur together, with one following the other in time, that the first event *caused* the second event. Here is an obvious and rather silly example. My husband and I live in the country, with the closest home located about a mile away. Living in a secluded area surrounded by farmland has many benefits, and one of these is being woken each day to the sound of roosters crowing just before dawn. If our windows are open, we hear this every morning, so the evidence is consistent and repeatable: rooster crows, and 15 minutes or so following his announcement, we see the sun peaking over the horizon. Sunrise follows rooster crowing. So, does the rooster *cause* the sun to rise? Of course not; it is silly to think this. Yet, for many other things in life, this is exactly the error that we make. One event preceding another, even if the relationship is repeatable and consistent, does not prove that the first event *causes* the second event. This error is sometimes referred to in a broader sense as "correlation does not prove causation."

Examples of the post-hoc fallacy in the field of pet health abound. We are especially prone to these in nutrition precisely because we can easily change the food that we feed and because we tend to change foods only when our dogs experience a problem. Think about it this way. If your dog is healthy, thriving and happy, switching her to a new food does not typically enter your mind. Everything is rolling along fine, so why would anyone choose to rock the proverbial boat and change something that does not need to be changed. Makes sense, of course. However, when a dog's coat becomes dry, when persistent itchiness shows up or when cancer strikes, many owners consider diet as a cause. Because changing foods or adding a nutrient supplement is a simple solution and does not require oversight by a veterinarian or extensive medical tests, focusing on dietary change in the face of a health problem is a common reaction. Here's the catch…if the dog's condition improves after changing her food (and the timeframe encompassed by "after" may be days, weeks or even months), then the improvement is immediately attributed to the change in food. A win-win situation is set up because of the highly variable post-event timeframe and because multiple variables are typically in place with an individual dog's case. However, if no positive change is observed, diet is still not eliminated as a cause. Rather the change may not have been the *right* diet. The owner moves on to another food, another supplement and another dietary approach. (Because of confirmation bias the misses are also often not noticed, while the hits are celebrated.) This example does not mean that a diet change was *not* helpful, simply that a diet change followed by a health improvement over a variable span of time and in the presence of multiple variables (i.e., medications, other treatments, seasonal changes) does not prove causation. When an individual dog is the entire case study, the placebo effect plus a lack of multiple cases means that we can conclude nothing about diet from this scenario.

Illusion of control

It is human nature to feel most comfortable with certainty, simple and neat explanations, and the feeling that we have at least a modicum of control over what happens to us and to our beloved dogs. Because of this deep-seated need, we tend to overestimate our ability to control events upon which we, in reality, have little or no influence.

Choice is also a key component of the **illusion of control**, because having a variety of options to choose from supports the fallacy that choice always leads to control. Using a lottery example, a series of studies conducted by social psychologist Ellen Langer showed that people who chose their own lottery number believed that they had a greater chance of winning than people who had their number randomly assigned to them. More dangerous behavior can also be caused by an illusion of control. A study conducted with students at Pomona University found that participants who were rated as having a naturally high tendency towards the illusion of control were more likely to use a cell phone while driving and also had exaggerated beliefs regarding their abilities to drive effectively while talking on the phone.

Because as owners we actually *are* in complete control of what our dogs eat and when they eat it, the jump to assuming (hoping) that we can control our dogs' health entirely by what we feed to them is pervasive. Proponents of nutritional trends that make extravagant claims exploit our deeply ingrained desire to be able to control health changes in our pets through what we choose to feed them. They offer simple and neat solutions that will "make everything better" without the need for extensive medical testing or expensive veterinary bills. It is no wonder that we fall for these claims, given our strong desire to help our dogs and the natural tendency of our brains to convince us that we have a universal ability to do so. The illusion of control is seductive because it allows us to feel that we can do something for our dogs in situations where in reality (and sadly) we may have little or no control.

Availability error

The **availability error** has its roots in our natural tendency to attach greater significance to events that are easily brought to mind or remembered (i.e., are "available"). Like most cognitive biases, the availability error has its roots in a heuristic that our brains use for speed and efficiency when evaluating incoming information. It can lead to errors in judgment when we would be better served to take our time and evaluate information more objectively. Examples of the availability error include the belief that shark attacks, child abductions and plane crashes are far more common (and present much greater risk to individuals) than they actually are. Extensive and sensationalist media coverage make these events highly salient (available) to our minds, so that when we consider going to the beach this summer for vacation, an image of a shark pops into our brains; when we think of a small child at the mall, we think of stranger-danger; and when we think of flying to that conference next month, we may think of the danger of a terrorist attack. While these events can and do happen, an examination of the actual risk (statistical analysis that determines the probability of an event occurring) is much lower than our perceptions lead us to believe.

The availability heuristic is also deliberately used by marketers to convince us to purchase things. For example, let's again look at the lottery business. You may have noticed that advertisements for lotteries never report the statistical odds that you will *lose* the lottery. The odds of *not winning* are of course extremely high, typically in the 50 million to 1 range. You can view this in the opposite way, in which you have 1 in 50 million chances of winning, but the odds are just the same. Having this discouraging statistic readily available would naturally lead people to spend their money on something much more useful (such as a new dog toy). Rather, marketers know that if recent winners are repeatedly promoted in their advertisements, the appeal of this information to potential players will sway them into believing that they too could win the lottery. You are more likely to buy a ticket if the first thing that comes to your mind is winning rather than losing, and the image of an ecstatic winner standing next to an enormous check is one that we see with almost every lottery advertisement. The availability error is also a powerful influence in the dog world. An unfortunate but common example occurs when people believe that all Pit Bull Terriers are dangerous because of sensationalized media coverage of dog bites that focuses repeatedly only on this particular breed or breed type.

Negativity bias

Negativity bias refers to the psychological phenomenon in which we naturally pay more attention to and give more weight to negative rather than positive experiences. It is this unconscious bias that causes people to be more hurt or discouraged by insults or poor work performance reviews than they are pleased or encouraged by compliments or shining performance reviews. For example, a study conducted by Susan Fiske gave subjects both moderately positive information and moderately negative information about a stranger who they met in person several minutes later. Afterwards, the participants' overall judgment of the person was significantly more negative than positive, even though they had equally positive and negative information about the individual. Interestingly, studies conducted by John Cacioppo at Ohio State University have shown that this bias appears to be "hard wired," since there is evidence of its occurrence at the neurological level. The brain actually experiences stronger neural activity when reacting to negative information than to positive information. In other (rather depressing) words, we are naturally predisposed to pay more attention to negative information than positive information; painful experiences are much more memorable to us than pleasurable ones. This tendency is most likely a trait that evolved to help keep us and those we love out of harm's way. The negativity bias can be thought of as "the buzz-killer bias" and helps to explain why people love to gossip, as well as why we have a tendency to remember (and sometimes repeat) negative information about others.

The negativity bias rears its ugly head in our interactions with dogs when we react only to "bad" (undesirable) behaviors and ignore the "good" (desirable) behaviors that our dogs offer during the day. It is common for owners to wait until their dog engages in unwanted behaviors, such as jumping up, chewing or excessive barking, which of course then puts the owner into the position of having to do something (react) to stop, change or redirect the unwanted behavior. And yet, the same owner neither notices nor reacts to the dog when he is sitting (not jumping), enjoying his own chew toy (not destroying the TV remote) or lying quietly at her feet (not barking). Many trainers, including myself, encourage our clients to train *themselves* to attend to the desired/good behaviors that their dogs are engaging in and to positively reinforce those things throughout the day. However, this is a lesson that we must repeat again and again because of the negativity bias—dog owners are naturally more sensitive to negative experiences with their dogs than to positive experiences. And of course, this bias can also affect the attention that we pay to our dog's health and wellness. We tend to wait until we see a change in weight, the development of itchy skin or the onset of a serious health problem before we react. In human medicine (and increasingly in veterinary medicine), efforts to train ourselves to focus on wellness and disease prevention as opposed to disease treatment are a reflection of recognizing and trying to combat negativity bias.

Jane's claims

These are just a few of the ways in which our mind's tendency to think rapidly, use shortcuts to form opinions and rules of thumb to make decisions can lead us to make errors in judgment. Let's return for a moment to Jane's insistence that her diet and supplement would cure Bruino's cancer. Upon further investigation, Pam discovered that one of Jane's dogs had died of cancer several years previously and that Jane had changed the dog's diet several months prior to the diagnosis. This led Jane to believe that "diet causes cancer," examples of both *post hoc* and *availability* errors. Because she spent many hours and a great deal of effort in the development of her nutritional supplement, Jane understandably was highly invested in believing in the efficacy of her approach. Therefore, these feelings could lead her to pay more attention to dogs who responded positively (or did not suffer from it) and to ignore cases in which the dog's condition worsened (confirmation bias). And, an additional *post hoc* fallacy was committed when she assumed that a dog's change in status was due specifically to her remedy because the change in condition *followed* feeding the remedy chronologically (regardless of how long that time period was and ignoring the effects of other treatments that a dog may have been receiving). The fact that Jane's remedy (and her beliefs about it) had not been shown to be effective through controlled scientific study does not discount the fact that her remedy *might* be helpful or effective. *The point is that we just don't know.* The claims that Jane made for her nutritional approach had never been tested and the risks of succumbing to a variety of potential biases make her claims at the very least unfounded, and at the most highly suspect.

So, what is a dog person to do? Are our minds, while highly efficient at processing loads of information and helping us to react quickly to changing circumstances, at the same time sabotaging our attempts to weigh evidence and make well-reasoned decisions? Well…yes. But when it comes to our dog's nutritional health and well-being (as well as to many other important decisions in our lives), there is a rational and reliable tool that can help us to avoid these traps, evaluate information objectively and choose well. This tool is available to us all. It is called science.

What IS science (and why do we need it?)

Let's begin by softening up the word **science** a bit. Remember that dog owners don't typically think of nutrition as science. Rather, we are more apt to consider providing for our dogs' nutritional needs in terms of nurturing, love and caretaking. But, nutritional care can be both. While our emotional mind is necessary for us to *care* about choosing well for our pets, our rational brain (often called our reflective mind) is needed to carefully evaluate information, weigh choices and make informed decisions. And this is where science comes in. In line with Richard Feynman's famous quote, "Science is a long history of learning how not to fool ourselves," we should think of the science of pet nutrition as protecting us from ourselves, specifically from our tendency to make emotionally influenced choices that are susceptible to those pesky and pervasive cognitive biases.

At its most basic, science refers to a systematic approach to acquiring knowledge. The system of science uses observation and experimentation to describe and explain the natural world. And—this is important—science is specifically and intentionally designed to prevent the biases and cognitive traps that come along with being human, traps that will almost always trip us up in one way or another if we simply go about willy-nilly making decisions in response only to how we *feel* and without any type of system or plan. One of the best things about science is that, by definition, it is testable. Science is designed to evaluate the validity of the stuff that you think/ponder/learn to make sure that your beliefs actually reflect reality as opposed to being flawed, misleading or an outright falsehood.

In most disciplines, including nutrition, science is put into practice through use of the **scientific method**. Most of us learned the steps to this method in high school, and some of us have had the opportunity to put it into practice later in college and in our careers. Just in case the steps to the scientific method have not yet percolated up to your conscious brain, let's give these a quick review. There are four primary steps to the scientific method:

Step 1: The investigator notices a natural phenomenon or a problem and takes the time to observe it closely, trying to learn as much as possible about it.

Step 2: The investigator considers one or more possible explanations or causes for the phenomenon and typically selects a favorite for testing: her hypothesis. Now the fun begins.

Step 3: This is the essence of the scientific method. A study is designed, data are collected and analyzed and conclusions are drawn. The results of the first study may suggest a second, and understanding grows.

Step 4: Following study replication (preferably by unrelated groups of researchers) the hypothesis is either rejected as false (and you start all over again), accepted or judgment is withheld pending still more study.

The scientific method
Step 1: Observe
Step 2: Conduct studies, collect and analyze data
Step 3: Observe a bit more, replicate studies
Step 4: Accept, reject or withhold judgment

Figure 2.1 Steps in the scientific method.

A key difference between the scientific method and other ways in which we learn about the world is that it is designed to protect us from inherent biases and mistakes in reasoning. In the following chapter, we will see how the use of well-designed studies can support or refute claims that are made about a particular pet food, ingredient, nutrient or feeding method. Before we start to examine those details, let's return one more time to the issue of diet and cancer in dogs.

The scientific method in practice: Can diet influence the progression of cancer in dogs?

The scientific method provides a systematic approach to testing ideas about "how things work" that protects those doing the work (and those who stand to benefit from it) from making errors in judgment. Jane promoted a feeding approach and nutritional supplement that she was convinced would slow the progression of Bruino's cancer. Her convictions, while sincere, were based not upon scientific evidence but upon personal experience. As we have seen, personal experience can lead to flawed conclusions. Yet, as I mentioned, we did change Bruino's diet. What made Pam choose the food that she selected rather than the approach that Jane promoted?

The food that Pam chose for Bruino included an increase in fat and reduced levels of digestible carbohydrate (starch). Protein was moderately increased. The type of fat was also modified to include a high proportion of a class of fatty acids called the omega-3 fatty acids. These are commonly found in certain types of fish. When included in the diet in proper amounts, omega-3 fatty acids have varying degrees of anti-inflammatory benefits to different tissues in the body. The reasons for these changes have to do with changes in the way that animals with cancer are able to use energy-containing nutrients from their diet (fat, carbohydrate and protein) and also how being affected by cancer influences body weight, body condition and an animal's interest in eating.

Most animals, including humans, experience certain changes in metabolism (the way in which the body digests and uses nutrients) during cancer. These changes become most pronounced during the later stages of cancer and can also be influenced by cancer treatments such as chemotherapy and radiation. It is known that most tumor cells preferentially use carbohydrate as an energy (fuel) source and use fat and protein far less efficiently. Therefore, feeding an animal who has cancer a diet that shifts its energy balance away from carbohydrate and towards fat is designed to *feed the patient while starving the tumor.* Because tumors grow fastest when using carbohydrate for energy, depriving them of this form of energy may slow their growth and slow the progression of the cancer. An additional benefit to increasing dietary fat is that fat improves a food's energy density and appeal to dogs, which will both encourage a dog to eat and will help to maintain body weight during treatment. Increasing omega-3 fatty acids in the diet has anti-inflammatory benefits in the body and may also help to limit tumor growth. Finally, many dogs with cancer lose weight and specifically show a loss of muscle mass and strength. Increasing protein helps to conserve the body's lean tissue and reduce this decline in body condition.

The recommendations made for Brunio arose from an understanding of both canine cancer and nutritional science. Still, an approach to feeding dogs with cancer that uses this nutrient matrix must be *tested* (scientific method, remember) if we are to accept that a diet switch could help Bruino. Is there scientific evidence? Indeed there is. Although there are not mountains of it, there is enough to suggest that dietary modification may be beneficial for dogs with cancer. I will briefly review the published research, with each statement followed by a superscript number. The number corresponds to the number of each of the published studies that are listed under the References heading on page 25.

First, a study of dogs with lymphoma showed that patients who were fed a high-fat diet successfully shifted their nutrient use (metabolism) away from digestible carbohydrate and toward dietary fat, a shift that is expected to reduce tumor cell growth and that supported body weight and condition in the dogs.[1] In a second study of dogs with the same type of cancer, dogs fed a high-fat diet that was supplemented with omega-3 fatty acids and an amino acid called arginine had improved blood glucose tests and had increased disease-free intervals and survival times when compared with dogs who were not supplemented.[2] In addition, studies in other species (including humans) have shown that increasing long-chain omega-3 fatty acids can limit tumor growth, prevent harmful changes in the patient's metabolism and increase the susceptibility of cancer cells to chemotherapy drugs.[3,4,5,6] Another study of dogs with nasal tumors that were receiving radiation therapy showed that dogs fed a therapeutic food containing increased fat plus the omega-3 fatty acids EPA and DHA showed reduced radiation-induced tissue injury and were reported by their owners to have improved health performance compared with dogs who were fed a control diet.[7] Finally, although few studies of dietary treatment of dogs with Bruino's specific form of cancer have been conducted, one investigation did show that dogs with osteosarcoma (bone cancer) demonstrate the same metabolic changes that are associated with other types of cancer.[8] This information supports feeding a diet that contains reduced digestible carbohydrate and increased dietary fat and protein to dogs with osteosarcoma.

This set of eight studies (plus additional studies that are not cited here that were conducted in laboratory animals or using cell cultures) provide the science that was needed to make a decision for Bruino's wellness and quality of life during cancer treatment. They all followed the scientific method of observing, developing a hypothesis, testing the hypothesis using controlled studies, retesting and finally coming to a conclusion. In addition, all of these studies were published in peer-reviewed, scientific journals (more about this in Chapter 3). To date, several other nutrients, such as certain amino acids (arginine and branched-chain amino acids) and antioxidant nutrients (lutein, beta-carotene and vitamin E) have shown some effectiveness at slowing the growth of tumor cells. However, not all studies show benefit and these nutrients have not been studied specifically in dogs with cancer, so we cannot currently make a recommendation about their use.

Happily for Bruino, the knowledge that we did have at the time provided him with a diet that at the very least supported his body condition and muscle mass during his treatments. Bruino experienced a high quality of life for almost a year following diagnosis. While we cannot know if the dietary intervention slowed his cancer progression as an individual case, we do know that a dietary matrix that includes increased fat and protein, reduced carbohydrate and increased omega-3 fatty acids has the potential to do so. And, because the food that he was fed was formulated to be nutritionally complete and had been tested, we also know that we did not harm him by feeding it. This is something that we would not have known had Pam chosen to feed him the recommended concoction of Jane's. Now that we have seen the type of information that science *can* tell us (and why it is important), let's examine types of scientific (and not so scientific) evidence that are available about dog nutrition along with critical thinking skills that you can use to make evidence-based decisions for your dogs' health and wellness.

> ## Nutrient matrix—diet for dogs with cancer
> Foods that are designed (formulated) for dogs with cancer should account for nutritional changes that are associated with cancer. These include weight loss and changed in body condition, reduced appetite and metabolic effects caused by tumors. Recommended diets include:
>
> - Increased fat
> - Reduced digestible carbohydrate (starch)
> - Increased omega-3 fatty acids (specifically EPA and DHA)
> - Moderately increased protein
> - Quality ingredients that are highly digestible

Figure 2.2 Recommended nutritional modifications for dogs with cancer.

References

[1]Ogilvie GK, Walters LM, Fettman MJ, and others: "Energy expenditure in dogs with lymphoma fed two specialized diets." *Cancer* 71:3146-3152, 1993.

[2]Olgilvie GK, Fettman MJ, Mallinckrodt CH, Walton JA, Hansen RA, Davenport DJ, Gross KL, Richardson KL, Rogers Q and Hand MS: "Effect of fish oil, arginine, and doxorubicin chemotherapy on remission and survival time for dogs with lymphoma." *Cancer* 88:1916-1928, 2000.

[3]Lowell JA, Parnes HL, Blackburn GL: "Dietary immunomodulation: beneficial effects on carcinogenesis and tumor growth." *Crit Care Med* 18:S145-S148, 1990.

[4]Ramesh G, Das UN, Koratkar R, and others: "Effect of essential fatty acids on tumor cells." *Nutrition* 8:343-347, 1992.

[5]Begin ME, Ellis G, Das UN, and others: "Differential killing of human carcinoma cells supplemented with n-e and n-6 polyunsaturated fatty acids." *J Nat Cancer Inst* 77:2053-2057, 1986.

[6]Plumb JA, Luo W, Kerr DJ: "Effect of polyunsaturated fatty acids on the drug sensitivity of human tumor cell lines resistant to either cisplatin or doxorubicin." *Brit J Cancer* 67:728-733, 1993.

[7]Anderson CR, Ogilvie GK, LaRue SM, and others: "Effect of fish oil and arginine on acute effects of radiation injury in dogs with neoplasia: a double blind study." *Proc Vet Cancer Soc*, Chicago, Ill, 1997.

[8]Mazzaferro EM, Hackett TB, Stein TP, Ogilvie GK, Wingfield WE, Walton J, Turner AS, Fettman MJ: "Metabolic alterations in dogs with osteosarcoma." *Am J Vet Res* 62:1234-1239, 2001.

3

The Critical Consumer—Evaluating the Science

"No way of thinking or doing, however ancient, can be trusted without proof."

Henry David Thoreau

"Never ignore a gut feeling, but never believe that it's enough."

Kermit the Frog

Henry David Thoreau, author of *Walden*, was a strong proponent for clear thinking. It appears that Kermit the Frog was too. As we have seen, our emotions provide us with rapid and unconscious responses to events that occur around us—our "gut feelings." While these feelings help us to react quickly and stay safe, they can also lead us to make some glaring errors in judgment. In this chapter, we listen to the wisdom of Thoreau and Kermit and learn to use our critical thinking skills to ask the right questions and to objectively evaluate information prior to making decisions. Because we are interested in dog nutrition and feeding, we will specifically look at how scientific practice provides usable information and how we can differentiate between reliable and unreliable evidence. This is an important skill because testimonials and anecdotes abound among dog enthusiasts and are also used regularly by pet food companies to promote their products. Let us begin by asking why, exactly, is it so important that we attempt to base our decisions on scientifically acquired information about nutrition rather than on personal experiences, anecdotes and what Joe next door (who happens to know a lot about dogs) tells us about dog nutrition?

Rosemary extract—a cause of seizure disorder?

Last year, while attending a conference to present a nutrition lecture, I chatted with a woman who owns a doggie day care and training business. Because the conference was just a few hours drive from her home, she had brought one of her dogs, a young Papillion, along with her. She told me that the Papillion had recently experienced several seizures and she wanted to keep her close at hand. We talked a bit about nutrition, but also about potential genetic, neoplastic (cancer) and toxin-related causes of seizure disorders in dogs. The following day, she approached me again and asked if I knew anything about a connection between the herb rosemary and seizure disorder in dogs. She said that she had read recently on a dog-related website that rosemary in dog food could cause seizures. Because the food that she fed contained rosemary extract, she was concerned that this might be the cause of her dog's illness. I had not heard anything about this claim, but did tell her that rosemary is included as a naturally derived preservative in some dog foods and that it is typically present in very small amounts. Rosemary extract contains a mixture of oils that have moderate **antioxidant** effects in foods. Antioxidants function to protect dietary fat, certain vitamins and other food components from the damaging effects of oxidation that occur during storage. In addition, the oils have a sharp odor and rather displeasing flavor, so large amounts in food are generally not well accepted by dogs. After returning home, I decided to research the claim about a connection between rosemary and the onset of seizures in dogs to discover what evidence, if any, there was for it.

Rosemary is an herb that is derived from the leaves of the rosemary plant *(Rosmariunus officinalis)*. It has culinary uses in human foods and its oils are also used as a fragrance in body lotions, soaps and cosmetics. Rosemary is also used in human complementary and alternative medicine (CAM), with claims that its essence improves memory and reduces anxiety (aromatherapy), that applying it topically will stimulate hair re-growth and that consuming it can relieve muscle aches and pains. A search of the available literature showed that there is some, albeit limited, evidence that human subjects who were exposed to rosemary oil during aromatherapy showed improvements in some forms of memory and had reduced stress prior to taking an exam. None of the other CAM claims have been studied and there is no published evidence either supporting or refuting beliefs that rosemary promotes hair growth or reduces muscle pain.

Rosemary extract however, does have proven antioxidant properties when used as a food additive. Specifically, it functions to retard fat oxidation, which is a major cause of food rancidity and production of off-flavors. In one study, J.B. Sebranek and co-workers at Iowa State University found that rosemary extract was equivalent in function to the synthetic antioxidant BHA when used to preserve pork sausages (Sebranek et al., 2005). There is also evidence that rosemary extract has antimicrobial and antifungal properties in foods, which may be an added benefit of its use as a naturally derived preservative in dog foods. And, although not yet studied in either animals or humans, studies using cancer cell lines have shown that carnosic acid, a compound found in rosemary extract, increased cell death in leukemia cells. In recent years, rosemary extract has been used with increasing frequency in commercial dog foods, especially in those that advertise to be preserved using naturally derived compounds. Interestingly, current regulations disallow pet food manufactures from making a claim about the antioxidant properties of rosemary because as an ingredient it is classified only as a spice or seasoning.

What about safety? Is there any evidence of a causative association between rosemary extract and seizure disorders? Published toxicity studies conducted with rodents have shown that rosemary extract is tolerated at very high levels when fed to animals for long periods of time. Although no safety/toxicity studies have been conducted with dogs (or humans, for that matter), for ethical reasons it is common to conduct toxicity tests with rodent species and extrapolate the results to humans and other species. In this case, given the high doses that have been fed with no ill effects, rosemary extract is presumed to be highly safe.

This information begs the question—where did the belief that including rosemary extract in pet foods can trigger seizures in dogs come from? It appears that this claim originated with a small study stating that some types of essential oils used in aromatherapy have been implicated (but not proven) to be triggers for epileptic seizures in human patients. Peter Burkhard and others reported the occurrence of seizures in three human subjects who had been treated with a variety of essential oils that included eucalyptol and camphor oils (Burkhard et al; 1999). No subsequent cases have been reported, nor have any controlled studies been conducted in humans or any other species. Here are two important points: (1) The original study did not include rosemary oil; and (2) no cases at all exist in the published literature that identify an association between rosemary extract and seizure disorder in dogs. If one had to speculate, it is possible that the purported CAM uses of rosemary to boost memory and cognition (i.e., neurological effects), coupled with the 1999 paper (that did not specifically use rosemary) led (albeit via a tortuous path) to this belief. Add a dose of social media, and you have a potent and lasting rumor that starts to sound more and more like fact. A quick search of the internet pops up countless dog-related websites, email messages and blogs that warn against rosemary in dog foods because of its role in seizures. However, when we add up the science and examine the type of support behind the claims that are being made, we can make an educated decision that given the demonstrated safety of rosemary, the lack of data showing it to be a risk and the complete lack of cases of seizure disorder being caused by this food additive, it is highly doubtful that rosemary extract was the cause of seizures in my conference companion's Papillion.

I would like to close this example with one more piece of information that will serve us all well as we begin to hone our decision-making skills. There is an old medical proverb that applies equally (well better, really) to issues of animal health. It advises: "When you hear hoof beats, don't look for zebras." In other words, when you observe symptoms that are consistent with something that is relatively common and frequently observed *(horses)*, do not first look for something that is exceedingly rare or even impossible *(zebras)*—assuming you are not living in Africa, of course. There is a scientific version of this proverb called the **principle of parsimony** that cautions researchers to apply the simplest and best supported explanation to any set of observations. The principle of parsimony is intended to prevent us from leaping to explanations that are highly unlikely and ignoring or discounting those that are perhaps mundane, but are more probable. This can be applied to the case of the charge that rosemary extract in a dog food caused a dog to seizure. Let us review what is known about seizures in dogs. Seizure disorder has been shown to have a genetic component, with certain dog breeds having a higher incidence than the general population of dogs. Other potential causes include exposure to toxins and development of a brain tumor. In most cases (80% by some accounts), an underlying cause for the seizures is never identified and the disorder is treated symptomatically. These cases are classified as idiopathic seizure disorders. However, *not* being able to find an underlying cause cannot not be taken as license to decide that there is a connection between a dog's seizures and the presence of rosemary extract in the dog's food!

Our inclination to jump at dietary explanations for health disorders that confound us is understandable. In the case of seizure disorder, the alternative explanations are not appealing. For example, one obviously cannot do anything to change a dog's genetic make-up—it is what it is and you live with (and love) who your dog is. Contemplating a brain tumor is a frightening diagnosis and is certainly something that we all want to consider as being far down on the list of potential causes. And, the word idiopathic is just simply maddening. "What do you mean, they don't know?!?! How can there be no explanation for this!?" So, it is not surprising that we are inclined to latch on to information that impugns diet as a potential cause, since the food that we select is something that is easily changed and provides us with the sense that we can fix this problem. Here we see confirmation bias and the illusion of control working hand in hand. And of course, correct or not, this is what we all are naturally inclined to do. This is why we must train ourselves as "citizen scientists" to attend to information that *informs us* rather than *misleads us*.

Scientific studies, testimonials or anecdotes—who to listen to?

As a species, humans are programmed to react strongly to experiences and events that have an emotional impact. We enjoy stories that personalize experience and that share information that is relevant to our own lives and to our dogs. And of course, we learn valuable life lessons from our family members, friends and from the dog enthusiasts and professionals we trust. Accordingly, we also have a strong tendency to make decisions based upon memories and experiences that have a strong emotional impact on us. Animal shelters and advocacy groups are well aware of this bias. They use heartrending stories of an individual dog, cat or family to capture our attention and evoke our sympathy. By contrast, statistical data are numbers. Statistics are dry, boring and completely lacking in emotional punch. For example, take a look at Figures 3.1a and b. In Figure 3.1a, you learn about Jack's terrible start in life, near death due to extreme neglect, his rescue by Animal Helpers and his subsequent rehabilitation and adoption into a loving, forever home. In Figure 3.1b, you see current dog relinquishment and euthanasia statistics, reporting an estimate of the number of dogs who were released to shelters and killed in 2011. This advertisement reports a degree of animal suffering and death that is magnitudes greater than the first, which describes just a single dog. Yet, which advertisement do you respond to strongly and which would be more likely to lead to your decision to donate money to Animal Helpers? If you are like most people, you naturally respond to Jack and his story and are much more likely to donate to the sponsoring organization of Jack's ad rather than the dry, statistics-yielding advertisement, even though the statistics convey a much larger degree of suffering and need than the single story about Jack.

Animal helpers—call now to donate!

Meet Jack. He was abandoned in the yard of his former owner, left tied to a tree with no water, no food and no love. Lucky for Jack, a concerned neighbor called Animal Helpers, who rescued Jack and nursed him back to health. This week, Jack met Sally Smith, his forever mom. Sally tells us "I fell in love with Jack the moment I looked into those eyes. Thank you Animal Helpers for bringing this wonderful dog into my life!" Animal Helpers, in YourTown USA, helps all pets who are unwanted or neglected. They are with us now, waiting to meet you and go into their forever homes.

Fig. 3.1a Jack's story.

Animal helpers—call now to donate!

- Five to seven million animals enter animal shelters nationwide every year, of which three to four million dogs and cats who could be in homes are euthanized.*

- Shelter intakes are about evenly divided between pets relinquished by owners and those picked up by animal control.*

- Animal Helpers, in YourTown USA, takes in approximately 25 dogs and 40 cats each week who are unwanted or neglected. They are with us now, waiting to meet you and go into their forever homes.

*2012 Statistics provided by the Humane Society of the United States (www.humanesociety.org).

Fig. 3.1b Shelter statistics.

We respond in a similar manner to information about the foods that we select for our dogs. Pet food commercials provide images of healthy dogs interacting with loving owners (often in a green field, with flowers and harp music playing in the background). Websites include owner testimonials and photos of happy dogs. These stories have a strong impact upon our reaction to a product. If a commercial presented the results of a scientific study, would it capture your attention and your interest in the food to the same degree? Probably not, because we are not wired that way. There is no reason that you should *not* enjoy the anecdotes and the testimonials of dog food websites. However, we must avoid making the next leap: assuming that these stories provide conclusive evidence of the claims that are being made for a product's quality, appeal or superiority. For this, we need the boring and dry data collected from scientific studies. It is this information, unspectacular as it may seem, that allows us to make evidence-based decisions for our dogs.

Evidence-based decision making

The term **evidence-based medicine** (EBM) was first coined in the early 1990s and has its origins in human clinical medicine. There are three elements of evidence-based decision making in veterinary medicine:

- **Research evidence**
- **Clinical expertise**
- **Owner values/needs**

Research evidence comes from the publication of nutrient requirement and feeding studies with dogs (more about this later). The second element, clinical expertise, comes from the knowledge and experience of various pet professionals such as veterinarians, animal nutritionists, breeders, trainers and shelter professionals, among others. The dog owner's values and how much he or she is willing and/or able to care (and pay) for their dog's nutritional care makes up the third component of the relationship (Figure 3.2).

EBM has gained acceptance in both human and veterinary medicine and can also be used as a framework for making nutrition and feeding decisions for our dogs. The illustration below shows how the three elements in EBM overlap and interrelate to each other.

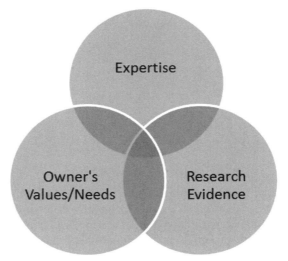

Figure 3.2 The three elements of evidence-based medicine.

Jessica and Jax—evidence-based medicine in action

Let's look at an example of making evidence-based nutrition decisions for a dog's health. Jessica is a talented young trainer who works for me at my dog training school and teaches group and private agility classes. In addition to training and competing in agility trials with Grace, her Australian Shepherd, Jessica also lives with and loves Jax, her 4-year-old rescued Greyhound. Jax gets along well with Grace and is a great dog, silly and energetic some of the time and a total couch potato the rest of the time. Shortly after he was adopted, Jax began to have intermittent bouts of diarrhea. Episodes were usually related to some type of environmental stress, but Jessica also noticed that Jax tended to have frequent defecations and voluminous fecal output even on his "good days." After multiple veterinary visits and consultations with an internal medicine specialist, a tentative diagnosis of canine inflammatory bowel disorder (IBD) was made for Jax (clinical expertise component). IBD is a general term that encompasses a group of intestinal disorders that are characterized according to the type of inflammatory reaction that the dog experiences, the area of the intestine that is affected, and the cause (if known). Because an underlying cause could not be identified, Jax was treated with anti-inflammatory medication and his diet was switched to a veterinary prescribed food.

Jax's diet was changed because research studies of dogs with IBD have shown success when dogs are fed a highly digestible diet containing a single protein and a single carbohydrate source. If possible, novel (new) protein and carbohydrate sources are selected.

In addition, recent research shows that feeding a food that contains a hydrolyzed (partially digested) protein source may also be effective when the underlying cause of IBD is related to an adverse food reaction (research evidence component). Jax was prescribed a food that contained salmon and potato as the protein and carbohydrate sources, respectively. He liked the food and tolerated it well. Over time, Jessica was able to wean Jax from the anti-inflammatory medications and maintained his GI tract health by feeding just the prescribed diet. However, after several months, the expense of feeding the veterinarian-prescribed food to a 70 pound Greyhound became increasingly difficult for Jessica to manage (client needs and values component). Knowing that published studies have shown that limited ingredient or hydrolyzed protein foods can manage symptoms for dogs with IBD, Jess and I began to research over-the-counter foods that met these criteria but were less expensive than the prescription diet that Jax was being fed. Luckily for Jessica and Jax, the concept of limited ingredient foods has become increasingly popular in recent years and several pet food companies have developed brands that are formulated specifically to this concept. Jessica found a food that was less expensive, contained single protein and single carbohydrate sources that generally conformed with the food she was feeding and gradually switched Jax to the new food. Jax tolerated the change in food and is doing well on his new and more affordable feeding regimen.

All nutrition evidence is not created equal!

How does the approach that Jessica used with Jax differ from the example of the seizing Papillion? The difference lies in the types of evidence that were selected and used to form an opinion and make a decision. A core principle of EBM is the premise that all evidence is not created equal and that a hierarchy of reliability exists. In life we are faced with all types of evidence coming from all sorts of sources. While some pieces of information are emotional, highly suggestive and seem compelling, they are often unreliable. Anecdotes and testimonials typically fall into this category. Conversely, other evidence may make comparatively moderate claims yet be trustworthy and well supported. Scientific studies and clinical case studies generally fall into this category. As we have seen, we need science to counteract the biases that are inherent in our thinking. Nowhere is this more evident than when we seek out new information about nutrition and health. What are some of the types of evidence that we encounter as we attempt to evaluate information about pet health and nutrition and how can we differentiate among them?

Opinions, anecdotes and testimonials

We often pay attention to the **opinions** of others when seeking information about our dogs' care and nutrition. It is natural and human to listen to the viewpoints of friends, family, co-workers and sometimes even Joe next door who happens to know a lot about dogs. A primary reason for this is that, as a social species, we crave the support of others who have experienced similar challenges or health problems with their dogs. In some situations, these experiences are helpful. They provide emotional support and can also suggest options that lead us to additional sources of information. Additionally, opinions that are provided by professionals or colleagues who have years of experience and are considered to be credible sources can be of invaluable help in our decision making. However, we also know that our memories are continually influenced by emotions and that the many cognitive biases that our brains are prone to will skew and change the "facts" that we recall and share with others. Furthermore, we are usually unaware of how these biases influence our opinions. For these reasons, while helpful as a source of emotional support and for constructing potential options, a single person's opinion should not be accepted as irrefutable proof for any type of health care or nutrition claim, no matter how emphatically given or how invested the person may be in his or her beliefs.

Another form of evidence that we are inherently drawn to and interested in is personal **anecdotes**. These are the stories that people tell, which relate their life experiences, usually in a way that is both engaging and entertaining. We all know people who are marvelous story tellers and who can keep a group of friends captivated and entertained as they relate their latest adventures or mishaps. Because anecdotes are typically recalled and related to others on numerous occasions, they are prone to the same errors and distortions that all memories are susceptible to. With the passage of time, some details are omitted, others are inserted, events are exaggerated and time sequences become jumbled. And, without question, anecdotes are impossible to test for accuracy or to control for biases. Interestingly, it is popular for proponents of complementary and alternative medicine to quip "The plural of anecdote is data." This is an untrue and quite misleading statement. The plural of anecdote is *anecdotes*. Simply having *more* unreliable evidence does not add up to reliable evidence. Other than contributing emotional support and perhaps entertainment, we must view anecdotes as inherently problematic in terms of providing reliable information for decision making.

Testimonials are a bit different from opinions and anecdotes, and actually have the potential to be more misleading and harmful. In the pet realm, these are stories that dog owners provide to pet supply companies that relate their experience with the company's products. Testimonials are not controlled in any way and are subject to the same biases that we see with opinions and anecdotes. By definition, testimonials also contain a strong persuasive message (i.e., they "*testify*"). They are used precisely with the intent of persuading others to view a product favorably and then to purchase it. A second failing of testimonials is that they are subject to the "attention-seeking bias" that comes along with seeing one's name (or one's dog) on a website or in an advertisement. This is powerful stuff to those who are chosen to participate and to those who view the testimonial. They provide the "personal experience" and story-telling that we all crave.

And, last but certainly not least, the testimonials that are selected to be included on a website or in an advertisement are without question skewed toward the positive. Think about it. When was the last time that you went to a pet food company's website, clicked on the "dog owner's stories" page, saw a photo of Joe (from next door) and his dog Gypsy, with a caption of Joe's quote that reads: "Yeah, my dog seemed to like his food okay; it did not make him sick, he eats it, and it is pretty cheap. I think I will still keep buying it." People (and marketing agencies) generally do not provide testimonials unless they are trying to convince you of something, and this in itself should raise a few red flags. Moreover, only those testimonials that proclaim extraordinary praise for a given product make it onto the website or into an advertisement. Mediocre endorsements need not apply. Although they make up the most emotionally compelling kind of evidence that is used to promote dog foods and all sorts of health products for our dogs, testimonials are simply not trustworthy as a source of helpful

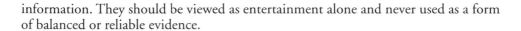

information. They should be viewed as entertainment alone and never used as a form of balanced or reliable evidence.

Scientific evidence

Scientific evidence can come from several sources; these include direct evidence from results produced by nutrition research studies, published reviews of original research in academic journals or journalistic reviews published in the popular media. When we read an **abstract** or the complete paper of an original research study in a science journal, this is referred to as a **primary source**. Because you are reading results as written by the researchers who conducted the study, the chance of the results being misrepresented should be low. An additional safeguard is in the form of something called **peer review**. Most academic journals that publish original research studies require that submitted papers are subjected to complete review by a panel of scientists prior to publication; in our case this means other animal nutritionists. The panel scrutinizes the study's design, execution, statistical analysis, results and conclusions. In a typical scenario, the paper is either accepted without revisions (rare), is returned to the author for a series of revisions that are suggested or required by the panel of peers, or is rejected outright. This "vetting" is a way to ensure that the studies that are published in the journal present information that was obtained using proper scientific method and that can be trusted. Think of peer-reviewed studies as those that are receiving a "Scientific Seal of Approval" from their field of study. (Keep in mind that this seal of approval does not mean that the conclusions are infallible or that new evidence will not come along that challenges the conclusions of the study. It *does* mean, however, that the study met the standards of good scientific practice and the scrutiny of other nutritionists.)

Today, many academic journals provide full-text articles online as PDF files, and almost all journals provide abstracts to their articles online. As an example, Figure 3.3 shows a citation for an original research article reported in the journal *Veterinary Therapeutics,* Figure 3.4 shows the abstract for this paper, and Figure 3.5 summarizes the format that all scientific journals use to report results of original studies. Abstracts are typically restricted to around 250 words and provide an overview of the study's objectives, methodology, results and conclusions. For many people, reading the abstract can provide enough information for their needs; for others, an abstract can determine if you need (or want) to read the entire paper. Keep in mind that all scientists use the jargon of their academic field, which means that there may be technical words in an abstract that are unfamiliar to you (and others that read as if they must be written in an alien tongue). Make it a practice to keep reading along, as the important results are almost always evident, even if some meaning is muddled by the jargon.

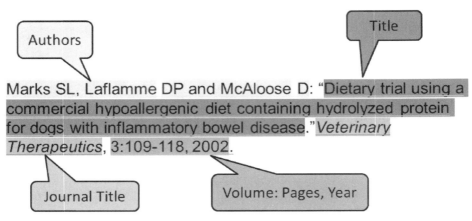

Figure 3.3 Citation example of an original research study
published in a scientific journal (peer-reviewed).

Example of original research study citation and abstract (Figure 3.4)

Marks SL, et al: "Dietary trial using a commercial hypoallergenic diet containing hydrolyzed protein for dogs with inflammatory bowel disease." *Veterinary Therapeutics*, 3:109-118, 2002.

Abstract: Six dogs with inflammatory bowel disease (IBD) received a commercially available hypoallergenic diet containing an enzymatically hydrolyzed defatted soy globulin as the only protein source. Five of the six dogs had been refractory to a variety of controlled diets, and four dogs had failed to respond to previous medical therapy. All dogs were fed the test diet twice daily for 10 weeks. Dogs not showing adequate improvement in clinical signs after 2 to 4 weeks on diet alone had appropriate medical therapy added to the dietary regimen. Gastroduodenoscopy and biopsy were performed on Day 0 and repeated at the conclusion of the study. Intestinal biopsies were evaluated by a pathologist using a numeric grading scheme to describe histologic alterations and mucosal architecture. Dietary therapy alone provided adequate clinical improvement in four dogs, and concurrent medical therapy was required in two dogs, one of which had exocrine pancreatic insufficiency. Mean fecal scores improved after therapy. Five dogs showed mild to moderate histologic improvement in duodenal biopsies after therapy. The clinical improvement observed cannot be solely attributed to the hydrolyzed nature of the protein source because the diet tested was highly digestible, contained cornstarch (rather than intact grains) and a source of medium-chain triglycerides (23% of fat), and had an altered ratio of omega-6 to omega-3 polyunsaturated fatty acids. Nevertheless, the resolution of clinical signs and improved biopsy scores demonstrate the importance of conducting further studies to critically assess the role of diets containing a hydrolyzed protein source for the management of dogs with previously refractory IBD.

Original scientific paper organization (Figure 3.5)

TITLE: The paper's title must be concise and must clearly describe the scope of the study (i.e., what was measured and in what animals).

ABSTRACT: The abstract is a short paragraph, typically limited to 250 words, that identifies the objectives of the study, methods used, significant results and the primary conclusions. (Note: Almost all scientific journals provide article abstracts, free of charge, online.)

INTRODUCTION: A brief section that reviews relevant information about the topic and reviews previous related research. The introduction typically concludes with one or two statements of the current study's objectives.

MATERIALS & METHODS: This section describes the experimental design, study sample and data collection techniques used in the study. With dog nutrition research, this section includes a description of the source of animals (i.e., kenneled dogs or client-owned dogs living in homes), adherence to animal welfare guidelines and regulations, diet composition information (ingredients and nutrients) and the types of statistical tests that were used to analyze data.

RESULTS: Describes but does not interpret the results of all measured comparisons in the study. The results section typically includes one or more tables and graphs that represent data means (averages) and results of statistical tests.

DISCUSSION: Provides the interpretation of the results along with a complete review (and comparison) of previous studies that are relevant to the current study. Clinical or practical significance of the study results are presented, when appropriate.

So, what can a pet food consumer learn from the abstract presented in Figure 3.4? Well, first we notice that the study was small, including only six dogs. Although these numbers are definitely low, it is not unusual to have fewer than twenty dogs included per treatment in a dog nutrition study, especially in a clinical trial such as this. The dogs in this study were client-owned dogs living in homes (as opposed to kenneled research dogs). They were also dogs who had been previously diagnosed with inflammatory bowel disease and whose owners agreed to enroll them in a nutrition study. Given all of these constraints, it is not surprising that the treatment group numbered fewer than ten dogs. Five of the six dogs had not responded to previous dietary changes and four had not responded previously to medical treatment. The experimental diet in this study was a hydrolyzed protein diet that was highly digestible and also included a novel carbohydrate source and a fatty acid profile intended to dampen inflammatory response. (Hydrolyzed refers to a protein source that has been partially digested to reduce size and to attempt to reduce its potential to induce an adverse response.) All of the dogs were fed the test diet for a ten-week period (i.e., there was no control group of dogs in this study). During the treatment period, four of the six dogs responded favorably to the new food. In addition, improvements in dogs' fecal scores (i.e., a reduction in diarrhea) was seen, as well as signs of intestinal healing. A notable weakness of this study was that a control group that did not receive treatment was not included. Although each dog's initial state of health was used as a control, an experimental design such as this cannot account for changes that may have occurred over time regardless of treatment (i.e., a post hoc error might occur in a study that is designed in this way). A strength of this study is that it was conducted using owned dogs, living in homes, who were affected by inflammatory bowel disease. Such studies are difficult to set up, to recruit patients for and complete, and are enormously expensive to conduct. For this reason, this study (primary source) may be helpful information to a pet professional who is trying to determine how to feed a dog such as Jax.

A second reliable source of nutrition information is review papers that are published in academic journals. Like original research papers, these articles are subjected to peer review prior to publication. As such, review articles can provide an excellent source of information for dog professionals, because most journals will only publish reviews that are written by experts in the field. For example, Figure 3.6 presents an abstract of a paper that was written by Dr. Joseph Wakshlag, a veterinarian and professor at Cornell College of Veterinary Medicine. His review of nutritional agents that are being used in cancer treatment in dogs was published in the *Compendium for Continuing Education for Veterinarians* in 2011. In this paper, Wakshlag reviews the safety and toxicity studies of these compounds and makes recommendations for their use. This paper is a reliable source of information for three primary reasons: (1) Wakshlag is a credentialed expert in both internal medicine and animal nutrition; (2) His paper reviews studies that were published in peer-reviewed journals; (3) *The Compendium* is a nationally recognized and respected journal of veterinary science.

Example of review paper citation and abstract (Figure 3.6)

Wakshlag, JJ: "Flavonoids: Not just for cancer anymore." *Compendium of Continuing Education for Veterinarians* 33:E1-E4, 2011.

Increasingly, veterinary clients are using nutraceuticals as adjuvant treatment for a variety of ailments in their pets. Recent evidence suggests that more than 50% of clients who have companion animals with cancer are using a nutraceutical and/or supplement as part of the treatment plan, and 65% of these clients say their veterinarian approves. This trend does not extend to healthy pets, of which only 10% receive routine supplements. Unfortunately, few resources regarding the safety of nutraceutical use exist, and recent evidence has shown that doses of human-formulated supplements such as lipoic acid can be toxic to cats. Veterinarians need a better understanding of the metabolism and safe upper limits for commonly used nutraceuticals because many clients are giving these products to their pets, often in human formulations. This article focuses primarily on two flavonoids: epigallocathechin-3-O-gallate (EGCG), a flavanol found in green tea, and genistein, an isoflavone found in soy.

This leads us to the third and most frequently used source of scientific evidence for dog nutrition information: popular media. In addition to being easily accessed, the type of information that popular press media provides is also the most diverse and thus difficult to judge. For dog folks, several widely popular magazines that publish information about nutrition include the *Whole Dog Journal, The Bark* and *Dog Fancy*. Online sources of nutrition information that dog owners and professionals may use include PetMD (www.petmd.com), VetInfo (www.vetinfo.com) and WebMD Pets (pets.webmd.com). Some of the articles that are published in dog magazines and on websites are well researched and contain scientifically sound information. As a rule of thumb, articles in popular press media that are written by either an animal nutritionist or a veterinary nutritionist are most reliable. If a pet journalist (usually a layperson, not a trained scientist) wrote the article, it should include primary source information—this means either direct interviews with experts or reference to studies that have been published in scientific journals.

Conversely, articles written by dog enthusiasts who have no formal training in science or in nutrition must be viewed with a critical eye, even if they have the look and feel of a scientific paper. A primary problem with magazine pieces is that they exist to sell magazines and they are typically short summaries of information that may or may not include the biases of the writer. In all spheres of popular media, the underlying motivations of grabbing the two-second attention span of internet surfers and boosting readership cause writing to tilt towards sensationalized headlines and misleading claims. If overtly persuasive speech or the denigration of alternative approaches are used, consider this form of hyperbole to be a red flag. Put on your skeptic's hat, and continue your search for complete and well-supported information. As we will see, asking a few key critical thinking questions when reading online articles and researching a topic using the internet can help you to differentiate between information that is evidence-based and information that is biased, intended to mislead or that is just plain wrong.

The "Evidence Pyramid" of dog nutrition studies

In addition to considering the source of nutrition information, you must be a critical consumer in terms of the studies themselves. Science-based evidence can be viewed as the sum of multiple research investigations, preferably from different investigators. A single study (or article or blog) should never be used as irrefutable proof for a given nutritional claim. Let me repeat this: *A single study (or article or blog) should never be used as irrefutable proof for a given nutritional claim.* This is vitally important in an age of proliferating claims accompanied by dwindling evidence. Because it is now easier than ever before in our history as humans to repeat and disseminate information, we often seen the same opinion/anecdote/testimonial repeated over and over and over again through different internet sources. And, of course, this can lead to the availability error, that heuristic that tells our brain *if you see it often, it must be true.* Nowhere before in our history is this less true than it is today. Just because I tell you over and over again that the moon is made of green cheese makes this no less false the 1,000th time that I tell you this than it was the very first time! Yet, we have an unconscious bias toward believing things that we see/hear/read often over those that are less "available" to us. And as we will see later in this book, pet food marketing folks know all too well how to exploit the availability heuristic!

There is a simple **pyramid** that is used in evidence-based medicine to rank scientific evidence. Figure 3.7 (on page 41) shows a modified version that can be used to rank nutrition studies regarding their relevance and importance as evidence. At the base of the pyramid are **studies** that are typically the impetus for researching a particular nutrient or ingredient or diet. Within the field of dog nutrition, these have historically been studies with other species such as humans, laboratory animals or farm animals (usually pigs) whose results were used to develop a hypothesis for application with dogs. Also at the base, but somewhat less common in nutrition, are studies that are conducted **in vitro** (in the laboratory) that suggest a benefit or a need for a particular nutrient or ingredient. The wide base represents a general trend that the initial studies are most numerous, while being on the bottom of the pyramid tells us that these studies also should be viewed as being relatively low in practical importance to dog feeding. As you move up the pyramid, you see "**case studies and case reports**" at the second level. Many dog folks are surprised that case reports are not regarded as stronger scientific evidence. While these reports can provide support for a hypothesis, case studies also have serious flaws, most importantly the lack of control groups. Cases are often collected anecdotally and can lack the objectiveness that is required by the steps of the scientific method.

The next level up is "**controlled and randomized feeding trials**." In dog nutrition, these are usually the most important type of supporting evidence and are considered to be the "Gold Standard" of scientific evidence. These generally include studies that are conducted at universities (typically at either veterinary schools or in animal sciences departments) and those that are conducted by pet food companies. The dogs who are used in these studies are either kennel (research) dogs owned by the university or company or they are client-owned dogs living in homes. At the apex of the pyramid you see the phrase "**systematic review.**" This refers to a specific type of review in which an expert in the field conducts an assessment of all of the relevant studies that address a particular topic. A specific set of criteria is used to locate, organize and assess the entire body of literature on a particular hypothesis or clinical application. Because this type of review often also includes a quantitative pooling of all data (called a meta-analysis), it is considered to be the most reliable type of evidence. That said, because systematic reviews require enormous commitments of effort, time and money, and because they are only possible once a hypothesis has been studied in depth, these studies are few in number.

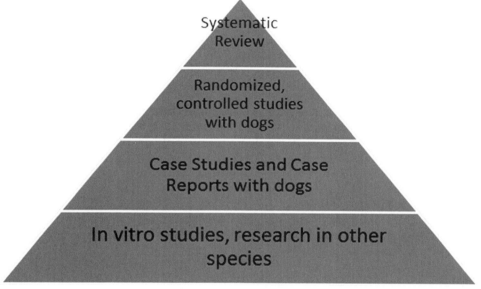

Figure 3.7 Evidence pyramid of dog nutrition studies.

The evidence pyramid in practice: Should you feed prebiotics to your dog?

Let's take a look at an actual dog feeding example. Prebiotics are specific types of dietary fiber that, when included in the diet, can support intestinal health. Examples of prebiotics that you may see included on a dog food label include fructooligosaccharide (FOS), soybean oligosaccharides (SOS), lactulose and inulin. Of the large group of prebiotic fibers (and sources), FOS has been the most extensively studied using feeding trials with dogs. The prevailing hypothesis is that prebiotics can provide benefit to the gut by influencing the number and type of microbial populations that reside there. Prebiotics have been shown to promote bacterial populations in the intestine that are beneficial to the gut and inhibit microbes that are not beneficial or are even potentially pathogenic. They exert these effects by acting as a food source for these bacterial species. While the "good" bacteria can digest (ferment) prebiotics, the "bad" bacterial cannot, which (theoretically) leads to a situation in the gut in which you are "feeding the good bugs and starving the bad bugs." So, let's follow our evidence pyramid to help us decide if including prebiotics in a dog's diet might be beneficial (or not).

The original impetuses for a hypothesis regarding prebiotics for dogs were studies showing a benefit of prebiotics when fed to production animals such as pigs, and a few studies showing benefits in human subjects. A young graduate student named Greg Sunvold was studying comparative nutrition at the University of Illinois during the early 1990s. He became interested in prebiotics and their intestinal action in different species. As part of his PhD work, Sunvold developed a laboratory technique (in vitro) that essentially mimicked the microbial environment of the dog's large intestine. Using this "model" he was able to follow the digestion (which is actually fermentation for fibers) of various types of prebiotic to determine which might be beneficial to dogs and which either did nothing at all or were potentially harmful (i.e., could cause diarrhea). Following the initial set of in vitro studies, certain prebiotic fibers that looked promising were selected for additional study. These were incorporated into a complete and balanced dog food at various levels and fed to dogs in controlled feeding trials. The first series of dog studies was conducted with dogs living in research facilities to allow careful control of each dog's diet, environment, health and exercise. These studies allowed nutritionists to refine the prebiotic fibers into "fiber blends" that provided the best benefit to dogs' intestinal health while still supporting diet digestibility and normal stool quality (an important diet characteristic for dog owners).

At this point in the game, many pet food companies were jumping on board as Sunvold's work was published and his results disseminated, with each company studying its own particular prebiotic blend or individual source of prebiotics such as chicory or beet pulp. Most conducted feeding trials with dogs and many patented prebiotic fiber blends to use in their foods. Collectively, these studies support the benefits of some types of prebiotic fibers in the diets of dogs and definitely show us that dogs *do* need to have fiber in their diets, with most benefit coming from a blend of fiber types. Figure 3.8 shows our pyramid of evidence once again, with a sampling of the published studies within each category that examined prebiotics and gut health in dogs. (For a list of the papers plus their abstracts, see Appendix 1).

Are there any weaknesses or red flags in the "prebiotic pyramid"? Perhaps a few. First, you will notice that (as of late 2012) no in-home feeding trials of the effects of prebiotics with client-owned dogs have been published in the literature. This means that we do not have evidence of intestinal health benefit to a variety of dog breeds, ages or activity levels of dogs who live in homes with owners. This is a weakness for these data and should be considered. In addition, a review of the actual papers will show us that at least one study failed to show a benefit of prebiotics in terms of changes to gut microbe populations. That study, along with those that report a benefit, must also be considered when evaluating all of the evidence. Finally, because it is a relatively new area of study, a systematic review of prebiotics (with dogs) has not yet been conducted. When one looks at the cumulative evidence for including prebiotics in the diet of dogs, it appears that these are probably healthful fiber sources in terms of providing the gut with needed substrate for the production of short-chain fatty acids (a fermentative end product that is beneficial to cells of the intestine), but may or may not impact microbial growth and health conditions that are affected by changes in intestinal microbe populations. In other words, prebiotics probably provide a healthful fiber source for dogs but they should not be viewed as a dietary treatment for intestinal diseases because there is not ample evidence that supports this type of use or claim.

Faber TA, et al: Galactoglucomannan oligosaccharide supplementation affects nutrient digestibility, fermentation end-product production, and large bowel microbiota of the dog, J Anim Sci 89:103-112. 2011

Barry KA, et al: Low-level fructan supplementation of dogs enhances nutrient digestion and modifies stool metabolite concentrations, but does not alter fecal microbiota populations, J Anim Sci 87:3244-3252, 2009.

Middelbos IS, et al: Evaluation of fermentable oligosaccharides in diets fed to dogs in comparison to fiber standards, *J Anim Sci*; 85:3033-3044,2007

Flickinger, B, et al: Nutrient digestibilities, microbial populations, and protein catabolites as affected by fructan supplementation of dog diets, J Anim Sci 81:2008-2018, 2003

Sunvold, et al: In vitro fermentation of selected fiber sources by dog fecal inoculum and in vivo digestion and metabolism of fiber-supplemented diets, *J AnimSci* 73:1099-1109, 1995.

Sunvold GD, et al: In vitro fermentation of selected fibrous substrates by dog and cat fecal inoculum: influence of diet composition on substrate organic matter disappearance and short-chain fatty acid production, J Anim Sci 73:1110-1122, 1995

Figure 3.8 Study evidence pyramid for the use of prebiotics in dog foods.

The science sleuth—finding the evidence

So, how do pet professionals and pet owners *find* the science-based evidence that they need to make well-informed decisions for their dogs? If you do not work at a university or are personally engaged in a research field, you may feel that it is difficult or impossible to locate this type of information. But remember—this is the information age! Many types of evidence are available to everyone, well at least to everyone who has access to a computer and the internet. Let's explore a few of the fastest and easiest ways to become a Science Sleuth for your dog's nutritional health.

Canine nutrition on the internet

The internet is truly an information highway; and like a highway there are careful drivers and there are crazy and irresponsible maniacs! As you ferret out information for your dog's (and your clients' dogs') nutritional health, it is important to find the careful and reliable sources and to ignore the crazy ones. Let's begin with a few easy distinctions. The origins of a website can tell you a lot about reliability. For example, sites that end with .edu are educational institutions. If the site is a veterinary college or animal sciences department at a major university, they are likely to provide science-based information that comes from primary sources. Similarly, sites that end in .org are non-profit organizations. These can provide balanced educational information about canine nutrition, but may also have biases that are in line with their mission. Sites that end in .gov are government websites. In the case of nutrition information, these sites are typically those that are involved with regulatory oversight of pet food and pet food safety (more about these in Chapter 11).

A few recommendations

When you are looking for published research reports, the best place to start is with either a search engine that specializes in scientific information or with academic journals that regularly publish peer-reviewed papers about canine nutrition. Online academic paper search engines that are free and easy to use include Medline and Science Direct (see Figure 3.9). Abstracts of nutrition articles are available online and can be found by selecting search words that capture the topic that you are interested in. Using our previous example, a search on Google Scholar using the phrase "dog nutrition prebiotics" will provide you with a selection of articles. These can be used as a starting point for additional searches. For example, selecting the "cited by" link on a particular article will find more recent related papers that referenced the selected study. Although many journals provide only abstracts for free, some do provide full text articles as PDF files and some authors make their work available online. (Here is a tip: Once you have found an article that you are interested in, try copy/pasting its title into a Google search—not Google Scholar—to find out if a full-text version of the paper is available elsewhere. Often, you will be pleasantly surprised!)

Recommended search engines

- Google Scholar: www.scholar.google.com/

- PubMed/Medline: www.ncbi.nlm.nih.gov/pubmed/

- Science Direct: www.sciencedirect.com/

- Scirus: www.scirus.com/srsapp/

Recommended peer-reviewed journals

- Journal of Nutrition

- Journal of Animal Science

- Journal of Veterinary Research

- Journal of the American Veterinary Medical Association

- Journal of Animal Physiology and Animal Nutrition

- International Journal of Applied Veterinary Research

*Figure 3.9 Internet search engines and peer-reviewed journals
as sources for science-based nutrition information.*

Internet sources to be wary of

While the internet is a great resource, it is also a source of misinformation, exaggeration and outright lies. Anyone can publish a blog on the internet and can say just about anything that they like. This poses an obvious problem with using a blog as a research source, as there is often no way to know the credentials of bloggers or to obtain an understanding of a writer's level of expertise. So, first and foremost, ignore blogs and websites of unknown or un-credentialed writers, except for entertainment or social value. Today, people also use various types of wiki websites for their information. While some wiki sites and topics are well researched and can be informative, they can also be untrustworthy. Wiki sites allow groups of people to add and edit the information contained on the pages with little or no oversight. (Remember how important peer review is!) Last, generally speaking, television and print news sources can be used to provide a general overview of a topic but should never be relied upon exclusively, especially when making health-related decisions for your dog. Both network and cable news stations are involved in entertainment and are motivated by the need to increase viewership and readership. In all cases, for all information, the bottom line is: *check the source*. An internet article that is published by a reputable research organization, nutritionist or veterinarian, or the scientist who conducted the research provides the most reliable sources of nutrition information.

Putting it into practice: asking the right questions

So, you know where to look for information about dog nutrition, you know the types of studies and journals to use, and you have an idea about the types of studies that are important to look for. Let's finish up with a few essential guidelines to follow and questions to ask as you make your way through the mountain of information that is available as you become a critical consumer for your dog's (and the dogs of your clients) nutritional health.

Be skeptical of sensational claims

Most of us are emotionally invested in giving our dogs the very best of care to keep them healthy and to treat them when they are sick. Because nutrition and diet are something that we can readily modify without extensive testing or even a visit to the veterinarian, and because there are a plethora of ingredients, nutrients, additives and preservatives to target and identify as problematic, sensational and unsupported claims abound in the field of dog nutrition. It is prudent and just downright smart to be skeptical of claims that either promote spectacular health results or condemn a particular ingredient or nutrient as a cause of illness. Moreover, given the environment of online social media today, remember that stating the same piece of information on 100,000 different blogs or websites does not make that piece of information any more or less true than it was the first time it was posted. There exist a set of regulations that limit the types of claims that pet food companies are allowed to make on their package labels and in advertisements (more about these in Chapter 10). However, because of the very important right to free speech, no such restrictions exist regarding claims made by individual dog owners who write blogs and promote their pet nutrition theories (pun intended). This does not mean that the claims that an individual may make are necessarily false; rather it means that the onus must always be upon the claimant to support his statements with reliable scientific evidence. It is this second step that is often severely deficient or altogether absent when we read spectacular claims about nutrition. As my grandfather, Poppy, used to quip *"If it sounds too good to be true, it probably is."*

Watch the language

A difference between information that lacks scientific support and information that has it can often be found in the nature of the language that is used. The scientific method, by definition, requires precise language. And once again, this language can be dry, unemotional and well...sometimes a tad boring! (At least it seems boring when compared with the extravagant claims and highly emotional testimonials that are used as marketing hooks when solid evidence is lacking.) Conclusions that are made from the results of a research study must address only what the experiment measured plus prior related study results. Conversely, proponents of a diet or supplement who are not reporting scientific evidence or who are simply trying to sell you something are under no such obligation. This is an important distinction. Prudence is a fundamental feature of the scientific method and this caution results in gradual progress as understanding expands. Conversely, claims that are made in overstated language, that boast of 100% confidence or that make outrageous promises are to be viewed with a critical (or even suspicious) eye.

Use original sources

Whenever a claim is made, especially if that claim refers to a study, always search for the original source of the information. In the case of scientific research, reputable journalists always identify the name of the investigator and the place that the study was conducted. Secondary sources can provide excellent overviews and are a nice shortcut for learning about a new topic, but should always be viewed critically, keeping in mind that crucial information may have been left out or results may not be presented exactly as they occurred. When in doubt, find the original source.

Ask questions

Whenever you read about a new ingredient, a claim about a food or nutrient or a study showing the benefits of a new product, put on your critical thinking hat and ask questions before you accept the information as valid. When reviewing nutrition and feeding studies with dogs, here are a few important questions to ask:

Who conducted (and funded) the study? Research studies in companion animal nutrition are primarily conducted by either animal nutritionists or veterinarians in academia or by nutritionists who work for pet food companies. The studies are conducted either at veterinary colleges, in animal science departments at universities or at animal facilities that are owned by the pet food company. The major funding agencies for pet nutrition studies are pet food companies, most typically large companies that have robust research and development departments. Some funding is also available through government agencies and from non-profit animal organizations, but these groups generally make up a much smaller portion of study funding. The situation is not unlike the current pharmaceutical or human nutrition industry. Without a doubt, pet food companies have biases and vested interests in study results that will support sale of their products or allow them to make a label claim for a new ingredient or diet matrix. We must also be aware that, just as these biases affect the consumer's ability to make decisions and interpret information, so too do they influence researchers. These facts further emphasize the importance of using peer-reviewed journals as primary sources of information. (And remember, if no research is being performed or reported in journals, you have no evidence at all for claims that are made!). Knowing that a pet food company either conducted a study directly or funded a study is important information, but by itself does not automatically discredit the information that is obtained from the study. Knowing the source of funding and where a study was conducted is paramount, as it helps to keep our critical thinking caps firmly in place.

How many animals were included in the study? Several years ago, I attended a training course for users of the statistics program that I use in my nutrition consulting business. At that time I was working with a pet food company's nutritionists who had a series of in-home studies in progress that were examining the effectiveness of using diet to help to control several forms of allergic skin disease in dogs. The study groups that I had in my data sets generally included between 30 and 40 dogs per treatment group (i.e., that were being fed either one of the test diets or a control food). I sat next to a gentleman who worked for a pharmaceutical company and we chatted briefly about the studies that we each brought with us to use as examples during the training course. His study groups, comprised of human patients, numbered over 2,000! (We had a little "statisticians chuckle" when I commented wryly that I was experiencing major "data envy" comparing my tiny dog treatment groups to his.) By and large, numbers are always a challenge with dog nutrition studies, especially when in-home studies are conducted. Therefore, controlling these studies is of utmost importance, so that when differences are real, we can pick them up statistically (see below). Without question, bigger study groups are always better than small study groups. Dog nutrition studies that include ten or more dogs per treatment group are common; if the study includes more than 20 to 30 dogs per treatment group, consider it a rock star.

Are the results statistically significant? Statistical analysis of data and the conclusions that can be made from statistical tests are essential for evaluating scientific information. Despite the many jokes about statistics and their purported ability to skew results to say whatever the researcher wants the statistics to say, this is simply not true. Statistics are essential for distinguishing between results that are *real* (i.e., the new diet really was helpful) and results that are meaningless. The best way to think about statistics is that they provide a mathematical method for determining whether the results that you find in a study reflect a true effect or if the results that that you find were simply due to random chance. A frequently used statistical barometer of this is called the P-value, with "P" standing for "probability." For example, when a P-value of 0.05 is used, this means that when a statistically significant difference is reported between the test diet and the control diet, the probability that chance alone will produce such findings is just 0.05, or 5%. The flip side of this is that the researchers would be *95% confident* that the observed (significant) effect was real and due to a true effect rather than due to chance alone. Therefore, in a nutshell, statistics provide us with confidence in the validity of study results. As a rule of thumb, studies that do not report results of statistical analysis should not be trusted, and when statistics are reported, only those results that are "statistically significant at P-values of 0.05 or less" should be considered reliable.

Were the study results replicated by other researchers? Another advantage of using the scientific method and publishing in academic journals is that the format journals use is designed to enable other investigators to repeat the experiment that is described. Most journal articles are divided into six primary sections; these include the title, abstract, introduction, materials and methods, results and discussion section (see Figure 3.5 on page 37). This standard format helps other investigators to replicate part or all of a study's design when attempting to provide additional evidence for a theory or when conducting a similar study. A key feature to demonstrating whether or not something really works is repeated testing by different investigators in different populations. In the case of dog nutrition studies, it is common for a new diet to be first tested in research dogs living in kennels and eventually to be tested clinically, with client-owned dogs living in homes. Preferably, although not always the case, results that support a particular theory will come from different sources and different funding groups.

Do the study's conclusions fit with what we already know and understand about canine nutrition? Finally, are the results of a study consistent with other findings in the field? Carl Sagan once famously quipped "Extraordinary claims require extraordinary evidence." This is true in all areas of study, including dog nutrition. If an extravagant claim is being made for a new diet or approach to feeding, and if that claim does not fit well with what is currently known and understood, then the bar must be set quite high to prove that the claim is valid. Consistency and the preponderance of evidence are the cement of scientific knowledge. A study whose results seem to refute an entire body of research is not necessarily wrong, but must offer strong (and statistically significant) evidence in its support. Is there corroboration with other nutritionists? Have the findings been checked by other experts? This is one of the most important questions that you can ask when looking at a study or evaluating a claim that someone makes to you about nutrition.

Be aware of cognitive biases and logical fallacies (your own and others)

Congratulations! You are now properly prepared to be a critical consumer for your dog's nutritional health! You are aware of how your brain naturally gravitates toward and responds to emotional experiences and information as well as the cognitive biases that influence the ways that you process information and make choices. In addition, you are able to distinguish between information that is reliable and that which is not and to identify information that is evidence-based through use of the scientific method. It is now time to jump into the fray of canine nutritional science. We will begin by looking at what we actually *know* from research about how to feed our dogs well, and how you can use this knowledge to inform the choices that you make for your dogs, throughout their lives.

4

What's So Special About a Dog's Nutritional Needs?

During my years of teaching canine nutrition to college students, teaching training classes to dog owners and providing educational materials and training programs to staff in the pet food industry, I have come to believe that, as a profession, companion animal nutritionists have generally done a poor job of educating dog lovers regarding *exactly what we do know* about dog (and cat) nutrition. It is my hope that this book will bridge this gap and provide you with both the tools for critical thinking and enough nutrition information about dogs to help you to make well-supported and informed choices for your dog's nutritional health. For those of you who are pet professionals, this information will help you to guide and advise your clients when they ask you the most frequently asked question: "What should I feed my dog?" (This is typically followed by "What do you feed your dogs?")

As we have seen in earlier chapters, when compared with hyperbole and extravagant health claims, the evidence that science provides seems to plod along at a snail's pace and often is about as exciting as watching paint dry. The fact that science-based evidence does not scream at us in sensationalist language or excite emotion to the same degree that someone claiming to cure cancer with a nutrient elixir might does not mean that we should throw in the towel, give up and just listen to Joe next door who seems to know a lot about dogs. Rather, we need (and should demand) solid, science-based sources of nutrition information that both inform and motivate us to choose well for our dogs. However, I also realize that nutrition can be dry as dirt and that most nutrition books are not considered to be great bedside reading material. So, here's the deal: I am going to provide as much nutrition-packed information as possible in the next several chapters while at the same time giving you plenty of examples and stories. (Uh oh—anecdotes! You know to now place your skeptic's hat squarely upon your head!) My hope is to make the process a lot more palatable (tasty!) as well as to provide examples that will help this information to "stick" given that we now know that humans best remember events and facts that are associated with some type of experience or story. Let's begin with an examination of what we know versus what we may believe or wish to be true about a dog's nutritional needs. First, a basic and oft-discussed question about dogs: What are they—carnivores or omnivores?

Dogs are carnivores, right?

There is a great deal of confusion (and opinion) today regarding how to classify the domestic dog. Those who identify dogs as **carnivores** (meat-eating) animals tend to focus on the predatory nature of the dog's closest cousin, the wolf. Conversely, those who are inclined to classify the dog as an **omnivore** (consumes both plants and meat) rely upon the dog's scavenging nature and ability to consume and digest a wide variety of food types. So, which is it? And perhaps more importantly, why does what we call the dog, carnivore or omnivore, seem to matter so much to us?

First, some confusion can arise from the dual use of the term "carnivore." This term is used as both a taxonomic classification and as a description of a species' feeding behavior and nutrient needs. Both dogs and cats are classified within the taxonomic order of *Carnivora* (Figure 4.1), a diverse group of mammals that includes over 280 different species. While many of the species within *Carnivora* hunt and consume meat, not all are predatory or nutritionally carnivorous. The *Carnivora* species vary considerably in the degree of dependency that they have upon a meat-based diet. For example, all of the cat species, including our domestic cat, *Felis catus,* are obligate carnivores (see definition below). In contrast, bears and raccoons consume both plant and animal foods, while the giant panda subsists on a vegetarian diet. Therefore, while all of the species within the order called *Carnivora* can eat meat, their typical feeding behaviors exist along a broader spectrum, ranging from the obligate carnivores at one end to animals that are almost completely herbivorous (plant-eating) at the other end. Where does the dog fall along this spectrum?

Taxonomy of the dog and cat		
Taxonomic Group	**Dog**	**Cat**
Phylum	Animalia	Animalia
Class	Mammalia	Mammalia
Order	Carnivora	Carnivora
Family	Canidae	Felidae
Genus	Canis	Felis
Species	Familiaris	Catus

Figure 4.1 Taxonomic classification of the domestic dog (Canis familiaris) and cat (Felis catus).

Let's consider this question by comparing our two best animal friends, the dog and the cat. The label "obligate carnivore" (sometimes called "true carnivore") means that the cat is incapable of surviving on a vegetarian diet and must have at least some meat (animal tissue) in its diet. This means that a diet that comprises all plant materials cannot meet all of the cat's essential nutrient needs. Specific nutrients that are problematic if Fluffy is fed a vegetarian diet include vitamin A, a type of amino acid called taurine, and an essential fatty acid called arachidonic acid. All three of these nutrients are found in forms that cats can use in meat products and but which are *not* found in plant foods. During evolution, cats either lost or never developed the ability to produce these nutrients in the body from the precursor forms that are found in plant foods. In contrast, all of the canid species, including the domestic dog, are more generalist in their eating habits and subsequently in their nutrient needs. In the wild, wolves and coyotes exist as opportunistic predators, hunting and eating the type of prey that happens to be available. In addition to the flesh of their prey, wild canids readily consume viscera (stomach, intestines) which contain partially digested plant matter. Canid species also scavenge carrion and garbage and regularly consume fruits, berries, mushrooms and a variety of other plant materials. Similar to its wild cousins, the domestic dog is a predatory species that also consumes plant foods and scavenges, and is capable of consuming and obtaining nutrition from a wide variety of food types.

Not only does the dog naturally choose a wider variety of foods to eat than do cats, the dog is capable of deriving needed nutrients from plant foods more efficiently than cats. Let's look at the three nutrients that we mentioned earlier: vitamin A, taurine and arachidonic acid. First, like other omnivores (such as humans and pigs) the dog can produce vitamin A from a pigment called beta-carotene, which is found in plants (think carrots). Arachidonic acid (AA) is an essential fatty acid that is found as part of the cell structure in almost all cells in the body. Cats, but not dogs, require this fatty acid in the diet because they are unable to make enough of it in the body to meet their daily needs. Therefore, they need to get this nutrient from their diet. Arachidonic acid is found only in meats, not plant sources. By contrast, the dog does *not* need a dietary source of AA because the dog can produce this nutrient from another essential fatty acid called linoleic acid. And, you guessed it, a major source of linoleic acid is plant foods. Last, taurine also is found only in animal tissues. The cat has an unusually high demand for taurine while dogs have both a lower requirement and are able to use alternative compounds in the body when taurine is lacking, for example when they are fed a plant-based diet. Finally, anatomically, dogs' gastrointestinal tracts, from their mouths to their intestines, are consistent with other predatory species (i.e., meat-eating) that consume a varied diet. They have some ability to grind food (molars), and possess a small intestine that is longer in length (relative to body size) than that of obligate carnivores, but that is shorter in relative length than that of herbivorous species. Altogether, the nutrient, metabolic and anatomical characteristics of dogs place them on the omnivorous side of the spectrum within the wide range of species that hunt prey, scavenge and consume plant foods (Figure 4.2).

Essential nutrient	Cat	Dog
Vitamin A	Requires preformed active vitamin A (retinol), which is found only in animal tissue	Can convert beta-carotene from plants to active vitamin A (retinol) to meet requirements
Arachidonic acid	Has a dietary requirement for arachidonic acid, an essential fatty acid supplied only by animal tissue	Does not have a dietary requirement; can produce enough arachidonic acid to meet needs from its precursor, linoleic acid, which is supplied by plants
Taurine	Has a high metabolic requirement for taurine, which is found only in animal tissue; cannot use metabolic alternatives	Does not have a high metabolic need for taurine during most life stages; can use metabolic alternatives

Figure 4.2 Essential nutrient comparison.

When we look at the evidence, we see that both nutritionally and taxonomically, the dog is best classified as an omnivore, an animal that consumes and derives nutrition from *both* animal and plant food sources. More specifically, the dog evolved from a species that made its living primarily through hunting and consuming prey but that also consumed whatever was available through scavenging. (Anyone who lives with a Golden Retriever is well acquainted with the scavenging part…more about this later.) So, why is it that we read multiple websites and listen to certain "*experts*" who insist that the dog is a carnivore? Indeed, not to put too fine a point on it, many proponents of the "dog as carnivore" hold on to this conviction like a dog with a meaty bone. One may wonder: why is this distinction even important, except perhaps for academic interest? My own opinion is that the keen interest that we see in recent years is caused by an unusual and somewhat unprecedented focus on a desire to "feed dogs naturally." Oddly enough, prior to the development of commercially prepared dog foods in the early 1900s, domestic dogs were fed naturally—they were fed scraps of human food—in other words, they scavenged. So, we appear to have come full circle, with the only difference being that the fervent adherence to a mantra of "feeding dogs naturally" now focuses on the dog's hunting and meat-eating history rather than on its equally significant existence as a proficient scavenger.

The naturalistic fallacy

Proponents of the "dog as carnivore" theory often use identification of the dog as a carnivore as an argument for feeding dogs "prey model" or "raw meat" diets, promoting what they believe to be a natural diet for dogs. These arguments are more emotional than scientific in nature, however, and fall prey (pun intended) to one of those pesky cognitive errors. In this case, the error is a logical fallacy called the **naturalistic fallacy**. The naturalistic fallacy refers to claims that something is better or more healthful because it is either a natural behavior or because it is a product that contains only natural ingredients. In the case of dog nutrition, both of these claims are frequently made. The first pertains to our present discussion of the dog's history as a hunting species. The second has to do with the types of ingredients that are included in commercial pet foods. Let's examine these claims and how they relate to the naturalistic fallacy.

We know that the dog's closest relative and ancestor, the wolf, is a hunting species. It is also without question that most dogs have retained at least portions of the wolf's predatory behaviors. They stalk, they chase, they grab and some even shake and kill (albeit fluffy stuffed toys for most). The naturalistic argument maintains that because of this history, domestic dogs are therefore *best* fed as if they were still a hunting animal. Proponents of this argument state that because hunting is a natural behavior for dogs, obtaining food that is similar to prey that was hunted is more healthful. A second and related naturalistic claim has to do with the type of ingredients that are included in a particular food. In recent years, pet food label claims of "All Natural Ingredients" have become popular with many pet owners. This naturalistic assertion usually refers to the type of preservatives that are used to protect nutrients in processed foods as well as to the avoidance of artificial colors and additives. Most commonly, naturally-derived antioxidants such as vitamin E (mixed tocopherols), vitamin C (ascorbic acid) and rosemary extract are used as preservatives in foods that carry a claim of "all natural."

Two specific logical flaws are made when a claim of natural behavior is put forward as an argument for the superiority of a feeding approach. The first and most important has to do with the notion that identifying something as natural is synonymous with it being superior to other things that are identified as being "less natural." Certainly, when asked, most people would say that they would prefer to take a "natural" remedy over an "artificial" or synthetic treatment. Similarly, a substantial number of people prefer human foods that have "all natural" ingredients and also prefer to feed their dogs foods that contain naturally-derived ingredients. However, these beliefs only can follow from the assumption that "goodness" or superiority *automatically* follows from naturalness. Though this *may* be true, it is not necessarily so. Let's look at a different example. Let's say that you came over to my home for dinner one evening. While sipping drinks on the deck prior to our meal, you comment about the beauty of my flower garden this summer, in particular a plant that has a pretty starfish-shaped leaf and fuzzy red flowers. "Oh yes!" I reply, "That is a castor oil plant. The neat thing about it is that it also produces beans. I have made a castor bean salad for our dinner this evening. Everything in it is fresh and natural—right out of my garden!" If you had your wits about you (and have not fallen for the naturalistic fallacy), you would excuse yourself immediately and run for the hills, seeing that your hostess (me) appears to be trying to poison you. The castor oil plant (*Ricinus communis*), in particular the seeds (beans) that it produces, is the source or ricin, one of the most toxic and deadly neurotoxins known to man. Ingesting just four to five castor beans is a fatal dose for an adult human. Natural? You bet! Good for you? Not so much. As you are bolting out of my yard, you faintly hear me calling after you "Wait, wait, you are leaving before the main course, raw red colobus monkey, the prey that our closest relative, the chimpanzee hunts and eats! Isn't our ancestral diet so very healthful?!'"

So, putting my cooking skills aside for a moment, even if we agree that hunting is a natural behavior for dogs (it is), as is eating raw meat (and carrion and garbage—remember they scavenge too), and that certain dog food ingredients are more natural than others, what follows from this knowledge? The answer is: *Nothing at all.* There is no rational reason to believe that, just because something can be classified as *natural* for dogs (feeding raw, feeding only a diet that includes naturally-derived preservatives), that it without question follows that these things are *better* for dogs. A claim for providing superior nutrition, for promoting health or for being safer does not follow from a claim of naturalness without *evidence* of such benefit. Something natural *can* be better, no doubt at all. However, the benefits must stand on evidence, not simply on a classification of being natural. If feeding raw or feeding only foods that are preserved with vitamin E has health advantages, then we must demonstrate those independently, not through a general claim of being natural.

A second problem with naturalistic claims for our dogs' health is a pervasive lack of consistency. We cherry pick specific behaviors and diet components that we choose to use as examples of natural while we conveniently ignore others. There are numerous ways in which we care for and feed our dogs that cannot be construed as anything close to natural. We confine them for their safety, we subject them to surgeries that remove their reproductive organs to prevent unwanted breeding, we vaccinate them to prevent illness and we treat them with synthetic (artificially produced) medications to help them to recover when they are ill. Similarly, feeding a dog a food that contains raw beef or chicken that was raised using today's intensive agricultural methods or that includes fruits that are imported from Central America cannot hold up under a knife of naturalistic scrutiny. Yet, these inconsistencies are conveniently ignored or discounted when we choose to use a naturalistic argument to support a cherished belief (remember our old friend, the confirmation bias?).

So here is the bottom line. Something being identified as natural is *not by itself* sufficient evidence for that thing being desirable or better than an alternative. This does not mean that the particular thing is *not* healthful or better; it very well may be. Today, many people prefer to select foods that contain natural ingredients in their own and in their dog's diet and try to avoid overly processed foods and artificial preservatives. This is understandable and often desirable, given the evidence of the harm that we have witnessed in recent years of processed ingredients such as trans fatty acids and the ubiquitous use of high fructose corn syrup in processed foods. A general approach to reducing processed foods and increasing fresh foods is definitely healthier in perception and may indeed be beneficial in many ways. Still, we cannot use the "it's natural" argument alone as proof of superiority or healthfulness. We must think of hanging the "natural" label onto something as a descriptive term, unless or until there is actual evidence that it actually does support superior health or provide better nutrition. The merits of the approach to feeding dogs a raw food diet or selecting certain types of dietary ingredients must be shown to stand on their own via actual evidence of benefit in order to win this argument.

Nutrients versus ingredients

All introductory nutrition courses begin with a few definitions. Let's start with **nutrients**: A nutrient is any component in the diet that is required to sustain life and that has specific functions that contribute to growth, maintenance of normal tissues and organs and health. The seven categories of nutrients for all animals are water, energy, protein, fat, carbohydrate, vitamins and minerals. In addition, within these categories, nutrients are further classified as either "essential" or "non-essential." The essential label is a rather confusing one, to be sure. One might ask, aren't ALL nutrients "essential"? Yep, they are all essential to *the body* to sustain life. The nutritional terms **essential** and **non-essential** actually refer to whether or not a nutrient must be included in the diet. Essential nutrients are those that *must* be present in the diet in order to meet an animal's (in this case a dog's) daily nutrient needs. This occurs because the dog cannot produce the nutrient internally at all or cannot produce enough of the nutrient to meet daily needs. In contrast, the non-essential nutrients are nutrients that animals can produce in the body. These can *either* be consumed in the diet *or* produced in the body. Therefore, non-essential nutrients, while present in the diet, are not essential to a complete and balanced diet.

It is also important that we make the distinction between the nutrients that a dog requires and that are provided in the food and a diet's **ingredients**. Although many people intuitively understand the difference between these two things, this distinction can get muddled when we are addressing some of the important controversies that exist about pet foods today. Just like human foods, all dog foods are composed of ingredients. A food's set of ingredients is the various foodstuffs that were combined to make the final product (just as a cake is composed of ingredients such as eggs, flour, sugar and chocolate). Each of the ingredients that go into a dog food contains a unique set of nutrients that it contributes to the final product. For example, some ingredients, such as chicken meal, provide primarily protein (and some fat, minerals and vitamins), while other ingredients, such as corn meal, tapioca or potato, contribute primarily digestible carbohydrate to the diet. In a nutshell, dogs require nutrients (not ingredients), but pet foods are made up of ingredients that provide the essential nutrients.

Fillers: ingredients, but not nutrients?

If ingredients supply the nutrients in a food, is there ever a case in which an ingredient supplies, say, nothing? Is this possible? Anyone who has been working with dogs for any period of time has almost certainly heard this advice: "Oh, don't buy that dog food. It contains [insert ingredient of choice here] and that is just added as filler." And dog enthusiasts are not alone in using this disparaging term. Many pet food companies use it as a marketing strategy when making claims about a particular ingredient that is *not* present in their food (and, gee, by coincidence just happens to be found in their competitor's product!). But what exactly does the term **filler** mean? On the face of it, the intent is to imply that the particular ingredient provides nothing of value to the food, other than taking up space. Some may believe that fillers provide only "empty calories," a phrase taken from human nutrition, which suggests that the ingredient in question provides calories but is lacking in all other essential nutrients. While the use of the term filler seems to function as a red flag telling dog owners what to avoid, it has a serious flaw in that it has been and continues to be applied to such a wide variety of different ingredients as to make the term virtually meaningless. In recent years, some of the ingredients that have earned this unsavory distinction include corn, rice, wheat, corn gluten meal, beet pulp, rice bran, soy, citrus pulp and even chicken meal.

The allegation that a particular ingredient serves only as a filler in a food contends that the ingredient is included by a pet food company with the sole intent of adding bulk to the food at the expense of ingredients that are presumably more nutrient dense and more expensive. Fillers are presumed to provide no nutritional value to the food and by extension to the dog who is eating the food. The problem with this term and with its use is that it is an emotionally charged label that tells us absolutely nothing. First, all ingredients contribute nutrients to a food. Unless the manufacturer is adding something that is completely unusable by dogs, say shoe leather or ground up rebar (which, even the most cynical among us have to agree is unlikely), the ingredients that are included in dog food are all contributing one or more nutrients. For example, ground corn is a source of digestible carbohydrate and so supplies dietary energy. It also contributes small amounts of vitamins and minerals and the essential fatty acid linoleic acid to the diet. Citrus pulp and beet pulp are sources of fiber, specifically a type of fiber called fermentable fiber that is important for intestinal health. Other forms of fiber, such as wheat bran, contribute primarily non-fermentable fiber which, just as in human diets, is the type of fiber that contributes to stool bulk and normal intestinal passage. Energy is an essential nutrient (without it, your dog will starve and die). In all cases, these ingredients *do* contribute nutrients to the diet. You may not wish to see a particular ingredient in a food that you select for your dog and you may have a very good reason for avoiding that ingredient. For example, you may decide not to feed a diet that contains corn to your dog because you prefer to select a food that contains a non-grain source of carbohydrate, such as potatoes or peas. (Although corn is often identified as the cause of food-related allergies in dogs, food allergies are less often caused by corn than by beef, dairy or soy proteins). Similarly, you may decide that you prefer to feed a food that contains primarily animal-source protein rather than plant-source protein and so make a decision to avoid foods that contain corn gluten meal.

Affixing the "filler" label onto one or more pet food ingredients is an example of a common cognitive distortion called **mislabeling**. Mislabeling occurs when someone describes an event or object with language that is highly colored and emotionally charged. Although it is often unconscious, mislabeling has the effect of provoking an emotional response in the listener and typically encourages the person to form biased opinions. For example, let's say a friend of yours has decided to switch his dog to a food that contains increased dietary fiber and reduced calories. He tells you that the food is advertised as a weight control diet and while he knows the dietary fiber is very high, he is hoping that the reduced calories will help his Labrador Retriever to lose weight. (Increasing non-fermentable fibers in food is one approach that is used in weight control formulations and may have some benefits; however the research does not show consistent results in terms of weight control.) You may have an opinion about the effectiveness of using fiber to dilute a food's energy (calories) as an approach to controlling energy intake. However, if you respond to your friend with this state-ment: "Oh, that food contains cellulose, which is just added as a filler. I would never feed my dogs a food that contains a filler like that," you will almost certainly stop the conversation in its tracks (and may even find yourself experiencing an uncomfortable silence). Rather, if you responded with something to the effect of: "Oh really? I see that cellulose is included in the food as the source of fiber. Have you read anything about how that works to control weight?" you would most likely encourage further discussion. You may ask your friend questions such as these: "How are your dog's stools on the food? Does he seem to be satisfied after eating? Have you seen any change in weight yet? Have you considered any other approaches to weight loss, such as increasing his exercise, reducing portion size or feeding a food that has reduced calories but normal amounts of fiber?" Regardless of your personal opinion about increased fiber in a food, the purpose of this example is to illustrate the uselessness of the filler label and the negative consequences that occur when we use mislabeling to express our opinions.

Remember that all ingredients provide nutrients to a diet; some are simply more nutrient-rich than others. If you feel the "f-word" starting to slip out when discussing a dog food with a friend, a training colleague or client, stop talking. Think. Then, if you know, discuss the reason that the shunned ingredient is included in the food, the nutrients that it does (and does not) supply, and why you disagree with its use in pet foods. If you do not know these things, keep your mouth firmly closed, excuse yourself and use your science sleuth skills to gather more information. Then come back and discuss. To aid in purging the f-word from your vocabulary, Figure 4.3 provides a list of common ingredients that have been denigrated as "filler" by *both* pet owners and pet food companies, along with the nutrients that they provide to foods.

Ingredient	Provides:
Corn (ground)	Digestible carbohydrate, protein, fat (linoleic acid)
Corn gluten meal	Protein, small amount of digestible carbohydrate
Beet pulp	Dietary fiber source (moderately fermentable)
Soy flour	Protein, fiber (prebiotic, fermentable)
Citrus pulp	Dietary fiber source (soluble, moderately fermentable)
Chicken meal	Protein, fat, linoleic acid
Antioxidants such as BHA, BHT	Synthetic antioxidants that protect fat, vitamins and other diet components from breakdown

Figure 4.3 Ingredients commonly identified as "filler."

Nutrients to pay attention to (and why)

Let's now move on to examine what it is that we know about the domestic dog's basic nutrient requirements and how this knowledge helps to inform the choices that we make for our dogs' health. We must have this base of understanding in order to move on to what nutritionists refer to as **applied nutrition**, which means how we actually feed dogs during the various life stages. Let's begin with the two most essential nutrients—and the two that are typically ignored altogether by many pet owners and pet professionals—water and energy.

Water (What is it good for? Absolutely everything!)

Although it is often overlooked as a nutrient, **water** is, in fact the *most important* essential nutrient for all animals, including our dogs (see Figure 4.4.). More than two-thirds of your dog's body is water. To illustrate its importance—a dog can lose most of her body fat, approximately half of her protein (lean muscle tissue), but if she loses more than eight percent of her body's water, she becomes severely dehydrated and will die. While animals can survive for extended periods of time without other nutrients, they will perish within a few days when deprived of water. To support normal water balance, dogs consume water from both drinking and from the water that is found in their food. The body also produces a small amount of water through digestion. Canned foods and raw diets provide much more water to dogs than do dry dog foods. Still, all dogs must be provided with an unlimited source of clean, fresh water each day. And keep in mind that not all water is created equal. Untreated water and water that dogs drink while playing outdoors or swimming can harbor bacteria, viruses and parasites. (Some owners choose to give their dogs bottled water if their source is questionable.) Remember that a dog's water needs increase during periods of warm and humid weather, when exercising strenuously and during illness.

Water—what is it good for?

Well, lots of things, in fact. Here is just a short summary of the many roles that water plays in our dogs' health:

- Regulates and maintains normal body temperature

- Needed for the digestion of food and absorption of nutrients into the body

- Necessary for the transport of nutrients within the body

- Involved in many of the body's essential chemical reactions

- Removes waste (urine and feces) out of the body

Figure 4.4 The functions of water in a dog's diet.

Energy

Several years ago at an obedience trial weekend, the subject of dogs' energy levels came up with a group of trainers. One of the competitors had a young Border Collie who he had just started showing in the open classes. Knowing that I was a dog nutritionist, he asked me how best to feed his dog to "boost her energy level." A bit confused by the question, I asked him, "Do you mean how to best feed her to provide her with energy for the activities that you do with her—to feed her as an athlete?" He replied "No, I mean she is not always as energetic as I would like and so I need to find a food that will improve her energy level." At the time, I was teaching companion animal science to undergraduate students and this question often also came up with my students. I finally realized that the confusion lies with the word "energy." While dog trainers and many owners generally think of **energy** as *how a dog behaves* (i.e., is or is not energetic), when the term is used in nutritional science it refers to something entirely different. A food's energy (more correctly, its energy density) refers to number of **calories** that the food provides in a given volume or weight of food. The typically used units for a food's energy density is calories per cup, pound or kilogram (kg) of food. Energy is the fuel, measured as calories, that is supplied to the body by the chemical bonds found in certain nutrients. After water, dietary energy is the most essential nutrient because it is necessary to keep the body running. Not to put too fine a point on it, but without energy (calories), a dog loses weight and starves. Food energy is supplied by just three nutrients in the diet: protein, fat and digestible carbohydrate (also known as starch). Food energy is measured (and reported on food labels) in kilocalories (kcal). You will see this expressed as either kcal or as a capital C. (For comparison, the "calories" that you see on human food labels are also kilocalories; manufacturers report this as calories because human nutritionists have amended kcal to calories.)

Choices to consider—expanding calories (and expanding waistlines). Without question, the most important energy-related feeding problem in dogs today is the over-consumption of energy, leading to overweight conditions. As we will see throughout this book, general trends in pet nutrition closely follow trends in human nutrition, usually by a year or two lag period. So, just as our own waistlines and body weight have increased during the last twenty years, so too have those of our dogs. Numerous studies have shown (and veterinarians agree) that obesity is the most commonly diagnosed chronic health problem in dogs today. Although there are multiple underlying factors that contribute to this change, one important factor for dogs is poor diet selection: mismatching a food's caloric content with the dog's lifestyle and activity level. The lifestyle of most dogs has become more sedentary as their role in our lives has changed from working partner to companion. In addition, an important change has taken place in the foods that are marketed and sold to pet owners as adult (maintenance) foods. To understand these changes, let's go back a few years to a time when the concept of "adult maintenance foods" was first developed.

During the 1970s and 1980s, most pet food companies produced and sold just one or two brands and a handful of products. Typically these included a puppy food for growing dogs and an adult maintenance food for mature dogs. The science that was available at the time supported this age division as we were beginning to understand the important differences between these two major life stages (more about this in Chapter 5). Regardless of the company and the quality of the food, the adult maintenance foods were formulated to meet the needs of the typical adult dog living as a pet in a home. The energy (calorie) content of these fell within a relatively narrow range of between about 350 and 380 kilocalories per cup of food (kcal/cup). From the point of view of the dog owner, this meant that you could be pretty certain that a cup of adult food would supply about the same number of calories to your dog, regardless of the brand that you chose to feed. This is an important consideration because, just as with people, changes in daily energy intake in dogs lead to changes in body weight. Increased calories = weight gain; decreased calories = weight loss. So, if Susie Brown was choosing the food that she fed to her Beagle Buster Brown based upon the current sale price in the grocery store, she was pretty safe to feed the same volume of each food to Buster to meet his energy and nutrient needs. (Putting aside some of the other problems that might arise from frequent changes in foods, of course.)

Beginning in the 1980s and continuing today, pet health research began to provide a flood of new information about life stage and life style nutrition for dogs. In addition, dogs were becoming increasingly important to our lives and an entire new industry of dog-related activities, services and products was developing. Similarly, the pet food industry (and the products that it produces) began to expand. Dramatic examples of product **segmentation** occurred, leading to the creation of multiple new pet food niches and the proliferation of dog food brands. Although it is debatable whether or not all of these segments are supported by good science (for example, do the nutritional needs of a Fox Terrier really differ enough from those of a Tibetan Spaniel to warrant different foods?), some are supported by solid research. Examples include performance dog foods, large breed growth diets and some of the foods that are formulated for healthy senior dogs or weight control. At the same time, segmentation of adult maintenance foods resulted in a variety of products such as those that include various types of protein sources, limited ingredient diets, grain-free foods, low carbohydrate foods and organic products. Today, rather than a single food for adult dogs, most companies have two or more brands and multiple product lines of adult maintenance foods for owners to choose from. (We discuss this expansion in detail in Chapters 7 and 8.)

The point that is important to our current discussion is the fact that these foods also vary markedly in energy content, in other words in the number of calories that they provide in a given volume of food. Although a small number contain fewer calories than the traditional adult maintenance diet, most provide substantially more calories per cup. This is important because *energy always determines how much food will need to be fed* (and by extension, how many calories get into the dog). While a hard-working agility dog who trains daily may thrive on a food that provides 440 kcals per cup, the same food can rapidly lead to obesity if selected for a pet dog who receives a single walk around the block each day. We will explore the many reasons behind these changes later in the book—for now, take a look at Figure 4.5 to see an example of the range of energy densities found in ten different dog foods that are currently marketed for adult dogs. Keep in mind that none of these foods is promoted (marketed) as a food for highly active dogs. Just looking at this small selection of foods, if you compare the Nutro Natural Choice food to Evo's Turkey and Chicken Formula, you see a difference between calories per cup of almost 100 % (278 versus 537). If an owner switched her dog from the Nutro food to the Evo food without considering this difference, she could easily *double* her dog's daily intake of calories if she did not reduce the volume of food that was offered. The lesson here is that, in today's market of proliferating choices, it is important to pay attention to the calories per cup that a food provides. As a general rule of thumb, a food that provides between 340 and 380 kcal/cup is suitable for most adult dogs who are low to moderately active. If your dog runs, swims or trains hard daily, a more energy-dense food, such as one that provides 400 to 480 kcals per cup may be more suitable.

Brand of adult dog food (dry)	kcal/cup
Nutro Natural Choice Wholesome Essentials (Chicken)	278
Pedigree Adult Complete Nutrition	335
Eukanuba Adult Maintenance	347
Science Diet Ideal Balance Grain Free Adult	360
Newman's Own Organics Adult Dry Dog Food	397
Blue Buffalo Wilderness Chicken	410
Wellness Core Grain Free	421
Innova Adult Dry Dog Food Red Meat Large Bites	468
Canidae Grain Free Pure Elements	498
Evo Turkey & Chicken Formula Dry Dog Food	537

Figure 4.5 Energy (calorie) content of ten commercial dog foods sold for adult dog maintenance.

Protein

Dietary **protein** is necessary for the growth and maintenance of almost all tissues of the body. For example, protein is the major structural component of hair, skin, tendons, ligaments and cartilage. The enzymes that are needed for all of the body's chemical reactions, the hormones that act as the body's messengers and the antibodies that comprise the immune system are all proteins. Amino acids are the building blocks of protein. Think of protein as the major building material of the body. All proteins are made up of small molecules called amino acids, which are linked together to form long and complex chains. The protein that is consumed by dogs in their diet is digested by the body into these individual amino acids, which are then absorbed in the small intestine. Because animals consume protein, not individual amino acids, we speak of a "dietary protein requirement" rather than an amino acid requirement (even though it is amino acids that the body actually requires and uses). Like other animals, the dog has a metabolic requirement for 22 amino acids. However, twelve of these, the **non-essential amino acids**, can be produced by the body in adequate amounts to meet needs. The remaining ten amino acids, called the **essential amino acids**, cannot be made by the body in sufficient amounts and must be supplied by dietary protein. (For a list of the essential and non-essential amino acids for dogs, see Appendix 2.)

Dogs require a daily intake of new protein because the body's protein stores are not static, but rather are in a constant state of flux, as cells and tissues wear out and are replaced. However, any excess protein that is consumed and is not needed for these functions is not stored for later use in the body. Rather it will be used as an energy source and will provide calories, or will be converted to fat and stored. This is an important point because many of the foods that contain very high protein are not contributing to muscle development (despite many beliefs about this), but instead are a rather expensive source of calories for the body. A goal should be to provide the optimal amount of dietary protein that is needed to meet a dog's daily needs and not too much extra.

The most frequently used animal-source proteins in commercial pet foods are various forms and grades of chicken, lamb, beef, pork (meat meal) and fish. The most commonly used concentrated plant-sources of protein are corn gluten meal, soybean meal and most recently, pea protein and potato protein. Most of the protein-containing ingredients in dry (extruded) dog foods are added in a dry form called a "meal." When meat that is not in a meal form is included, the high proportion of water contained in the ingredient (60 % or more) is cooked off during processing, so that the whole meat actually contributes a very small amount of protein to the end product. The protein quality of protein-containing ingredients refers to an ingredient's ability to provide digestible and usable essential amino acids (and nitrogen) to the dog. In commercial pet foods, the protein quality of ingredients varies tremendously. And, unfortunately, there are only limited methods for discerning among sources and evaluating the protein quality of commercial foods. We discuss this issue in detail in Chapter 8. For now, let's turn to another choice issue that dog folks frequently face today when selecting a dog food.

Choices to consider: exotic protein sources. In recent years, the use of exotic and game animal meat sources in dog foods has become increasingly popular. Numerous brands offer protein ingredients such as salmon, bison, rabbit, venison, duck, ostrich and pheasant. There are even dog foods made with alligator, kangaroo meat and Australian possum (Brushtail). Salmon is worth a special mention because it appears to be going the way of lamb meat. When first introduced, lamb was used as a **novel protein** source in diets formulated for dogs that were suspected to have either a food intolerance or allergy. Because lamb had not been used previously in dog food, it met the requirements of being "novel," an ingredient that most dogs had not been exposed to. However, over a period of 15 years or so, more and more pet food companies began to use lamb as a meat source, leading to a loss of its function as a novel protein for most pets. Today, salmon appears to be experiencing a similar explosion in popularity. This is occurring probably because of wide availability of farmed salmon as an ingredient and because of its role in providing a source of omega-3 fatty acids. However, given the large number of foods that are salmon-based today, chances are that within a few years this protein source will no longer be a good choice for dogs whose owners are seeking a novel protein source to feed.

There are multiple reasons that dog owners may choose a food that contains an unusual or exotic protein source. Some of these make sense, while others fall prey to one or more of those pesky cognitive errors. First a little history. Single and novel source protein diets were originally developed as **limited ingredient foods**, which means the food contains a single protein and a single carbohydrate source and that these sources were presumably "novel" or new to the dog. The theory (which has some support in research) is that feeding a dog who has a suspected food allergy or food intolerance a diet that contains ingredients that the dog has never been exposed to will not evoke an adverse response (i.e., itchy skin in most cases, diarrhea in fewer). So, some owners who have itchy dogs may select a food with an unusual protein source with this benefit in mind. However, the problem is that not all of the exotic protein foods that are sold in pet supply stores (i.e., over the counter, non-prescription foods) contain a single protein source. While the exotic animal source may be listed on the label with great fanfare, the food can and often does contain other protein sources, such as chicken, beef or fish, some of which may cause an allergic or intolerance response in the dog. So, many of these foods are not suitable for this type of use. This illustrates the importance of reading labels—more about this in later chapters.

A second and unrelated reason that owners may choose a food with an exotic protein source is a decision to avoid sources of meat that come from confinement animal feeding operations, the euphemism for the "factory farmed" environments that produce virtually all of the poultry and meat products that are included in commercial dog foods today (and which produce most of the meats in the human food chain as well). Because exotic meats are perceived as being more natural (they may or may not be) and are believed to have been acquired by means other than factory farms (this is true for some, but not all of these sources), owners may choose these foods hoping for more ethically sourced ingredients. While this may be true for some products, it is not necessarily so. For example, most if not all of the salmon that is included in dog food comes from farmed salmon, not wild caught sources. Similarly, while the image on the bag may show a wild bison grazing in a wide open plain, in reality bison are farmed on ranches and in feed lots and are slaughtered using the same methods used with most beef cattle for consumption as food. Kangaroo from Australia are hunted, but this is also a controversial source of pet food meat and is opposed by some animal welfare groups because of the lack of regulation and the hunting methods that are used. Therefore, if your goal is to feed a food that includes ethically sourced and/or locally obtained ingredients, simply choosing a food that uses an unusual source of protein is not the answer.

What is the bottom line regarding your choices when considering exotic protein sources? First, be aware that a food that is advertised with an unusual protein ingredient may or may not reduce signs of food allergy or intolerance. To do so, the food must contain a protein that is novel (for example, has Rusty ever eaten ostrich before?); it must contain no other protein source (i.e., Rusty's food must have ostrich, but no chicken, beef, lamb, etc.); and Rusty must actually be afflicted with a true food allergy or intolerance. Without question, we know that atopic disease (atopy), which refers to allergies caused by pollens, grasses and other environmental allergens, is responsible for the majority of itchy dog problems, rather than food allergies. Second, if your goal is to feed your dog a food that contains ethically- or locally-sourced ingredients, you must find out where the exotic meat originated and how it was kept prior to ending up in dog food. Companies are not often forthcoming with this information, since many of these animals are farmed using modern day confined systems, while others may come from sources that are not well regulated or that raise animal welfare concerns. In other words many of these animals did not necessarily live a pleasant life in the wild prior to ending up in dog food (despite what that attractive label wants you to believe). The best advice with these protein sources is to read labels and ask the tough questions—be a careful and critical consumer.

Carbohydrate

Digestible **carbohydrate** (starch) is the second energy-containing nutrient that is present in a dog's diet. As an energy source, starch provides the same number of calories per unit weight as protein, 3.5 kcal/gram. Although dogs do not have a dietary requirement for carbohydrate, it does provide a highly digestible energy source. For example, nutritionists commonly use the phrase "carbohydrate spares protein in the diet." This refers to the fact that when a body uses carbohydrate to provide its needed energy, dietary protein is "spared" from being burned as an energy source and is available to be used for the important functions of providing essential amino acids, building and repairing body tissues, and supporting a healthy immune system. Therefore, including at least some digestible carbohydrate in the diet of dogs is considered to be beneficial. Therefore, including at least some digestible carbohydrate (starch) in the diet of dogs is considered to be beneficial. The controversy about starch in dog foods revolves more around how much starch is in the food, and where that starch comes from, rather than its overall presence or absence from the diet.

A wide range of types of starch are used in commercial dog foods today. These include various forms of corn, rice, wheat, oats and potato. Other vegetables and fruits are also included but these contribute smaller amounts of digestible starch. In recent years, following trends in human nutrition once again, focus has been placed upon a distinction between starch that comes from grains such as wheat, corn, rice or barley and the starch that comes from other non-grain plant sources such as potatoes (a root vegetable) or peas (a legume vegetable). A further division may be made between the gluten-containing grains of wheat, barley and rye and other types of grain such as corn and rice.

Dietary fiber is also classified with carbohydrates. Fiber is a collective term used to describe the parts of plants that are poorly digested by the body. As such, fiber does not provide appreciable amounts of digestible energy to dogs. Like humans, dogs do not have a dietary requirement for fiber per se. However, research in recent years has shown that, also like humans, dogs benefit from the inclusion of some fiber in their diets. Specifically, non-fermentable fibers provide dietary bulk, may contribute to satiety (a feeling of fullness) and help to maintain normal gastrointestinal motility and function (i.e., fiber keeps things moving along at a normal rate). The fermentable fibers, which come from different plant sources, have an important role in supporting normal microbial populations in the intestines and for health of cells lining the intestinal tract. Most nutritionists agree that a combination of fiber types is best for dogs. In general, a dry dog food that contains between three and seven percent fiber (listed as "crude fiber" on the label) is considered normal and beneficial. A list of fiber sources that are included in pet foods, and the types of fiber that they provide is included in Appendix 2.

Choices to consider: Understanding "grain-free" versus "low-carb" foods. The development of foods that are advertised as being grain-free and/or low carbohydrate is a prime example of hyper-segmentation of the pet food market today. Although these foods can be formulated to be nutritious and balanced, it is important to recognize that they have been developed in response to pet owner demand rather than in response to scientific research that has demonstrated either a need or a health benefit. First, let's examine what these terms mean. Foods that are advertised as being "grain-free" are those that exclude grain sources of digestible carbohydrate. These include wheat, corn, rice, barley and oats. In replacement of grains, the grain-free products include digestible carbohydrate from other plant sources such as white potato, sweet potato, peas or tapioca (from the cassava plant root). Most grain-free foods provide digestible starch from these sources at levels that are lower than the amount of carbohydrate found in grain-containing foods, but still provide appreciable amounts of digestible carbohydrate as an energy source. In general, these foods tend to be slightly higher in caloric density than grain-containing adult maintenance foods. Similar to the trend in human diets, interest in grain-free foods appears to have its origins in increased recognition and diagnosis of gluten intolerance (called Celiac disease in humans) and its less severe manifestation, gluten sensitivity. In dogs, wheat has been identified as a potential allergen because of its gluten content. Corn has also been believed to be problematic. As a result, just as some people have done with their own diets, some pet owners have begun to avoid grain-containing foods for their dogs. (Interestingly, published studies of food allergy have shown that beef, dairy products and soy are the most common causes of food allergy in dogs. While allergies to wheat or corn can develop, they are significantly less common.) A very small number of dogs may develop a disorder called gluten-sensitive enteropathy, which is somewhat analogous to Celiac disease in humans. However, this is a rare, genetically influenced disease that occurs primarily in Irish Setters and is rarely diagnosed in dogs of other breeds.

Another approach includes foods that are formulated to contain very low levels of starch. These "low carb" products are also grain-free and replace carbohydrate with increased levels of fat and protein. The primary end result is that low carbohydrate foods are *very high* in calories. This occurs because something must replace the energy-providing carbohydrate and the two choices are fat and protein. Most of these foods are very high in fat and moderately high in protein content. Although a high fat diet is not a problem for dogs metabolically—they thrive on high fat diets and do not experience the cardiovascular problems with dietary fat that humans are more prone to develop—these foods can contribute to weight gain and obesity. When one considers the frequency of overweight conditions in dogs today, feeding a food that contains more than 400 kcals/cup means either that the dog must be fed a very low volume of food (which can lead to deficiencies of other nutrients) or that the dog is unintentionally overfed, leading to unwanted weight gain. So, if you select a grain-free or low carbohydrate food for your dogs, make certain that you consider the number of calories that a cup of food provides as well as the type and amount of carbohydrates that are included in the food.

Fat

Fat is the last of the three energy (calorie) contributing nutrients in your dog's diet. Fat provides a more concentrated source of energy than either protein or carbohydrate and also contributes to a food's texture and palatability. On a weight basis, a gram of fat provides about 2.5 times the calories to the body than a gram of either protein or carbohydrate (8.5 kcal/gram versus 3.5 kcal/gram). Similar to us, dogs love the taste of fat and most enjoy high fat foods more than low fat foods (compare French fries to a boiled potato, for instance). Nutritionally, fat aids in the absorption of fat-soluble vitamins from the diet and also is the source of the essential fatty acid for dogs, linoleic acid. Linoleic acid is found in both plant and animal products such as corn oil, soybean oil, beef tallow and chicken fat.

Choices to consider: omega-6 and omega-3 fatty acid content. Fatty acids can be classified into two major families, called the omega-6 fatty acids and the omega-3 fatty acids. Both types are important in the diet, but dog foods (like human foods) tend to contain an over-abundance of omega-6 fatty acids simply because of the types of ingredients that are produced by our modern agricultural system. Linoleic acid and arachidonic acid are both omega-6 fatty acids. Three fatty acids in the omega-3 family are important nutritionally. These are the parent omega-3 fatty acid called alpha-linolenic acid (ALA), which is found in flax seed, borage oil and some nut oils. Alpha-linolenic acid can be converted to two larger omega-3 fatty acids; these are eicosapentaenoic acid (EPA) and docosahexaenoic acid (DHA). Although most mammals can convert some ALA to EPA and DHA, the most efficient converters are algae. For this reason, certain types of fish and fish oils are the best concentrated sources of EPA and DHA in the diets of both humans and dogs. Dogs benefit from having both omega-6 and omega-3 fatty acids present in their diet. Efforts to increase omega-3 fatty acids have come about primarily because of a known reduction in this family of fatty acids in a typical Western diet (both for humans and for dogs).

So, what is so special about the omega-3 fatty acids? Omega-3 fatty acids have important functions in the body that can contribute to dogs' health and vitality. Appropriate amounts of omega-3 fatty acids in the diet support normal neural development, the cardiovascular and immune systems, skin and coat health, and reproduction (pregnancy and lactation). Increasing omega-3 fatty acids in the diet may also have therapeutic benefits for some dogs. For example, increasing the proportion of omega-3 fatty acids in the diet has been shown to aid in managing certain types of chronic inflammatory disorders in dogs such as joint pain due to arthritis and allergic skin problems. Recent research indicates that DHA is important for development of a healthy nervous system and vision in fetuses and newborn puppies and may promote learning in young puppies who were exposed to an enriched DHA environment prior to birth and immediately following birth (i.e., their mother's diet was enriched with DHA). Like other species, dogs can convert ALA to EPA and DHA, but they do not do this efficiently enough to provide high amounts of the longer-chain fatty acids. As a result, most nutritionists agree that the best way to increase these beneficial fatty acids in dogs' diets is through the oils of salmon, herring, white fish and menhaden.

A current challenge regarding omega-3 fatty acids is that optimal levels to include in dog foods are not well defined and both the levels and the sources found in commercial foods vary enormously. In 2004, a group of researchers at the Norwegian School of Veterinary Science in Oslo, Norway measured the fat content and specifically omega-6 and omega-3 levels of twelve different brands of commercially available dog foods (Ahlstrom et al; 2004). Analysis of the foods showed a wide range of both types of fatty acids. While some foods were almost completely devoid of marine oils and the specific omega-3 fatty acids that they provide, others contained omega-3 fatty acids but primarily in the form of alpha-linolenic acid which was supplied by plant oils. This is an important finding because only omega-3 content is reported on the pet food label. If the omega-3 fatty acids are supplied primarily as alpha-linolenic acid, for example from flax, the health benefits that come from EPA and DHA are not provided by that food.

When your intent is to choose a food that provides benefit from omega-3 fatty acids (EPA and DHA) to dogs, a general rule of thumb is to select a food that reports a ratio (proportion) of omega-6 fatty acids to omega-3 fatty acids of between 7:1 and 5:1. (Remember that omega-6 fatty acids are always higher in foods; the goal is to increase omega-3 fatty acids while maintaining or slightly reducing omega-6 fatty acids.) In addition, because the most effective forms of omega-3 fatty acids come from fish oils, check the ingredients list. The inclusion of fish oil, certain types of fish or fish meal (salmon, white fish) will tell you that the right types of omega-3 fatty acids are present. Alternatively if you see no fish products and instead find flax, flaxseed oil or canola oil, this means that the omega-3 fatty acids that are in that food are in the form of ALA, which is important but provides less therapeutic benefit to dogs than fish oil sources.

Vitamins and minerals

Vitamins are organic molecules that are needed by the body in very minute amounts, but are essential for health. Vitamins have a wide variety of functions in the body and are typically classified into two groups: **fat-soluble vitamins** and **water-soluble vitamins.** The fat-soluble vitamins, A, D, E and K, can be stored in the body. The water-soluble vitamins include the B-complex vitamins and vitamin C. They are not stored in any appreciable amount in the body and so must be supplied daily in the diet. **Minerals** are inorganic elements that are needed for the growth, development and maintenance of all of the body's systems. Macro-minerals are those essential minerals that are found in greatest quantity in the body. These include calcium, phosphorus, magnesium, sulfur and the electrolytes sodium, potassium and chloride. The micro-minerals (also called trace elements) are also essential for health but are needed in very small amounts. Today, mineral deficiencies are rare in dogs. When problems do occur, they are usually due to dietary imbalances in which one or more minerals are supplemented in excess of others or when a mineral imbalance occurs secondary to an underlying illness. Summaries of the essential vitamins and minerals and their primary functions can be found in Appendix 2.

How dogs eat

My husband and I are lucky enough to live very close to a park and forest preserve that has miles of trails that we enjoy daily with our four dogs. Certain areas of the park are safe for off-lead hiking, so our dogs also have daily opportunities to explore on their own and to play together on the trails with us. Because they have daily off-lead time, there are two obedience commands that we consider to be essential. The first of course is a rock-solid recall—coming when called is trained starting in puppyhood using the highest value treats available and making certain that our pups and young dogs are always exceedingly motivated to come a runnin' (in other words, no "set ups" for failure). A basic "peace of mind" rule for me is also the "eyes on dogs" rule, which means that dogs are always in sight and within a few yards of us while we hike or run along. The second command, and the one that is of greater interest for *this* book, is the "Leave It" command. Also invaluable, this directive states, in no uncertain terms, *"Do NOT eat that!!"* We train this in a very controlled way, starting in our training center (not on the trails) with low value items, teaching our dogs to turn away from the target item and towards me (because I have something that is of much greater value!). The "Leave It" command is essential because all dogs, and especially the typical chow hound breeds such as Goldens, Labs and other sporting breeds, like to scavenge. They snort around, find stuff, sniff it a bit and if it appears at all likely to provide even a smidgeon of gustatory enjoyment, they snarf it down. We like to say that our oldest Golden, Cadie, who has never met a smelly bit of refuse that she was not willing to taste, lives by the rule of "if I can fit it into my mouth, it must be edible." Needless to say, teaching the "Leave It" command benefits both us (as it prevents us from having to reach into mouths to extract the smelly thing) and our dogs—who it keeps safe (usually—from eating the smelly thing).

So, dogs scavenge. And when they scavenge, they not only eat actual food items that they find, but they will consume things that we humans usually consider to be non-food items, such as the feces of other animals, rotting carcasses and scraps of pretty much anything that looks or smells interesting. As we discussed earlier in this chapter, this scavenging behavior is associated with a more omnivorous nature, is observed in other canid species, and may even have been selected for more intensely during the early years of the dog's domestication. (For a complete discussion of the role that scavenging played in domestication, see Ray and Laura Coppinger's seminal book, *Dogs: A Startling New Understanding of Canine Origin, Behavior and Evolution*.) Dogs also tend to eat rapidly. Although it has been suggested that rapid eating may be more common in some breeds than in others, there is little scientific evidence for this. Indeed, a wide range of feeding behaviors is observed among individual dogs, even within breeds. The tendency to eat rapidly can be a problem for some dogs because it may predispose them to choke or swallow large amounts of air. (It can also be a problem for us if the "Leave It" command has failed to have the desired outcome and we are attempting to extricate the smelly thing from a dog's mouth.)

Anyone who lives with multiple dogs also knows that the social environment when eating is important to dogs. For example, a phenomenon called social facilitation occurs when the presence of another dog (or even a cat) at mealtime stimulates a dog to consume more food or to eat more rapidly. Studies have shown that puppies and dogs usually consume more food when fed as a group, compared with when they are fed alone. If food is available at all times, these effects eventually become minimal. On the other hand, if dogs are meal fed and have not been trained to eat only from their own bowl (and not to steal from others), competitive interactions and resource guarding (food bowl aggression) may develop. Training dogs in multiple dog homes to eat only from their own bowls, or simply feeding dogs separately, are the best ways to prevent or manage this problem.

Finally, vestiges of the wolf's food hoarding behaviors are often observed in our domestic dogs. For example, some dogs frequently bury bones in their yard or hide coveted food items such as biscuits or chew bones in furniture or under beds. My friend Brad's Bassett mix, Harpo, would regularly bury half-chewed biscuits under bedroom pillows, which Brad had the misfortune of finding after turning in for the night. Unlike their wild ancestors however, most dogs rarely return to their hidden caches to dig them up. As with my family of four (and our need for the "Leave It!" command) related activities that are common in dogs include scavenging and coprophagy (stool-eating). Many dogs readily consume garbage, carrion, insects and feces that they encounter in the yard or while out walking. Plant eating, in particular grass eating, is also frequently reported by owners. Contrary to popular beliefs, there is no evidence that grass/plant eating in dogs is a sign either of illness or nutrient deficiency. Rather, grass-eating appears to be a normal canid behavior as it is widespread among wolves and has not been shown to be associated with gastrointestinal upset or the onset of vomiting.

The good news is that, as a species, dogs are very flexible and can adapt to several types of feeding schedules. Although dogs can be fed portion-controlled meals or free-choice, meal-feeding is preferred for most dogs because it allows close monitoring of intake and because many dogs will over-consume when allowed free access to food. For most dogs, feeding two meals per day supports gastrointestinal health and helps to prevent hunger-related behavior problems. It is important to remember that every dog has his or her own activity level, energy needs and food preferences. In multiple-dog homes with dogs of different ages, activity levels and health status, more than one food may be needed. Monitoring body weight and condition is essential, as is selecting a food that not only contains all of the needed nutrients that we discussed in this chapter but that is also suitable for your dog's age, life stage and activity level. Let's now turn to an examination of what nutritional science tells us about how to best feed your dog throughout his life and for his or her specific lifestyle and activities.

5

Age Matters

Like many people whose lives revolve around dogs, my love of animals began when I was very young. I was lucky enough to grow up in a very "doggy" family, with parents who modeled not just love, but also respect and compassion for all other animals. Judy was our family's first dog; she was a medium-sized Beagle mix who, if my memory serves me well, had the absolutely softest ears ever known to the canine world. Judy was adopted from our local shelter, which in those days (the early 1960s) was the town dog pound, a place where strays were taken and held prior to being euthanized. My mom adopted Judy when she was eight weeks old, a pup born to a pregnant dog who had been impounded. Judy came home loaded with fleas and intestinal parasites and was so sick during the first few weeks with our family that it was possible that she would not survive. Lucky for all of us, she did, and Judy grew to be the best childhood companion that a shy, bookish kid could ever hope for. My childhood was spent exploring the outdoors, wading around our neighborhood creek, snuggling on the couch and sharing dinner and bedtime snacks with my pal Judy.

So, since this is a book about nutrition, what did we feed to Judy, our family dog of the 1960s? Well, first, let's go back in time to see what was available to dog owners during those years. Up until the 1950s, commercial pet foods were still a relatively rare commodity, particularly when compared with the multitude of choices that are available to us today. Most people fed their dogs either a canned dog food or one of the few dry meals that that were sold. Throughout the 1950s, Ken-L Ration dominated the canned food market while Gaines dog meals held the major portion of the dry meal market. Keep in mind that the canned foods of the first half of the 1900s contained primarily horsemeat, a practice that finally and thankfully was outlawed in the 1970s (see Figure 5.1). The dry meals also differed significantly from dry dog foods of today. Rather than the extruded foods that we are familiar with today, these were a dense mixture of meat meals, various grains and cereal by-products.

This all changed in the late 1950s when two nutritionists with the Ralston Purina Company in St. Louis considered using the same technology that was used to produce Chex cereal and corn puffs to produce dog food. This processing technique, called **extrusion**, is used to make a wide variety of human foods such as breakfast cereals, dried pastas and corn-based snacks like cheese puffs. Extrusion effectively cooks the starch in grains, resulting in a tasty and crunchy product that allows breakfast cereal to stay crisp in milk (a decidedly positive advance in cereal technology, in my humble opinion). Some of us will remember Rice Krispies and their early slogan "Snap, Crackle Pop." (As a kid, my Dad and I sat together and timed how long it took for our noisy bowls of cereal to stop yammering and get soggy.) The Purina nutritionists wondered if this cooking process would enhance dog food appeal and digestibility if applied to the dry meals. They borrowed an extruder from the cereal people, and after three years of experimenting, enter Purina Dog Chow, which we chose as the food we fed to our dog Judy. The "chow" came in a box (not a bag) that was about the same size and shape as my Rice Krispies carton. And, like my cereal, Judy's food had a pleasing crunchy texture and she not only accepted it, she gobbled it down with relish. Unlike my cereal, Judy's Purina Dog Chow was also covered with a greasy coating that increased both its tastiness and its nutritional value (more about this later).

When age did not matter

What I find most interesting about the Purina Dog Chow of fifty years ago was that it was promoted by the dog food experts at Purina as *the only food that Judy needed* to remain a healthy, happy and active dog throughout her life! Each box came with a statement asserting that the food contained in the box would provide "complete and balanced nutrition." In other words, these uniform pieces of kibble were all Judy should need to thrive. The dog food label went even further, typically including phrases such as "throughout your dog's life" or "for all of your dog's life stages." Wow. These were ambitious claims. Such assertions certainly were not made for the Rice Krispies that I often ate for breakfast (and most definitely were not promoted about cheese puffs). However, the claim that feeding a single food would provide a "complete and balanced diet" to a dog, throughout his life, was included not only on the labels of Purina Dog Chow but on many other early foods, and was also endorsed by experts of the time in advertisements and promotions. The wide acceptance of this concept, indeed the delight with which such an idea was greeted, must be considered within the culture of the time during which it originated in the United States.

The 1950s saw the birth of consumerism and an unprecedented growth of the middle class. As the economy recovered following World War II, industrialism boomed and living the good life became associated with buying a house in the suburbs, complete with the brand new television set, refrigerator, washing machine and a few shiny appliances for the kitchen counters. During the 1960s we began to explore space, were developing a plethora of new medical drugs and advances, and were enjoying the technologies that brought all sorts of new household appliances and gadgets into our homes. These items, promoted via the rapidly expanding world of advertising, were purportedly designed to make our lives easier and happier. Many of the new technologies and the new (and improved) products that they produced were viewed positively and accepted without reservation. Even our entertainment reflected these ideals. A favorite television program of the early 60s was The Jetsons which portrayed the cartoon life of a space-age family, including George and Jane, their two kids, and their really cool dog, Astro. The Jetsons lived in the futuristic community of Orbit City, where they traveled in flying cars, had a robot maid named Rosie, and received all of their meals from food pills popped into a contraption that looked suspiciously like a present-day microwave oven. I am not sure if Astro's dog food came from one of these pills, but the underlying message of the Jetsons was that future world was going to be a place where all of our wants and needs were met through machine support and high technology. (Of course, the final scene each week of George miss-stepping while walking Astro on the treadmill, resulting in the classic cartoon disaster of George's two-dimensional body being repeatedly sucked around the machine's revolving belt, could be read as foreshadowing of the skepticism that was to come in later decades.) Regardless, at that time and against this backdrop of "better living through technology," the Purina kibbles that were reportedly going to be all that Astro (or our Judy) needed to thrive, seemed to most families of the 60s, including my own, to be a pretty neat trick! We accepted these claims without question and with great enthusiasm.

And, truth be told, Judy did thrive. She loved her Purina Dog Chow, came running whenever she heard those crispy kibbles rattling in the box, and enjoyed a very long, happy (although somewhat portly) life with us. To my knowledge, we fed Judy the same food throughout her life, and she lived to be almost 15 years of age. Living in a home with two kids and parents who adored her, Judy also enjoyed her share of human foods along with an overabundance of treats on her birthday and holidays! However, what we did not do for certain, because these foods did not yet exist, was switch Judy to a food that was formulated for "less active" dogs when she gained a few inches of middle-age spread, or to a food that was marketed for "seniors" when she reached her older years. Which all begs the question: What does the phrase "**Complete and Balanced for All Life Stages**" actually mean? And more importantly, is this a scientifically valid claim? Knowing what we do today about canine nutrition, should we feed different foods for different life stages? Are these foods necessary or are they simply marketing gimmicks? Let's begin by examining the science behind label statements that were made about Judy's dog food of the 1960s, and that continue to be used on many foods today: the "Complete and Balanced for All Life Stages" claim.

Development of dog foods in the 20th century

- 1922: Canned pet food containing horse meat was introduced in the United States by the Chappel brothers of Rockford, Illinois as a means to dispose of deceased horses. The name of their dog food? Ken-L Ration.

- 1930s: Ken-L Ration became such a success that the Chappels began the very controversial practices of breeding horses explicitly for dog food and rounding up and killing wild horses. They slaughtered more than 50,000 horses annually.

- By 1940, canned dog food held 90% of the pet food market and was dominated by Ken-L Ration. (Dry foods were fed rarely and consisted of heavy "meals" that were sold in 100 lb. bags).

- WWII War Years: The US government rationed tin and meat, leading to a rapid decline in canned dog food production. Dry dog food became popular again and most companies either switched to producing a dry dog food or went out of business.

- 1957: Nutritionists at Purina introduce the first extruded (kibble) dry dog food. Within two years Purina Dog Chow became the leading brand of dog food in the United States.

- 1960s: Growing public opposition to the use of horses for dog food led to legislation, passed in 1971, that prohibited the capture and killing of wild horses for use as pet food. This eventually led to the complete discontinuation of horsemeat in pet foods and the increased use of other meats such as chicken, beef and pork.

- 1970s to present: In the United States, dry dog foods continue to be more popular than canned (wet) foods. Many owners use a canned product as a supplemental treat or mix a small amount of canned with their dry diet.

Figure 5.1 Twentieth century dog food trends.

Complete and balanced for all life stages…really?

We are so accustomed to seeing the phrase "complete and balanced nutrition" on pet food labels that most of us do not consider the implications of such a claim. Interestingly, this assertion was first included on dog food labels many years before companies had enough knowledge about dogs to back it up with nutritional standards. Clarence Gaines, the founder of Gaines dog food, first used the phrase in 1928 to describe his newly developed dog meal. Clarence was an avid hunter who kept a kennel of Pointers. Frustrated with the quality of foods that were available at the time, he worked with his family's livestock feed company to create a dry dog food composed of a meat meal base, dairy products, soy and a variety of grains. Initially, Clarence fed his new food only to his hunting dogs and also gave it to friends for their dogs. However, the meal quickly became popular, especially when a local game farm began asking their members to test the food on dogs who were being exhibited in hunting trials. Within a year, Clarence's family feed company had added Gaines Dog Meal to their line of animal feeds and the food was being shipped to warehouses around the country.

Clarence went on to invent a number of new dog feeding concepts that led to his company's success and had a major impact on the burgeoning pet food industry. First, Clarence decided to package his food in paper bags rather than the burlap sacks that had been traditionally used with dry dog meals. He argued that paper was sanitary and could be securely closed with a glue-based seal. An added (and prescient) bonus to this change was that unlike burlap, paper could be easily printed on. This small change heralded the dawn of pet food advertising, a field that is booming today and that has enormous influence on our pet food selection habits. Clarence included a company logo on his paper sacks, plus his illustrious claim that Gaines meal provides "100 % complete and balanced nutrition." Pet food advertising campaigns and label claims took off and the industry has not looked back since. Over the next few years, Gaines cleverly designed several additional advertisements for his foods and began to place these in dog fancier publications. One of his most popular slogans was the enthusiastic "Gaines Complete Meal—Nourishes Every Inch of Your Dog!" Interestingly, although Clarence eventually went on to test his food scientifically, at the time that the "complete and balanced" label claim first appeared on his dog food packages there was no documented evidence to support his ambitious pledge.

Gaines was also the first pet food producer to attempt to pellet a dry meal. The early dry dog foods had a consistency similar to coarsely ground corn meal. Owners were instructed to add water to the meal to improve its consistency and increase its appeal to their dogs. Still, the meals were dusty and messy and many owners complained of the food's texture and of the fact that their dogs' stools were voluminous and soft. This latter effect reflected the low digestibility of the product. In response, Gaines began to pellet the dry meal and marketed this new version as a brand called Gaines Krunchons. While somewhat more functional than the meals, these pellets were not cooked in the same manner as extruded foods of today and so continued to have low digestibility and appeal.

Clarence also appeared to have been a man of integrity. While it is true that he initially claimed "100 % complete and balanced nutrition" before actually conducting research to support such a claim, he did eventually go on to attempt to do just that. Gaines is credited as the first dog food producer to use a scientific approach to studying a dog's responses to his food as well as the first to hire a full-time veterinarian to help with both testing and promoting his brands. The Gaines Company prepared some of the first dog owner educational pamphlets that were intended to inform and educate dog owners and enthusiasts. Given that this was still well before the years during which animal nutritionists began to actively study the nutrient requirements of dogs, Clarence seemed to have been well ahead of his time. In 1943, the Gaines company was purchased by General Mills, a company that went on to create one of the first semi-moist dog foods (Gaines Burgers) along with a line of biscuits and other foods. In the ensuing years, other pet food companies picked up the "complete and balanced" claim and whether or not such a claim was verifiable, it had found a place on the dog food label and there it has stayed.

Enter the Association of American Feed Control Officials (AAFCO), the agency that eventually required scientific support behind label claims. AAFCO was founded in 1909 and is an organization comprised of state and federal officials that regulate animal feeds and pet foods (more about AAFCO in Chapters 10 and 11). Although not yet very active when Clarence Gaines was making his original claims, AAFCO eventually stepped in and set both definitions and regulations for the "complete and balanced" label claim, among others. AAFCO first established its Pet Food Committee in 1959, but regulations that applied specifically to pet foods were not adopted until 1967. This means that a lot of pet food, including at least several years' worth of Judy's dog chow, was sold with a label claim of "complete and balanced" or "100 % nutrition" before there were any established standards to authenticate such claims! As it stands today, AAFCO defines the phrase as follows: "Complete and balanced means the product has all the required nutrients, in proper amounts and proportions, and *has been tested* to make sure it meets the complex nutritional requirements of a healthy dog or cat" (emphasis is mine). The complex nutritional requirements to which AAFCO is referring are a set of nutrient profiles that were produced by companion animal nutritionists and published initially by the National Research Council and eventually, starting in the early 1990s, by AAFCO itself.

Today, in addition to "complete and balanced," the phrase "**all life stages**" is often found on dog food labels. When did this concept start to show up? During the 1970s and 1980s pet food companies used nutrient requirement levels that were published in the National Research Council's *Nutrient Requirements of the Dog* manuals. Using the NRC guidelines, the life stages requirement was somewhat ambiguous. A food was either identified as being suitable for "all life stages," meaning that the food met all of the published nutrient guidelines of the NRC or the food had a limited purpose, which meant that it should be fed only as a supplemental food and did not meet all of the NRC requirements. Needless to say, almost all foods tacked on the "all life stages" phrase to the already ubiquitous "complete and balanced" claim. Starting in the early 1990s, AAFCO refined the life stages requirement by publishing two sets of requirements: one set for growth and reproduction, and a second set for adult dogs during maintenance (i.e., normal activity level, not reproducing—your basic adult pet living in a home). If a food is formulated for (and has passed testing for) the highest nutrient requirements (i.e., growth/reproduction), it is assumed to meet needs for "all life stages" and so is legally allowed to carry that claim on the label. It is important to note here that these were (and continue to be) the only two life stages that are defined by AAFCO that are regulated in any way, and that have specific label (package) claims associated with them. To date, there exist no authorized set of nutrient profiles for other life stages, activity levels or lifestyles. This means that foods that are marketed for senior dogs, large breed puppies, less active dogs and for different breeds or breed groups are not required to comply with a predetermined or regulated set of standards such as nutrient profiles or feeding trials that specifically support the particular life stage or lifestyle niche (more about this in Chapters 9 and 10).

What exactly does it mean when consumers see the "Complete and Balanced Nutrition for All Life Stages" claim? Well, because the highest nutrient requirements generally occur during growth and reproduction, it means that when a food is formulated to pass the "all life stages" claim, per current regulatory guidelines, that food is in essence a puppy food. Practically speaking, this means that foods carrying this label may provide an excess of certain nutrients for most adult and senior dogs. Additionally, such a food may not be the best choice for a canine athlete who needs a food that is packed with energy or similarly for a couch potato who would benefit from a reduced calorie food. So, while the somewhat misleading label claim of "Complete and Balanced Nutrition for all Life Stages" does not generally pose a health risk to dogs, it also may not be the best that we can do for our dogs at each stage of life and activity level, knowing what we do today about the varied life stages and lifestyles of today's dogs.

Culturally, we have come full circle. What was first viewed as new and innovative (and really cool) during the early 1960s, now is (and should be) regarded with a healthy dose of skepticism. We know more today than we did 50 years ago about a dog's nutritional needs during different life stages. Just as human nutrient needs change as we age, so too do those of our dogs. We also know enough to formulate specific foods that target the nutrient and energy needs of dogs during different life stages, even though there are no AAFCO standards that must be met for such foods. So, while the claim of the 1960s that a single food provided all that Judy needed may have appealed to the "better living through chemistry" ideals of that age, the careful dog owners of today realize that such a food may not be the best choice for their dog. These advancements are reflected in the pet food market of today, albeit to excess. Most (but not all) pet food brands are now offered as a series of life stage and lifestyle foods. The typical line-up includes a growth (puppy), adult (maintenance), less active (or weight control), highly active (or performance) and senior diet. Other segments include foods that are size-specific or breed-specific or that manage a variety of health conditions.

Interestingly, some companies clearly are barking out of both sides of their mouths as they sell targeted life stage foods and at the same time market one or more brands or product lines within brands that carry an "all life stages" claim and promotion. Examples include the Purina's ProPlan brand and Diamond's Taste of the Wild brand. What is this about? Well, this little inconsistency reflects the fickleness of the free market and admonishes us once again to keep our critical thinking caps firmly in place. Generally speaking, the "all life stages" brands are designed to target pet owners who are most interested in convenience and simplicity and do not want to have to think too much about selecting a dog food. For those owners and professionals who *do* wish to choose carefully, this leads us to the question, what exactly do dogs need for life stage nutrition? Are there real differences, or are all of these different foods just marketing tactics designed to boost sales? Good questions—let's take a look at what nutritional science tells us about life stage nutrition for our dogs and what we can (and cannot) believe.

Puppy foods? Do our dogs need them or not?

We recently finished a session of training classes at my training school, AutumnGold. Like many trainers who promote methods that emphasize positive reinforcement, we use food treats as a primary reinforcer. For some owners, this can lead to unwanted weight gain in their dogs if they do not adjust their dog's daily intake carefully. To prevent this, we always include a short presentation about nutrition and feeding management. During this chat, Ruth, the owner of Ellie, a young Bernese Mountain Dog, asked about the suitability of feeding large breed puppy food. Ellie was six months old and Ruth said that she was feeding Ellie an adult maintenance food on the recommendation of the breeder. When I asked her why, she said that her breeder told her that puppy foods cause dogs to grow too rapidly and that rapid growth rates lead to bone problems in large breed dogs. Another student then added that he had always thought that the division of puppy food into two types, one for medium breed dogs and another for large/giant breed dogs, was just a marketing ploy that was designed to make people pay more for dog food. My initial response to these comments was a rather indecorous (coming from my emotional brain, most likely), yikes! Ruth's breeder had given her potentially harmful advice and the cynical comment about marketing was, while understandable, also false. Let's dig down and see why.

What does the science say?

Let's examine these two claims separately. The first is Ellie's breeder's belief that dog foods that are formulated for puppies cause a rapid growth rate that can lead to skeletal problems. Like many beliefs, this advice contains elements that are true and elements that are false. The true portion regards a connection between rapid growth rate and skeletal disease. Studies of the growth rate of large breed dogs date back almost 50 years, starting with a paper published by Riser and Shirer in the journal *Veterinary Radiology* in 1965 (see Figure 5.2). This was one of the first reports documenting the excessive growth demands that occur in large breed pups; this stress occurs simply because as adults, these dogs are almost *100 times larger* than our smallest breed dogs.

Despite this enormous difference in adult size, large breed puppies still attain their adult size in roughly the same amount of time as much smaller dogs, at about one year of age. This means that the *rate* of growth must be much greater in large breeds. It was hypothesized by researchers that this very rapid growth rate might be incompatible with healthy skeletal development.

Following publication of this initial report, a group of researchers at Cornell University explored this theory through a series of studies with growing Great Dane pups. Their studies provided support for the hypothesis; they reported that the rapid growth rates that are driven by a large adult body size put a great deal of stress on a developing skeleton and that this increases a dog's risk of developing skeletal diseases. This information is in complete agreement with Ruth's breeder's statement that dogs who grow rapidly are more susceptible to skeletal disorders such as hip dysplasia and elbow dysplasia. Additional studies after the Cornell series confirmed this, along with numerous case studies that have been reported in veterinary journals. Together, these studies have shown that large breed dogs are more prone to developmental skeletal diseases when compared with smaller breeds, at least in part because they have the genetic potential for excessively rapid growth, which is driven by their large adult size.

The second point that Ellie's breeder made had to do with feeding a puppy for rapid growth. Is there evidence that the type of puppy food that is fed influences growth rate and skeletal development? Again, nutritionists have studied this for over 30 years and continue to study it today. During this time, several theories were put forth about which nutrients play a specific role in both growth rate and skeletal development in large breed dogs. Studies examined the influences of dietary protein, fat, calcium, phosphorus, vitamin D and energy (calories). The accumulated results have shown that rapid growth rate is caused by overfeeding nutrient- and energy-dense foods, especially during the most rapid growth phase between three and six months of age. A second factor that appears to be important is the level of dietary calcium. Large breed puppies who consume too much dietary calcium are at increased risk of developing skeletal disease. The excess calcium does not affect the pup's growth rate, but rather has a direct negative impact on developing bones.

The solution? Feed a large breed puppy food that supplies all of the essential nutrients in their correct proportions and that contains reduced energy (calories) and slightly reduced calcium. In addition, all pups (not just large and giant breed puppies) should be kept lean (not plump!) throughout growth. Studies show us that there is a high correlation between feeding for a "plump" body condition and maximal growth rate. Today, dog foods that meet these criteria are being developed, tested and sold by a variety of pet food companies. Typically, a large breed growth (puppy) food provides between 300 and 340 kcals/cup of food and contains between 0.8 and 1.0 % calcium. To compare, growth foods that are formulated for medium and small breed dogs are more energy dense foods (i.e., provide more calories per cup) and do not control calcium levels. For example, typical growth diets for small or medium size dogs will provide over 400 kcals/cup and often have calcium levels that are over 1.1 %. Although we cannot state that such a food will definitely harm a large breed puppy, a food that is specifically designed to slow rate of growth and to supply enough but not too much calcium is a better choice for a large breed puppy.

Large breed puppy nutrition: research history

1965: Large and giant breed dogs have a rapid growth rate that can influence skeletal health: Riser WH and Shirer JF: "Normal and abnormal growth of the distal foreleg in large and giant dogs." *Veterinary Radiology*, 6: 50–64, 1965.

1974: Cornell studies with growing Great Danes showed a connection between over-nutrition, rapid growth rate and developmental skeletal diseases: Hedhammar A, et al: "Over-nutrition and skeletal disease. An experimental study in growing Great Dane dogs." IV. *Clinical observations*. Cornell Vet. 64:Suppl 5:32-45, 1974.

1980 to present: Studies that examined the influence of dietary energy (calories), protein, calcium and other nutrients upon skeletal health in growing large breed dogs were conducted. A partial list of these studies includes:

- Dammrich, K. "Relationship between nutrition and bone growth in large and giant dogs." *J. Nutr.* 1991; 121: 114S-121S

- Hazewinkel, HAW, et al: "Influences of chronic calcium excess on the skeletal development of growing Great Danes." *JAVMA* 21: 377-391,1985

- Tryfonidou MA, et al: "Intestinal calcium absorption in growing dogs is influenced by calcium intake and age but not by growth rate." *J Nutr.* 132: 3363-3368

- Kealy RD, et al: "Five-year longitudinal study on limited food consumption and development of osteoarthritis in coxofemoral joints of dogs." *JAVMA* 210:222-225, 1997

- Nap RC, et al: "Growth and skeletal development in Great Dane pups fed different levels of protein intake." *J Nutr.* 121:S107-113, 1991.

Current understanding: Excess caloric intake during growth in large and giant breed dogs promotes rapid growth which is associated with an increased incidence of skeletal disorders such as hip dysplasia and osteochondrosis. Feeding diets that are less calorically dense will not reduce adult size but will slow rate of growth so that mature size is achieved over a longer period. A slower growth rate is associated with fewer developmental orthopedic problems. In addition, both too much and not enough calcium can lead to developmental bone problems. For large breed dogs, this optimal range appears to be narrower than for other breeds, and excessive levels of calcium may contribute to bone disease. Therefore, moderately lower dietary calcium is recommended for the diet of growing large breed dogs.

Figure 5.2 Large breed puppy nutrition research.

Should some puppies be fed adult foods?

Alternatively, is it safe to feed a balanced adult dog food to a growing large breed puppy instead? To put it bluntly: no. The argument that adult foods are lower in caloric density than puppy foods and therefore are more appropriate for large breed puppies is not good advice. In fact, as we will see later in this chapter, the adult dog foods that are available today vary widely in calorie content, with some containing substantially more calories per cup than puppy foods. Adult diets are also not appropriately restricted in calcium content. So, the piece of advice that Ellie's breeder got wrong was her recommendation to "feed an adult food" to Ellie. While this advice may have been prudent 30 years ago, before nutritionists knew how to best feed large and giant breed puppies, it is not only unhelpful today, but potentially harmful.

What does nutritional science have to say regarding the second student's belief that puppy foods for different breed sizes are just a marketing ploy, designed to increase sales and profits? Well first, as we have seen, the science that is available supports a need for foods that specifically target the developmental health of large and giant breed dogs. Second, yes, dog food companies are interested in making a profit. And of course, this is true for almost everything that we purchase and use in today's consumer-based society. It is impossible to remove this bias and vested interest from a company's motivations and behavior, just as it is impossible to remove the profit bias from consumer products that we purchase for ourselves. Pet food label claims are regulated by state feed control officials and by the FDA; blatantly *unsupportable* claims of effectiveness or health benefit are prohibited, with violations leading to fines or extensive lawsuits. Therefore, although it is true that it is often the pet food companies themselves who are doing much of the research on pet nutrition today, the product claims that they make as a result of their research are subject to challenge (especially by other pet food companies) and regulation. However, these regulations are not tremendously stringent and have several limitations and weaknesses, as we will see in Chapter 10. Therefore, it is still our best option as critical (and skeptical) consumers to seek evidence in the form of published research and review papers when considering a food claim that may affect our dog's health. In this particular case—what to feed large breed puppies—the scientific evidence supports an approach of feeding a food that has reduced calories and calcium and supports a moderate, not maximal, rate of growth.

What else is important for our pups?

Well, most important is energy. We know that growing dogs have higher energy (calorie) needs than adults. These needs come about from the naturally higher activity levels of puppies (we all know about these!), plus needs for development and maturation. A general rule of thumb is that a growing pup needs twice the number of calories (kcal) per day as an adult dog who weighs the same amount. (For specific examples and calculations for estimating your dog's daily calorie needs, see Appendix 3). Most dog owners seem to have little problem providing their growing dog with *enough* food to meet his or her caloric needs. In fact, it is more common for owners to overfeed. Problems typically arise as a pup's growth rate and activity level naturally decline, which lead to lower daily energy needs as the pup reaches adult size. This change begins around six months of age for small dogs and at eight to ten months of age for large breed dogs. Unfortunately, owners often fail to recognize these changes and continue to feed their puppy as if he was still growing rapidly. This simple error is why we often see overweight conditions starting early in life. Without question, the best thing that you can do for your growing pup is to feed him or her to maintain a lean body condition (again, not plump!). Ribs should be easily felt but not seen and your pup should be exercised regularly (but not excessively) to support good muscle tone. Although some breeders continue to believe that keeping a dog lean during the growth phase will limit adult size (i.e., stunt growth), this is a false belief. Adult size is genetically determined; feeding for a lean body condition simply slows down rate of growth, it does not stunt growth. Dogs attain adult size at a gradual and healthy rate if fed with careful attention to their body condition.

We also know that growing puppies require a slightly higher proportion of dietary protein in their diet when compared to adult dogs. Some breeders and other dog enthusiasts mistakenly believe that increased dietary protein is the culprit that causes skeletal problems in large breed dogs. However, this is another false belief—as we discussed, excess energy consumption is the problem for large breed puppies, not protein. Growing puppies require higher protein to supply their needs for tissue growth. However, because they are also consuming more food overall (those high energy needs again), the actual *percentage* increase in dietary protein is moderate. For example, while the AAFCO minimum level of protein that must be included in adult diets is 18 %, the minimum level for growth is 22 %. And of course, the protein that is provided in the food should be high quality—this means that it supplies all of the essential amino acids that the growing dogs need and must be highly digestible. Because most animal-source proteins are generally of higher quality than plant-source proteins, foods that include an animal source protein as its primary protein source is recommended. Finally, optimal growth requires adequate, but not excessive levels of all of the essential minerals and vitamins. Some breeders focus unnecessarily upon calcium, thinking that a high calcium intake is needed for normal bone growth in puppies. As we saw earlier, this is not true, and in fact, excess calcium consumption poses as great a risk as insufficient intake.

Choosing well for your puppy

Many owners pay attention to the amount and type of protein in foods that they select for their growing dog, so let's end this section by comparing several commercial dry puppy foods in terms of protein level, protein sources and energy content (kcals/cup). Figure 5.3 shows a group of ten brands of commercial dog foods that are marketed for puppies. These were selected to provide a range of prices, ingredient sources and nutritional philosophies. (Note: A variety of brands are included as examples throughout this book. No single brand or company is intentionally represented more or less than others.)

Let's first look at protein content. Current label regulations require that pet food manu-facturers report nutrients on their label as a percentage by weight. Protein is reported as a minimum (i.e., contains no less that X % protein). As we stated earlier, the minimum AAFCO requirement for protein for growing puppies is 22 %. All of the foods in our set of brands contain more than the AAFCO minimum. As a rule of thumb, foods that are more energy dense (contain more kcals per cup) generally have a higher percentage of protein. For example, you will notice that food #1 provides 441 kcal/cup and has a relatively high protein content of 31 %, while food #7 provides 305 kcal/cup and has a lower level of protein at 27 %. Foods are *deliberately* formulated so that the percentage protein increases proportionately with calorie content. This is necessary to ensure that the food still meets an animal's needs. Although this relationship seems counterintuitive to us, it is indisputably correct because dogs will be fed a lower volume of a higher energy food when compared with a less energy dense food to maintain correct body weight. Since protein needs are the same regardless, the percentage protein in a higher energy food must increase proportionately. So, a general rule of thumb to remember is that if you are feeding a food that is energy dense (this comes up again when we look at feeding canine athletes), then the percentage (by weight) of all essential nutrients, including protein, must be slightly higher in more calorically dense foods.

#	Puppy food brand	Protein (%)	Energy (kcal/cup)	Primary protein source(s)*
1	Acana Puppy & Junior	31	441	Chicken meal, de-boned chicken
2	Authority Puppy Chicken	26	380	Chicken meal
3	Beneful Puppy Food	28	390	Chicken by-product meal, corn gluten meal
4	Blue Buffalo Wilderness Puppy	36	438	De-boned chicken, chicken meal, turkey meal
5	Castor & Pollux Natural Ultramix Puppy	28	330	Chicken, chicken meal, turkey meal
6	Hill's Healthy Advantage Puppy	31	384	Chicken by-product meal, corn gluten meal
7	Pedigree Puppy	27	305	Poultry by-product meal, corn gluten meal
8	Nulo Growth Diet	30	434	De-boned salmon, turkey meal, menhaden fish meal
9	Wellness Super-5Mix Puppy	28	450	De-boned chicken, chicken meal, salmon meal
10	Wellness Super-5Mix Large Breed Puppy	26	366	De-boned chicken, white fish, chicken meal

Figure 5.3 Proteins levels, energy content and protein sources in a selection of puppy foods (dry, extruded products).

Calories are also an important consideration, especially for large and giant breed dogs. Generally, dry foods that are formulated for growing puppies contain between 380 and 450 calories (kcals) per cup of food. Foods that are designed for large breed dogs should be moderately restricted in calories to support a moderate growth rate and lean body condition. For example, compare foods # 9 and #10. These are both Wellness brand foods; # 9 is formulated for medium size breeds, while # 10 is formulated for large and giant breed puppies. Notice that #9 provides 450 kcal per cup, while # 10, the large breed puppy food, provides almost 100 fewer calories per cup (360 kcal/cup). And notice that, while the protein sources are similar, the higher energy density food also has a higher *percentage* of protein by weight. Again, this is completely expected and justified and does not mean that these puppies will be consuming too much protein. I cannot state this enough: *a food that is higher in energy density must also contain a higher percentage of essential nutrients to meet needs.*

Last, we all know that protein source is an important consideration. This collection of puppy foods is a good illustration of the variety of protein sources that are included in dog foods today. We will examine ingredients in detail later in the book (see Chapters 8, 10 and 11), but a few tips are helpful here while we are looking at growth diets. In this table, I identified "primary" protein sources as the protein-providing ingredients that appear in the first items on the label's list of ingredients. You will notice that several foods list de-boned chicken or salmon as the first ingredient. In dry dog foods, protein ingredients that are not followed by the term "meal" are unprocessed and obtained as a frozen product. Because these frozen meats are listed first, they were added to the food in the greatest amount by weight. This looks like a great feature to us, since most people prefer to feed their dog a food containing unprocessed poultry or fish over feeding a food that contains a processed (dried) meal. However, while it is true that unprocessed meats are appealing (more about this later), finding these at the top of the ingredient list of a dry dog food is misleading and is a commonly used marketing ploy. This is true because of the amount of water that is present in unprocessed meats. For example, whole chicken is approximately 70 % water, which means that only a small portion of this ingredient provides protein to the food. Rather, it is providing the water that is needed for cooking and extrusion and which is eventually cooked off or removed from the product as it is dried. The end result is that only 30 % of the whole chicken added to the food contributes protein, which means that only a small proportion of the food's protein actually comes from this whole chicken that looks so great on the ingredient list.

When comparing dry dog foods, we must look primarily at the protein sources that are added in a dry form, as these are the ingredients that contribute the bulk of the food's protein. Knowing this, we can see that brands #1 and #2 supply protein from chicken meal, brands #4 and #5 supply protein as chicken meal and turkey meal, and brand # 9 provides protein as chicken and salmon. As a general rule, by-product meals are of lower quality than meals, and meals that do not identify the species of animal that they come from are considered lower quality than those that do. For example, brand #6 contains chicken by-product meal as its primary protein source and brand #7 has poultry by-product meal as its first ingredient, both indicators of lower quality protein sources (see Chapter 8 for a detailed discussion of by-product meals). This lower quality is usually, but not always, reflected in price. Finally, contrary to popular belief, corn gluten meal is a source of protein (not carbohydrate) in a food. It is generally a less expensive protein source than animal source ingredients and is considered to be moderate (not low, as many mistakenly believe) in protein quality. We will revisit protein sources and ways to choose among them in more detail in Chapter 8. Let's now move on to the stage of life in which our dogs, like people, spend most of their time, as adults.

Adulthood…why the heck are our dogs so fat?

The number one chronic health problem plaguing adult dogs in the United States is obesity. We explored some of the cultural elements of this phenomenon in Chapter 1. So, if we agree that this is a problem (and it is), how can we take precautions to keep our dogs' waistlines and weights where they should be once our pups reach maturity? It helps to begin with a few facts about dogs' actual energy requirements. Once a dog has finished growing and has reached his adult size, the most important nutritional change, and one that is frequently overlooked by owners, is a reduction in his daily energy (caloric) needs. It continually surprises me how often our training school clients do not realize this and fail to reduce the amount of food that they provide once their dog has matured. Oddly enough, as humans we certainly are aware of this type of change in ourselves. For example, when I was a teenager, I could consume a hot fudge sundae a day, and still stay rail thin. Today, now that I am well into my middle age years, it seems that simply looking at a jar of hot fudge on the grocery store shelf causes added pounds. This change has come about both because I stopped growing in my late teens and because my overall activity level gradually decreased as I aged. These two changes: cessation of growth and reduced activity, result in fewer calories being burned each day, which of course translates into my needing fewer calories each day.

So too it goes for our dogs, but at an accelerated rate. The young puppy who had an abundance of energy and never seemed to settle down, does in fact eventually mellow usually around one to one and a half years of age. Most dogs (Labrador Retrievers and Border Collies exempted), settle in to early adult life and reduce their activity to some degree. Although owners do tend to notice their dog's more relaxed demeanor as an adult, they do not always translate this change to an accompanying reduction in the number of calories that they provide to the dog each day. This disconnect can be further aggravated by training sessions that include plenty of positive reinforcement in the form of training treats. As dogs mature and we extend our training sessions to longer periods, we naturally use more training treats. Although dogs in training are often highly active, this activity does not necessarily offset the added treat calories.

Many dogs also experience another important change during adolescence that impacts their daily caloric requirement—they are neutered. For a long time, the belief of many owners that neutering causes dogs to get fat was considered to be an example of that common logical fallacy, the post hoc error. Because neutering is often conducted at the time in a dog's life when activity and growth rate are naturally declining, dogs would gain weight following neutering if food intake was not reduced. The operation was thus erroneously blamed for a weight gain that was in reality just due to reduced activity and overfeeding as the dog reached maturity. Interestingly enough, however, today there seems to be a bit of truth to this belief. Starting in the mid-1980s several different teams of veterinarians and nutritionists have studied the impact of neutering on energy balance in dogs. Although not a primary factor in weight gain, there is some evidence that intact dogs may naturally consume less food than neutered dogs and that the energy expenditure of neutered dogs may be slightly lower than that of intact dogs, irrespective of natural reductions in activity level. However, even in the face of these effects, the equation is still all about matching energy in (food) to energy out (activity). Knowing that energy needs decrease with maturity simply means that we must pay closer attention to how much we feed (and provides treats to) our adult dogs to avoid overweight conditions.

Choosing well for adult dogs

Food selection is an important matter for adult dogs, just as it is with puppies. As we saw in Chapter 4, the caloric content of dry dog foods that are formulated for adults varies dramatically today (see Figure 5.4). This is especially significant when looking at grain-free or low carbohydrate foods, as these products are generally much higher in calories than foods that contain a higher proportion of digestible carbohydrate. As we discussed earlier, in general, puppy foods have higher calories per cup (i.e., are more energy dense) than corresponding adult foods. This is important for puppies who have less volume available in their gastrointestinal tracts along with higher energy needs. However, it is a distinction that is important to be aware of, especially since some pet food companies encourage owners to feed their growing dog a puppy food for up to the first two years of life. With the exception of giant breed dogs (and large breed puppy foods), this is completely unnecessary and can contribute to overfeeding, simply because the puppy food will provide more calories per cup than an adult dog may need.

Figure 5.5 compares puppy and adult foods within five popular brands. Generally, adult foods are less energy dense than puppy foods (for medium breeds or smaller). The adult food within a brand provides 80 to 100 fewer kcals per cup less than its corresponding puppy food. A complicating factor is something that we discussed earlier—commercial adult foods today vary tremendously in energy content. In this short list alone, the adult foods vary between 278 and 504 kcal per cup! So, while brand #3 puppy food provides 384 kcal/cup, this is not much higher than the adult food of brand #1 (365 kcal/cup). And, oddly enough, not all adult maintenance foods contain few calories than the puppy version of the same food. In brand #5, the adult food supplies about 50 kcals per cup more than the puppy version of the same brand. These differences illustrate the importance of checking labels (and websites), paying special attention to the number of calories that you are providing as your young pup enters his adult years.

Brand of adult dog food (dry)	Kcal/cup
Nutro Natural Choice Wholesome Essentials (Chicken)	278
Pedigree Adult Complete Nutrition	335
Eukanuba Adult Maintenance	347
Science Diet Ideal Balance Grain Free Adult	360
Newman's Own Organics Adult Dry Dog Food	397
Blue Buffalo Wilderness Chicken	410
Wellness Core Grain Free	421
Innova Adult Dry Dog Food Red Meat Large Bites	468
Canidae Grain Free Pure Elements	498
Evo Turkey & Chicken Formula Dry Dog Food	537

Figure 5.4 Energy (calorie) content of 10 commercial dog foods sold for adult dogs.

#	Brand	Life stage	Kcal/cup
1	Eukanuba Naturally Wild	Puppy (Salmon & Rice)	433
		Adults (Salmon & Rice)	365
2	Nature's Variety—Prairie	Puppy (Chicken and Rice)	415
		Adult (Chicken and Rice)	319
3	Nutro Natural Choice	Puppy (Wholesome Essentials)	384
		Adult (Wholesome Essentials)	278
4	Royal Canin	Puppy (Medium Breed)	442
		Adult (Medium Breed)	327
5	Innova	Puppy	454
		Adult	504

Figure 5.5 Energy (calorie) content of puppy versus adult versions of the same brand (large breed puppy foods are not included).

Our beloved seniors…can nutritional science prevent or delay age-related illnesses?

I just finished writing a sympathy note to a running friend who recently lost her fifteen-year-old chocolate Lab, Brandy. I have known Brandy and her mom, Geri, for almost all of their 15 years together, seeing them both along the running trail near our home. The trail is an ideal place for runners and hikers who enjoy being out with their dogs and there is a nice community of trail regulars and their dogs. Geri kept Brandy in great shape, although, like many Labs, Brandy did enjoy her snacks and so carried a tad bit more weight than she should have. Still, she continued to run and hike well into her teen years, enjoying more leisurely strolls and sniffing outings during the final year of her life. When I talked with Geri last week on the trail, we both lamented the hard truth about our beloved dogs—their life spans are far too short. This is true even when a dog lives a healthy and long life, like Brandy. So, as I begin the final section of this chapter and ponder how best to feed our seniors, I am reminded that our goals are ultimately to feed our dogs, throughout life, in a way that will promote the very best of health and life quality well into their teen years. Do we know enough to do this? What does science tell us about the senior years for our dogs? And, can we use this knowledge to keep our dogs with us for many years and perhaps to even extend life?

First and foremost, we must remember that a dog's lifespan, just like that of all other species, is strongly dictated by genetics. Regardless of how well we feed or how excellent the medical care that we provide, we are constrained by the genetically determined biological clock of *Canis familiaris*. The maximum lifespan of the domestic dog is estimated to be about 27 years (don't we all wish for this?). However, very few dogs live beyond 18 years and the average lifespan of the domestic dog when all breeds are considered is about 13 years. Within the species, there is also a significant difference in lifespan among large and small breeds. Giant and large breed dogs have an average lifespan that is significantly less than 13 years, while most small and toy breeds tend to live longer than this. The shortened life span of giant breeds appears to be a result of selective breeding for extremely large dogs, the accompanying rapid early growth rates of these dogs, and the skeletal diseases that result. An additional factor seems to be the types of conformation and exaggerated body features seen in some of our dog breeds. For example, a 2007 study published in the journal *Research in Veterinary Science* reported that heavy but short in stature breeds experience a shorter lifespan due to the influence of inherited structural disorders in those breeds (Greer et al., 2007). We also know without question that purebred standards that require absolute reproductive genetic isolation (i.e., no dogs outside of the breed are added to the gene pool once a breed has been established) within breeds have led to inbreeding practices and the overuse of a small number of individuals (usually males) in an already limited gene pool. Over generations, this has contributed to the proliferation of the more than 500 identified inherited diseases of purebred dogs, many of which may contribute to a shortened lifespan in individual dogs. Although there are still some doubters among dog enthusiasts and breeders, the evidence speaks for itself and should serve as a wake-up call to all who are concerned about dog health and wellness.

When we consider the genetic constraints on lifespan plus the myriad of ways in which we humans have contributed to the dog's health and longevity, we must look at a dog with respect to his size and breed (or breed type) when trying to classify him as a "senior" dog. A helpful rule of thumb is to consider a dog to be in his senior years once he has reached the final third of his expected lifespan and when he has started to show some of the normal signs of aging. For example, a large breed dog with an average lifespan of eleven years may be considered to be a senior dog when he is about seven or eight years of age. Conversely, a small or toy breed dog with an expected lifespan of fourteen years may be classified as elderly when he reaches about ten years of age. Now, here is the catch. Although this is changing (slowly), many veterinarians (and pet food companies) continue to immediately classify *all dogs* as "seniors" when they reach the age of seven years! Because we know that breed, adult size and individual health all influence this, the best thing that we can do for our dogs is to assess them regularly, as individuals, for health-related changes that are associated with aging. Just as in people, dogs experience normal changes as they age. These changes may not be the same in each animal and they do not always significantly impact health or quality of life.

The most obvious age-related change in our dogs is a reduction in voluntary activity. This inevitably leads to a gradual reduction in lean (muscle) mass and an increase in the proportion of body fat. Many owners first notice changes in and around a dog's shoulders or rear limbs as well as the dog getting thicker around the middle while losing strength. Some dogs show signs of hearing loss and decreased visual acuity as they age. Changes in the sense of smell and taste can result in less interest in food. And of course, the risk of developing certain diseases increases as dogs enter their later years. These include mobility problems (most commonly, arthritis), periodontal (dental) disease, kidney or heart disease, changes in cognitive function and behavior, and cancer. In terms of nutrition, age-related changes that we may be able to influence through feeding practices include (once again) making changes to match the dog's lessened daily energy requirements along with providing seniors with the optimal amount of dietary protein and fat. There is some evidence that including functional ingredients such as antioxidant nutrients and chondro-protective (joint health) agents may provide health benefits. Let's start by looking at energy and fat.

Energy and fat requirements for seniors

Most dogs experience a slight to moderate reduction in daily energy (calorie) needs after a certain age. For example, a study of senior pets found that dogs older than eight years consumed approximately 18% fewer calories than breed-matched dogs who were less than six years of age. A decrease of this magnitude would definitely be seen at the dinner bowl level. Still, regardless of this trend, older dogs vary tremendously in their energy needs. Caloric intake should be carefully monitored in older pets to ensure adequate intake of calories and nutrients while at the same time preventing the development of overweight conditions. Most (but not all, as we will see) foods that are marketed for senior dogs have slightly reduced calories. And most (but not all) of these accomplish this by decreasing the amount of fat that they include. Because our older dogs may also benefit from the anti-inflammatory properties of omega-3 fatty acids, the type of fat in the food is an important consideration. Look for fish oils as a primary fat source, even when total amount has been reduced.

Should you reduce protein?

Let us return to one of those pesky cognitive errors, illusion of control. This is the belief that we have more control or influence over a particular phenomenon or situation than we actually have. When discussing nutrition, the illusion of control can lead us to believe that the food that we choose for our dog has more influence upon her long-term health (and lifespan) than it actually has. A common example of this error in senior dog nutrition is the incorrect belief that dietary protein *causes* kidney disease to develop in older dogs or its converse—that reducing the level of protein in an older dog's food will reduce a dog's risk of developing kidney disease. Contrary to its persistence, the belief that healthy older dogs benefit from reductions in dietary protein is incorrect (and has been shown to be incorrect by more than 20 years of research). In fact, not only should we not reduce protein for healthy older dogs, research has shown that healthy aging animals benefit from slightly higher levels of dietary protein. They need this to help to support lean body tissue and possibly also to support a healthy immune system. Dietary protein should only be reduced in the diets of dogs who are diagnosed with renal disease and when their disease has progressed to a point at which their symptoms can be managed by a reduction in dietary protein. Although this reduction can help to manage renal disease once it has occurred, this does not mean that dietary protein caused the disease in the first place. Most (but not all) pet food companies now formulate their senior foods to contain sufficient levels of protein, and do not automatically reduce protein in foods that are designed for older pets. Those foods that do contain reduced protein to manage renal disease are sold only through veterinary prescription and are not available as over the counter products. Finally, because some older dogs may have reduced digestive efficiency, the quality of the protein that is in the food is very important; we will examine the issue of protein (and food) quality in Chapter 10.

Antioxidants and functional ingredients

Older dogs have the same vitamin and mineral requirements as adult dogs. There is no evidence that suggests that they have unusually high or altered requirements. However, because of their antioxidant functions, some vitamins such as vitamin E, vitamin C and beta-carotene may be especially important for our seniors. We do know that these nutrients promote tissue health by reducing free-radical production, harmful compounds which may contribute to aging and the onset of chronic diseases associated with aging. There is also some evidence that providing a diet that is enriched with antioxidant vitamins and related compounds can support immune function and may improve cognitive function in older dogs. For diet selection, this means that it is helpful to look for foods that are advertised as having increased levels of naturally occurring antioxidant nutrients such as vitamin E, beta-carotene and vitamin C.

Another group of functional nutrients that are promoted in both human and canine nutrition are the "**chondro-protective agents**," a term that refers to agents that purportedly enhance joint strength and/or reduce joint inflammation. The two most commonly used supplements are glucosamine and chondroitin sulfate (CS). Many foods that are formulated for senior dogs include these as ingredients and will advertise their role in supporting joint health in older dogs. However, an interesting incongruity exists with these agents. While there is definite evidence that these compounds are effective in vitro (i.e., in a test tube or laboratory tests), there is very little evidence that these effects carry over to being effective when fed to animals—i.e., they may not actually reduce joint pain or increase mobility in dogs (or humans, for that matter). We have a pretty good understanding about how glucosamine and CS work within the joint capsule and there are also data from research studies showing that, in the test tube, CS functions to reduce the production of inflammatory agents and proteins that are involved in degradation of connective tissue in joints. However, when studied as a supplement or when incorporated into dog food, any positive benefits that are reported come almost exclusively from either case studies that did not include controls or even worse, from anecdotal reports. The few controlled studies with dogs that have been published have failed to show significant or consistent benefits. Still, this disparity between the test tube and the dog does not keep supplement manufacturers or pet food companies from using (and promoting) these compounds. They are most commonly included in foods formulated for senior dogs or for large breed dogs. While glucosamine and CS have been demonstrated to be safe, and while they have an impact on joint cells in test tubes, current science tells us that adding it may in reality mean very little for your senior dog's joint health and mobility.

Choosing well for senior dogs

Let me begin this section by stating that most healthy older dogs do not need a senior diet. The reason for this should be clear at this point. We know that senior dogs do not need reduced protein in their diets unless they have been diagnosed with chronic kidney disease and are at a point in their disease that reduced protein can help to manage their symptoms. We also know that older dogs have reduced energy needs and so may require a slight reduction in daily intake. This is often best achieved by simply reducing the amount of a high quality adult food that is fed to an older dog or simply switching to an adult food that contains fewer calories per cup. More important and more effective than reducing the amount of food is maintaining our seniors' daily activity and exercise, taking care to provide "age-appropriate" activities. For example, our oldest dog, Cadie, at thirteen, is lying at my feet as I type this, snoozing after a great hike with me this morning, followed by a swim (her very favorite activity in life!). Although Cadie does have some arthritic changes and is a bit stiff after longer outings, she still loves and benefits from her daily romps with us. And, while added antioxidants can be helpful to older dogs, these are also important for *all* dogs; selecting a food that contains natural or added vitamin E and beta-carotene is a good choice regardless of our dog's age. Finally, while many senior foods advertise as having added glucosamine and chondroitin sulfate, there is just not sufficient evidence that the demonstrated cellular/tissue benefits of these products translates into actual health benefits for our dogs. Altogether, these facts tell us that we can do just fine for our healthy seniors by continuing to feed a high quality food that is formulated for adult maintenance. Although senior dog foods are numerous and purport to provide benefits, they are probably not necessary. Let's look at a few of these.

Figure 5.6 compares ten brands of senior dog food. Interestingly, if you compare the protein and calorie contents of these foods to the adult foods in Figure 5.5, you will see that they encompass similar ranges of protein and energy. (Even more interesting, visits to the websites of these products will show you that most contain exactly the same ingredients as their adult maintenance versions.) This table also shows us that there is no uniform approach to senior diets, illustrated by the wide range in protein content alone. For example, compare food #7 (a grain-free product) which is very high in protein to foods #6, #8 and #9. While the latter three foods provide more than the AAFCO minimum of 18 % protein for adult dogs, they are lower in protein than most adult maintenance foods. Despite current evidence that protein restriction is neither helpful nor warranted for older dogs, the manufacturers of these products perpetuate the myth that older pets should be fed reduced protein foods. Similar to adult maintenance foods, the energy (calorie) content of these foods is all over the map. This range is validated by a recent survey study that was published in the *International Journal of Applied Research in Veterinary Medicine* of almost 40 different senior dog foods (Freeman et al, 2011). Veterinarian Lisa Freeman reported that senior diets had more than a two-fold range in calories; while some were severely restricted, others were similar in energy content to performance foods formulated for working dogs!

This information is a clear buyer beware signal. If you are considering changing to a senior food, it is important to compare the calories per cup of the food that you are feeding to the level in the food that you are considering switching to.

#	Senior food brand	Protein %	Fat %	Energy (kcal/cup)	Age rec.
1	Amicus Senior & Weight Management	30	10.5	400	NP*
2	Canidae—Senior & Overweight Formula	20	8.5	330	NP
3	Dr. Foster & Smith Senior	21	10	360	6-8
4	Eagle Pack Natural—Senior*	26	12	362	8
5	Eukanuba—Senior Maintenance	27	12	304	7
6	Nature's Recipe—Senior	19	8	NP	NP
7	Orijen—Senior Dog	38	15	395	NP
8	Premium Edge—Senior Dog*	20	19	320	NP
9	Science Diet Mature Adult Active Longevity	19.5	15.5	363	7
10	Wysong—Senior Dry Dog Food	18	10	NP	NP

NP—Data not provided by company website or label

Figure 5.6 Protein, fat, energy and age recommendations in senior dog foods.

Another intriguing detail that showed up with this list was that, of the ten foods in this selection, six of the brands *did not recommend an age for feeding*, either on their label or through the information provided on the brand's website. These brands simply referred to the targeted demographic as "seniors" or "older adults" without providing consumers with any guidelines that identified an actual age or age range. This is concerning given that the food is specifically being promoted for a particular life stage. Two of the products were also marketed as both a senior food and a weight management food, which suggests that the manufacturers are trying to increase the target demographic for the product. (Perhaps the strangest example is food #1, which is marketed on its label as a weight management food, yet provides 400 kilocalories per cup of food—an amount that is higher than many adult maintenance foods!) All but two of these foods also advertised as containing added glucosamine and chondroitin sulfate, an addition that is of uncertain benefit to our dogs.

Doing best by our seniors

Collectively, this information suggests that most healthy senior dogs will not experience any benefit from a dog food that is marketed for senior dogs. At this point in time, this particular life stage nutrition—more so than puppy or adult—seems to represent more marketing hype than reliable science. While we all desire continued health and the absence of disease in our older dogs, the nutritional elixir that guarantees eighteen healthy years does not exist. In fact there are several easy and more efficient ways to help our dogs to live long and healthy lives. First and foremost, we can maintain a healthy body weight *and* a toned condition as our dogs age by providing activities that stimulate both their physical *and* mental health. Regular and sustained periods of physical activity help to maintain muscle tone, enhance circulation, improve gastrointestinal function and prevent excess weight gain. The level and intensity of exercise should be adjusted to an individual dog's physical health. Many dogs, if healthy and maintained in good condition, can enjoy walking, running, swimming and playing active games well into old age (Cadie says "You go, dog!"). Though often ignored, proper care of the teeth and gums is probably one of the most important contributors to the long-term health of our dogs. Periodontal disease is estimated to be present in over 80 % of adult dogs today, a percentage that is truly shameful considering the devotion that we have to our dogs. Studies of periodontal disease in dogs tell us that the effects of gum disease are not limited to a dog's mouth and teeth. Rather, long-term gum disease contributes to systemic infections and to the development of chronic heart, liver or kidney disease in older dogs. Simply getting into the habit of brushing our dogs' teeth regularly can go a long way toward advancing health into old age. And of course, regular veterinary check-ups are essential for our seniors, as are attention to their daily behavior, the condition of their skin and coat and frequent massages to check for unusual lumps or bumps.

The greatest benefit to our senior dogs—and as a gift to ourselves—is to spend as much time together as possible. Although we may feel that time is short, every moment enjoyed together is a precious moment, one that celebrates all of the joy that our dogs bring to our lives. Now you must excuse me for a few moments—Cadie is awake and is asking for her second walk of the morning. When I return, we will examine questions of feeding for different lifestyles and activity levels, from the canine athlete to the canine couch potato.

6

Canine Athlete or Couch Potato?

When I was in my mid-twenties, a good friend got me hooked on running. He accomplished this not by extolling the joys of trail running (of which there are many), nor by modeling the health and fitness benefits of exercise (which of course are well documented), but rather by running every morning, bright and early, with his best friend, his dog Poncho. At that time, my husband Mike and I had three dogs, and we were involved in training and showing them in obedience trials (this was well before the explosion in popularity of agility). While I loved to hike and be outdoors with my dogs, I was not yet in the habit of running with them. That was all to change when, one weekend, Matt (a very speedy runner) invited me (a non-runner) to join him and Poncho for a run. My Golden, Fauna, and I met them at the crack of dawn at our local forest preserve to give this "running thing" a try. Well, Fauna loved it, I loved it, and shortly thereafter, Mike and Stepper too were bitten by the running bug. As soon as the youngster, Roxie, was old enough, she too hit the trails with the Case Clan.

Over the many ensuing years, Mike and I have continued to run with all of our dogs on trails here in Central Illinois. Every summer we travel to Acadia National Park in Maine to run the carriage trails there and to enjoy its very dog-friendly community. Although we no longer train and show our dogs competitively, we still run with them daily, currently with Vinny the Brittany, Chip the Toller and our youngest, Cooper, a Golden. Without question I consider running with my dogs to be one of the most enjoyable, energizing and bonding activities that we share together. We are challenged daily, experience the gift of seeing natural beauty, birds and wildlife, and have developed special friendships with other trail runners and their dogs. Simply put, I cherish every minute that I get to spend on the trails with my dogs.

So, what has all of this running meant for my dogs' nutritional needs? Well, mostly it affects calories. Just like people, dogs who exercise regularly burn more calories than dogs who do not. The old "energy in = energy out" equation means that dogs who exercise regularly consume more calories per day to maintain optimal body weight compared with dogs who are less active. However, as we will see, there is a bit more to it than this. As a species, dogs are highly efficient athletes. So, for many dogs, including my own, running five to six miles per day (i.e., for a period of 45 minutes to an hour) only *moderately* increases their energy requirements. Interestingly, but perhaps not surprisingly, we humans have a tendency to overestimate both our own needs and those of our dogs. This is a dangerous error, since one of the easiest roads to an exercise-induced injury in a dog is to allow her to carry too much weight. It is only when training becomes intense or prolonged that we may need to consider specific nutritional changes. For example, nutritional change may be called for if your dog runs with you when you are training for a marathon, when conditioning dogs for a season of hunting or herding work, or when conditioning and competing regularly with an agility or flyball dog.

Here is an example. Several years after I took up running, I decided to train for my first marathon —a race of 26.2 miles. Training involved building a solid running base of regular daily runs that gradually increased in distance, plus adding weekend long runs of up to 20 miles. At that time, my canine running partner was a dog named Sparks, a four-year-old field Golden who was also being trained and shown in obedience competitions. Sparks loved to run and thrived on our training together. He easily handled the increased distances as we ran together throughout the cool fall months. However, as our distances together increased to an average of 45 to 55 miles per week and entailed prolonged periods of running, Sparks began to lose weight, regardless of how much food I was feeding him. He was healthy, fit and happy—I just could *not* keep weight on him. At that time, I was working with a team of nutritionists at a pet food company who were studying the nutritional needs of racing sled dogs. I mentioned my marathon goals during a meeting one day and also that, while Sparks was having a blast training with me, he was too thin even by my standards. One of the nutritionists immediately jumped in, "Oh, Sparks may need our rocket fuel!" "Okay, I thought, here we go with a study of one dog...." I was a bit skeptical, but learned that the so called "rocket fuel" was an extruded, dry food that was a bump up from a normal, well-balanced (and well tested) performance food. It was formulated to be very high in fat and moderately high protein, had reduced carbohydrate (starch) levels and contained increased levels of naturally-derived antioxidants. Sparks was offered a trial bag of the stuff.

A 40-pound bag arrived at our home a few days later. The food looked similar to normal kibble pieces, but had a very distinctive fishy smell (this was the early days of discovering the benefits of omega-3 fatty acids), and was greasy to the touch. The "specs" on the food were that it contained 56 % of its calories from fat, about 32 % of its calories from protein and only 12 % of its calories from carbohydrate. This can be compared to a typical adult maintenance dry food that has a caloric distribution of fat:protein:carbs of 38:24:38. (Note—the term **caloric distribution** refers to the proportion of a food's energy that is provided by the three energy-containing nutrients of fat, carbohydrate and protein and should not be confused with the percentage of that nutrient as reported on pet food labels and brand websites). Each cup of food provided Sparks with 520 kcal of energy. Acceptance was not a problem—Sparks loved the food! (Thank goodness my dogs were all trained to eat only out of their own bowls as there was a lot of envious air-scenting and sideways glances toward Spark's bowl at meal times.) Within a few weeks, Sparks gained the weight he needed, continued to run well and had no GI upsets from the food. Although he was not allowed to compete in the actual marathon with me (silly human rules), we completed every single long training run together. I consider that he earned the same chops as a runner that I did when we completed our first marathon—we ran the distance while remaining injury free.

Like other canine athletes, Sparks needed more calories to meet his increased needs, and the best way to supply these calories (for dogs) was by increasing dietary fat. He probably also benefited from the high digestibility of the food, its slightly increased percentage of protein and perhaps from the additional antioxidant vitamins such as vitamin E. But, how do we know if/when our dogs may need a change in diet in response to work or increased exercise? Let's take a look at today's popular dog sports, the ways in which dogs work with us and what science tells us about how best we can feed hard working and exercising dogs.

Who are today's canine athletes?
We have been studying the nutritional needs of canine athletes for a relatively short period of time. The first studies took place during the 1970s and 80s and were conducted exclusively with two specific types of dogs—endurance racing sled dogs and sprint racing greyhounds. It makes sense that these dogs were used in early studies because both types of sport (ethical considerations aside) were highly athletic and involved large groups of dogs who were housed and managed communally. This allowed for the careful control of variables such as training regimens, feeding schedules and diet. We learned a great deal about the physiology, metabolism and nutritional needs of intensely exercising dogs through these studies. However, the problem is that the vast majority of canine athletes are neither racing Greyhounds nor sled dogs living in Alaska. Rather, they are dogs living in homes who work and play in a wide variety of ways that involve varying degrees of exercise intensity, duration and frequency. Agility training and competitions are one of the most popular of all dog sports today, attracting more than one million entries annually at AKC trials alone. Other popular dog sports that require fitness include flyball, dock diving, tracking, hunting tests and the higher levels of obedience work. Dogs also work today in search and rescue, as various types of service dogs, and with the police and military. So, do these working and exercising dogs have special nutrient needs? If so, what are these and how can trainers and owners select the best food, using evidence-based nutrition, for their canine athletes? Let's begin by looking at a few key differences between the two exercise extremes—sprinting (short and fast bursts of activity) and endurance (slow, steady and prolonged exercise).

How intense is your dog?
As in all animals, a dog's exercising muscles use nutrients for energy, which translates into increased calorie needs. The three nutrients that can be **metabolized** (burned) for energy by the body are fat, carbohydrate and protein. The degree to which a given activity that your dog enjoys increases his caloric needs is directly influenced by three things: the intensity of the exercise, its duration and the frequency with which the dog engages in it. These three factors directly influence the proportion of fat or carbohydrate (and to a lesser degree protein) that is used by muscles to fuel the activity. Exercise intensity is one of the most important factors for trainers to consider given the types of activities that we enjoy with our dogs.

Researchers who study exercise physiology use a measure called **VO2max** to estimate exercise intensity. VO2max is the amount of oxygen that is consumed when an individual is exercising at his or her maximum intensity. An individual's value for VO2max is affected by fitness level, age and health. To get a handle on how VO2max works, consider how your dog's rate of respiration and panting increase dramatically when he is exercising—this reflects the extra oxygen intake that he needs to burn fuel (fat and carbohydrates) for energy as he exercises. Using the VO2max as a standard, researchers have found that exercise intensity can be divided into three broad categories that are characterized by the type of nutritional fuel that muscles are using.

The first—high intensity exercise—occurs when the rate of oxygen consumption is greater than 75 % VO2max. The best examples are Greyhounds while racing, flyball dogs during a competition and agility dogs who complete a course at very fast speeds. At this level of intensity the body is using primarily glucose for energy and is also "burning" the glucose through primarily anaerobic (without oxygen) pathways. This means that even though the dog is taking in extra oxygen, energy is in such high demand by the intensely working muscles that it is produced through pathways that do not use oxygen. This is a pretty cool metabolic adaptation and one that animal species that survive by sprinting short distances excel at. The cost of this rapid burst of immediately available energy—there is always a cost—is that it very rapidly depletes the body's stores of glycogen, the storage form of glucose. Anaerobic work also rapidly increases lactic acid build-up in muscles. Together, these two side effects eventually lead to fatigue and muscle injury (not good).

The intermediate level of exercise occurs when a dog is exercising at 30 to 40 % of her VO2max. At this intensity, all of that extra oxygen that the dog is taking in has some time to actually do its job at the cellular level. This allows both carbohydrate (glycogen) and fat (free fatty acids) to be used to supply energy to working muscles.

The third category, low intensity exercise, is any activity that is above resting oxygen consumption but less than 30 % of VO2max. At this intensity, a dog's muscles are using primarily fat (free fatty acids) as an energy source.

Sprint athletes are the high intensity (and short duration) exercisers. Racing Greyhounds have been the traditional example of sprint athletes in the dog world and the group of sprinting canines that have been most thoroughly studied. Although their nutritional needs have not been directly studied, the world of canine sports includes a lot of sprinters—dogs engaging in flyball, lure coursing and agility sprint for a substantial proportion of their events. Let's contrast the intensity and duration of sprinters to endurance athletes, who engage in moderate or low intensity exercise (VO2max of 40 % or less) for long periods of time, with an occasional bout of higher intensity work. The best human example of an endurance athlete is the marathon runner, while examples in dogs are sled dogs training for long distances, some types of hunting dogs, dogs guarding livestock and dogs who run or hike long distances with their owners. Most exercising dogs fall somewhere in this intermediate category where the endurance exercise falls well below 75 % VO2max but which includes frequent or occasional bouts of high intensity sprinting.

We also must consider genetics when looking at exercising muscles. As a species, the dog is best characterized as a tireless runner (endurance), with an ability to sprint for short distances. However, selective breeding has resulted in some breeds that are physiologically and metabolically adapted for sprinting and others that are genetically adapted to thrive during endurance work. Our sprinters are the coursing breeds such as Greyhounds, Whippets and Salukis, among others. In addition to a conformation that is built for running like a gazelle, these breeds have also been shown through research studies to rapidly achieve a high VO2max. This ability is at least in part made possible by the fact that their leg muscles contain an unusually high proportion of fast-twitch muscle fibers, a specific type of muscle fiber that reacts rapidly, burns glucose efficiently and is designed for bursts of strength. Conversely, breeds that work all day long at low to moderate intensities, such as many scent hounds, possess a body type that is built for endurance and have a significantly lower proportion of fast-twitch muscles and a higher proportion of slow-twitch fibers in their legs. Most dogs fall somewhere in between, relying primarily upon slow-twitch muscles but having enough fast-twitch capacity for those bursts of speed when they are needed. For our purposes, when we think about nutrition, remember that fast/intense exercise uses glucose, moderate exercise uses glucose and fat, and low intensity (and endurance work) uses primarily fat. When I think about Sparks, trotting with me on our long runs, I envision his slow-twitch fibers humming along, consuming fatty acids, with the occasional burst of speed needed to jump into a pond to cool off or to run ahead to say hello to a friend from the trail. At those times, his fast-twitch fibers switch on, quickly gobbling up lots of glucose to support his burst of speed.

The third important exercise factor is frequency. The requirements of a dog who lounges on the couch during the week and goes swimming for 30 minutes or plays several games of fetch in the park on weekends are not comparable to a dog who is in daily training for dock diving or is conditioning for hunting tests. Just as with humans, the energy needs of our "weekend warrior dogs" are not increased above adult maintenance needs—a term used to describe the energy and nutrient needs of an adult, non-reproducing dog, living in a home. However, a service dog who walks for several hours a day at low intensity and is required to be mentally alert and engaged for a large portion of her day would have substantially increased energy needs. Similarly, hunting dogs who are in the field every day during hunting season have much higher energy needs compared with off-season periods. This difference is also seen in the wide variety of ways in which people enjoy agility, flyball and other sports with their dogs. If you train your dog once or twice a week in an agility class at your club, although he may be very active for short bursts of time during each class, his nutrient needs will not differ significantly from those of an average pet dog. In contrast, if you regularly condition your agility dog by running, biking or swimming him and if you train daily and compete on weekends, this level of physical and mental exertion will almost assuredly affect his energy and nutrient needs. Some estimates of where our different dog sports and types of working dogs fall in terms of intensity, duration and resulting energy needs are shown in Figure 6.1.

Activity	Intensity	Duration	Relative caloric requirements
Long-Distance Sled Racing	Moderate	Long	Very High
Livestock Guarding	Very Low	Long	Moderate
Livestock Herding (working dog)	Moderate to High	Long	High
Livestock Herding (trials)	High	Short	Moderate
Hunting (scent hounds)	Low	Long	High
Hunting (Pointers, Spaniels)	Moderate to High	Long	High
Hunting (Retrievers)	High	Short to Medium	Moderate
Search and Rescue	Low	Long	Moderate
Service Dog Work	Low	Long	Moderate
Agility Training/ Trials	Moderate to High	Short	Low to Moderate
Flyball-Frisbee Training/Trials	Moderate to High	Short	Moderate
Recreational Running	Moderate	Short to Medium	Moderate
Weight-Pulling Contests	High	Short	Low
Lure-Course Races	Very High	Short	Low

Figure 6.1 Dog sport intensity, duration, calorie needs.

One final point should be made about the intensity and duration of exercise and how these factors affect nutrition in our dogs. This has to do with the importance of conditioning. Physical conditioning for our dogs is absolutely necessary for successful participation in a dog sport and is also important in helping to reduce risk of injury. Naturally, a flyball dog who does not jump efficiently and cleanly will not be competitive, nor will a dock-diving dog who is not adept at running, leaping and swimming. However, it is easy to assume that more practice at the given sport is all that is needed for conditioning. In other words, if you are planning on competing in agility with your dog, then you just train agility more frequently and more intensely, right? Well…No.

Optimal conditioning not only involves a lot of training in the actual sport, but also includes conditioning that targets improvement of the canine athlete's overall strength and aerobic capacity. Human athletes know this, of course. As a runner, I understand the importance of including various types of aerobic cross-training exercise such as swimming, cycling and hiking with my training. These are all moderate VO2max activities, but use different muscles in different ways, thus helping to maintain strength while supporting overall (metabolic) fitness. For runners, this is the best insurance against injury, and the same holds true for our dogs. Giving your dog a variety of conditioning activities is not only fun for him, it reduces the risk of stress injuries from repetitive training and maintains or improves his overall fitness. This type of physical conditioning also has nutritional and weight management benefits for dogs because it has been shown to improve both oxygen use and metabolic rate. For example, a series of studies with dogs trained to run on treadmills showed that well-conditioned dogs had significantly increased VO2max (which signifies a greater capacity for producing energy for working muscles) and also they utilized fat for fuel more efficiently than unconditioned dogs. In fact, the dogs were unusually efficient at burning fat for exercise, which has important implications for feeding canine athletes.

Dogs are fat burners…or reasons not to carbo-load your canine athlete

As we have seen, like humans and other animals, dogs are able to use both glucose and fat to supply energy to working muscles during exercise. Glucose, the carbohydrate fuel, is an essential source of energy for many organs and tissues in the body. It is the preferred fuel of the brain and is why you get kinda dopey when you are really hungry and why a sugar-containing snack gives you a quick boost of energy. However, the body's supply of stored glucose, called glycogen, is quite small and runs out during periods of high need. This is a phenomenon called **glycogen depletion** and is something we want to avoid at all costs, both for ourselves and for our canine athletes. Glycogen depletion is strongly correlated with physical exhaustion, poor performance and even with mental fatigue and disorientation. This correlation is so strong and predictable that runners have a name for experiencing the dreaded depletion, "hitting the wall." I experienced this at about the 20-mile mark during my first marathon and learned immediately that it is a phenomenon that is aptly named. I went from thinking I was doing okay, that this marathon thing was not such a big deal, to suddenly feeling too exhausted to put one foot in front of the other and too mentally fatigued to care which direction my feet were going. (I did finish the marathon, but it was not pretty.) For our canine athletes, who are often required to both pay attention and respond to their handler's signals while performing a variety of athletic feats, hitting the wall can be devastating.

Therefore, an important goal when feeding canine athletes is to ensure that glycogen depletion does not occur. We know several things about the way that dogs burn nutrients for energy during exercise that can help us to do this. While engaging in high intensity exercise, a dog's muscles use primarily glucose as their energy source. While this supplies a dog's body with the rapid energy that is needed for chasing, turning, racing and jumping, it can also very rapidly deplete the body's stores of glycogen. In contrast, when engaged in exercise of somewhat lower intensity and speed, such as trotting or running for a longer distance or swimming, dogs switch from using glucose only to both glucose and fat. While fat takes longer to get going and get to the party, once up and running it has great staying power and will keep a dog active and alert for long periods of time. This is because, unlike glycogen, the body has an almost unlimited capacity to store fat, which can be mobilized and used for energy in times of need.

There are generally two nutritional approaches that we can use to avoid glycogen depletion during exercise. We can reduce the rate at which a dog's glycogen stores are used for energy during bouts of exercise so as to at least forestall and hopefully prevent glycogen depletion from occurring. Another approach is to ensure that the dog is highly efficient at "switching" to burning fat for use by muscles when needed (for example during periods of moderate activity), thus helping to spare glycogen from being used up too quickly. To accomplish these things, many human athletes engage in a strategy called "carbohydrate loading" or "carbo-loading." This strategy involves consuming a high carbohydrate (starch) diet at pre-determined periods of time prior to an athletic event, with the intent of "super-loading" muscle glycogen stores. This is beneficial during endurance events because if there is more stored glycogen at the start of the event, the athlete will be able to work for a longer period of time before approaching depletion. Although this has been shown to work well for many human athletes competing in endurance events (I did enjoy those pre-race pasta dinners, I must admit), we now know that carbo-loading is not an effective strategy for our canine athletes, who have been shown to be a different animal altogether.

Carbo-loading is not an effective nutritional strategy with canine athletes because metabolically dogs are naturally more efficient at using fat as a fuel for exercising muscles than carbohydrate (glycogen), even when exercising at relatively high intensities. I will try not to bore readers with the research details, but I think it is important to describe a classic study that first discovered this unique adaptation. In the 1970s veterinarian David Kronfeld conducted a study with racing sled dogs (Kronfeld, 1973). He initially fed a racing team a high-carbohydrate diet that contained moderate levels of protein and fat (a diet that was somewhat analogous to a carbo-loading diet for human athletes). He found that these dogs performed poorly during races and experienced an unusually high number of lameness injuries. When the dogs were changed to a diet that contained higher levels of fat and protein, performance improved and the observed lameness problems resolved. This study became the jumping-off point for subsequent research that looked at the importance of the balance of fat, carbohydrate and protein in diets of exercising dogs. All found that once fat is mobilized and being used as an energy source, it is the most important source, providing up to 90 % of needed energy to dogs' working muscles. Not only are dogs highly efficient "fat burners," but they also switch to using a higher proportion of fat much earlier than do human athletes (i.e., at lower intensities). This shift to using fatty acids early in exercise has a distinct advantage in that it helps to spare those limited muscle glycogen stores, preventing the dreaded "hitting of the wall." Although the majority of these studies have been conducted with pulling dogs and hunting dogs, Shay Hill, of Massey University in New Zealand, recently studied the importance of fat versus carbohydrate in the diets of sheep-herding dogs in her PhD dissertation research. Her results were in agreement with previous studies—she found that *a diet that was high in both fat and protein and low in digestible carbohydrate supported the best running and working performance in her group of hard-working herding dog*s.

How does this knowledge impact the way in which we feed dogs who are involved in dog sports? Can we even expect that studies of the nutritional needs of hard working or racing dogs can be used to help us feed dogs involved in sports? To explore this question, I spoke with Dr. Eric Altom, a canine nutritionist and researcher as well as an accomplished hunting dog trainer, competitor and AKC judge. He authored several of the first studies that examined the nutrient needs of hunting Pointers, of which one of the most interesting was a study showing that the type of fat that a diet contains can influence scenting and "finds" in hunting pointers (Altom et al, 2003). Eric reiterated the metabolic benefits of feeding a food that includes increased fat and calories to all canine athletes. He added that there are additional benefits to this type of nutrient mix, above and beyond the demonstrated metabolic advantages. Most important is that feeding a more energy dense food reduces the total volume of food that is fed and helps to regulate meal frequency and "gut fill" in working dogs. Dogs who are hunting for several hours at a time or competing at a day-long performance event should not be fed a large meal prior to or during their athletic event. Just as with human athletes, having a full belly is not conducive to being active and performing well. Small meals work best both to support food digestibility (large meals travel through the gut faster and reduce diet digestibility) and to avoid stress-related diarrhea. When competing with his dogs, Eric feeds twice a day, providing about one third of the dog's daily needs in an early morning meal and the bulk of the dog's food at the evening meal after all work is complete for the day. The second benefit to a performance food is palatability—tastiness. Some dogs, especially those who become nervous or hyper-stimulated while traveling, may be less inclined to eat when they are on the road or competing. Providing a food that is higher in fat is more palatable to dogs and so can encourage a finicky competitor to still eat when excited or nervous.

Feeding your canine athlete

Our current understanding of the metabolic changes and nutrient needs associated with endurance and high intensity exercise can be applied to many dog sports and working situations. This knowledge is useful to trainers and handlers who are trying to choose the best food and feeding regimen for their canine athletes. Let's look at the current set of evidence-based recommendations for nutrients and calories. We will follow this up with a review of a sampling of some commercially available foods that are marketed for hard working dogs.

Calories

Without question, all working dogs will have energy (calorie) needs that are higher than a comparable dog living a sedentary lifestyle. We also know that the duration and the intensity of the work determine the magnitude of this increase. Dogs working at low or moderate intensity for several hours at a time (hunting dogs, service dogs and military/police dogs) will require a consistent increase in caloric intake to maintain body weight and condition. My own best example is my dog Sparks, who easily maintained his body weight when running four to six miles a day with me (i.e., about 45 minutes to an hour of exercise), but needed a substantial "bump up" in caloric intake once we started to train for a marathon together and we were sometimes running for three hours or more at a time. Less obvious is the degree of increase that is needed for dogs who compete in various dog sports.

Research suggests that energy needs of exercising dogs typically increase by between 20 to 100 % above completely sedentary (pet on the couch) needs. Working in cold weather or swimming in cool conditions may further increase an individual dog's energy requirement. These estimates come from data collected with pulling dogs who were traveling short distances and from hunting dog studies and probably can be applied to dogs involved with dog sports who are training and exercising regularly. For most dogs involved in dog sports, an increase of 20 to 30 % above maintenance needs is a reasonable estimate. This is comparable to Sparks running with me during non-marathon training, for about an hour each day. (By comparison, studies of sled dogs running in distance races that take place over multiple days and involve hours of running each day have found higher calorie needs than in any other athlete measured—ever—including human ultra-marathoners! See Figure 6.2.)

The long-distance sled dog—a canine furnace!

Dogs trained for racing in long-distance sled races typically run 70 miles or more per day and travel at speeds of up to nine miles per hour. Studies show that the number of calories needed by these dogs exceeds anything ever before measured in exercising animals! Here are the facts:

- Racing sled dogs competing in a 300 mile race expended an average of **11,200 kcal per day** and consumed an average of **10,600 kcal/day!** (As a result, these dogs lost some weight during this race.)

- This is an enormous number of calories! It was observed that these values exceeded previously predicted maximal values for metabolic work for mammals of their size.

- When these data were first collected, researchers were incredulous and thought that some type of recording or calculating error had been made. However, double-checking data, plus repeating the studies showed that these numbers hold up.

- To date, no other canine (or other species) athlete comes close to the number of calories being burned daily by racing sled dogs!

Figure 6.2 Energy needs of long-distance sled dogs.

Let's use an example to illustrate what you might expect to experience with your own dog. My training school's agility trainer, Jessica, trains and shows her Australian Shepherd, Grace, in agility competitions. Jess exercises and trains Grace regularly and competes in agility with her throughout the spring, summer and fall. Jess adopted Grace during her third year of veterinary school. Because Jess was spending a lot of time studying and in clinics during the first few years of Grace's life, she did not have the time to train Grace with the same intensity and frequency that she does today. When I asked her about Grace's conditioning and weight, she laughed and told me that Grace, who now weighs in at a lean and fit 35 pounds, weighed almost 50 pounds during

Jess's final year of vet school! Jess explains, "There were a lot of stuffed Kongs being handed out at my house during study time or when I had to be on clinics…" When Jess realized that Grace was much too heavy for the running and repeated jumping that agility requires, she put Grace on a strict diet and fitness plan. Today, we can estimate Grace's daily calorie needs using a standard equation for active dogs (see Figure 6.3). For a 35 pound adult dog, this is about 1035 kcal per day. For comparison, if we calculated the energy needs of a 35 pound inactive dog (see Figure for equations), the estimate is 757 calories, a *27 % reduction*. Jess feeds a low carbohydrate dry food that has moderately increased fat and protein and that provides 408 kcal/kg. If this food made up Grace's entire daily ration, Jess would feed between 2 and 2½ cups per day. However, like most trainers, Jess uses a lot of "high value" treats in her training (and as "life rewards"), which Jessica deducts from this total. As a result, Grace is fed about 1 to 1 1/2 cups per day of this food, divided into two meals. These volumes (1/2 cup in the morning meal and ½ to 3/4 cup in the evening meal) are completely acceptable and what I would consider to be a target volume of food to feed an active 35 pound dog who is receiving daily training with food treats.

Inactive adult dog*: metabolizable energy (calorie) requirement = 95 x Wkg $^{0.75}$

Examples:

- ME requirement of a 10-kg (22-lb) dog = 95 x (10 kg)$^{0.75}$ = 534 kcal ME/day
- ME requirement of a 22.7-kg (50-lb) dog = 95 x (22.7 kg)$^{0.75}$ = 988 kcal ME/day
- Grace's requirement* = 95 x (15.9 kg)$^{0.75}$ = 757 kcal ME/day
- Volume to feed Grace: 757/408 = 1.85 (~ 1 ¾ cups per day)

Active adult dog*: metabolizable energy (calorie) requirement = 130 x Wkg $^{0.75}$

Examples:

- ME requirement of a 10-kg (22-lb) dog = 130 x (10 kg)$^{0.75}$ = 731 kcal of ME/day
- ME requirement of a 22.7-kg (50-lb) dog = 130 x (22.7 kg)$^{0.75}$ = 1352 kcal ME/day
- Grace's requirement* = 130 x (15.9 kg)$^{0.75}$ = 1035 kcal ME/day
- Volume to feed Grace: 1035/408 = 2.54 (~ 2 ½ cups per day)

*To convert lbs to kg, divide lbs by 2.2

* Estimates used equations provided by the National Research Council: Nutrient Requirements of Dogs and Cats, Nat Acad. Press, Washington, DC, 2006.

Figure 6.3 Calculating energy (calorie) needs for active and inactive dogs.

Fat

As we have seen, exercising dogs are efficient "fat burners." The best way to provide the extra energy needed by a canine athlete is to increase dietary fat and feed a food that is energy dense and highly digestible. Remember from Chapter 4 that fat is the most concentrated energy source in the diet—it provides 2.25 times more energy per gram than either carbohydrate or protein. Therefore, feeding a food that has an increased fat content is the best way to meet the increased energy needs of canine athletes. This is important not only because dogs efficiently (and preferentially) burn fat for energy but because of what it means to the volume of food that is fed (pay attention if you find that you regularly battle diarrhea problems with your exercising dog). If the energy content of the food is too low, the volume (cups) of food that must be consumed by a dog to meet his increased calorie needs may tax the physical capacity of the dog's stomach and intestinal tract (consider how uncomfortable you feel after eating too much at Thanksgiving dinner). Somewhat paradoxically, overfilling the GI tract results in *increased* rate of passage (i.e., things start to move along more rapidly than normal), which leads to a decrease in nutrient digestibility and the production of increased volume and decreased quality of stools (soft stools, frequent defecation, sometimes even diarrhea). Conversely, feeding a food that is energy dense (increased fat, high digestibility) allows you to feed a lower volume (fewer cups per day) for the same number of calories, will not tax your dog's gastrointestinal system, and will support nutrient digestibility—a win-win all around!

Protein

Hard-working dogs have higher dietary protein requirements because exercise increases the body's need for protein to build muscle, support increased blood volume and repair tissues. In addition, while it is best to not use protein as an energy source, certain amino acids are used for energy or to produce glucose during work and must be replaced through the diet. Most of the additional protein that working dogs need is supplied by their increased consumption of food as energy needs rise. However, performance foods that are energy dense must also include a higher *proportion* of protein (percentage) because energy dense foods must also be more *nutrient dense* to ensure that all essential nutrient needs are met. A nice rule of thumb is to choose a performance food that contains between 28 and 32 % protein and between 18 and 22 % fat, as reported on the label (i.e., dry food, weight basis, not caloric basis).

Carbohydrate

Although fat is the primary metabolic fuel for endurance dogs, and high-fat diets best supply this fuel, we must not forget the dreaded "hitting the wall" problem. Maintaining adequate muscle glycogen stores is important in all types of exercise. Hunting dogs and dogs who participate in certain types of canine sports such as agility and flyball work predominantly at low intensities for most of the day, interspersed with occasional bouts of high-intensity exertion. Although high carbohydrate in a working dog's diet is not recommended, some digestible starch is essential for replenishing and maintaining glycogen stores. All dry performance foods include some carbohydrate, even if they are grain-free, so this is not generally a concern. There is some research that indicates that providing a quick "carbohydrate snack" to dogs who are exercising intensely throughout the day can be helpful in replacing the glycogen that is lost and preventing depletion. This can be as simple as feeding a handful of biscuits (which all contain some type of starch).

Water

The importance of adequate water intake for exercising dogs cannot be overstated. Extra water intake is needed to keep the body cool and prevent overheating as excess heat is generated during activity. While humans use body sweat to dissipate much of this heat, dogs have very limited numbers of sweat glands (mostly in their feet) and dissipate more than 60 % of their excess body heat through respiration, i.e., panting. Fresh water should be available at all times during rest periods and should be offered as frequently as possible to working dogs throughout the day.

Antioxidants

In recent years, the role that antioxidant nutrients play in reducing oxidative stress during exercise and other types of physiological stress has been studied in both human and canine athletes. Strenuous exercise imposes significant oxidative stress that can lead to cellular and tissue damage. In addition, canine athletes who are fed high fat diets may be at increased risk because of an increased susceptibility to fatty acid oxidation in these diets. Vitamin E is the most thoroughly studied antioxidant to date. Two other naturally occurring antioxidants that may be important are beta-carotene (the vitamin A precursor) and a compound called lutein. A study with racing sled dogs found that the circulating lipoproteins of dogs supplemented with these three nutrients showed increased resistance to oxidative damage and reduced exercise-related DNA damage when compared with un-supplemented dogs (Baskin et al; 2000). More recently, the polyphenols and flavonoids that are present in certain fruits and vegetables, for example blueberries, have been studied (Dunlap et al; 2006). These compounds have strong antioxidant properties. A group of unconditioned sled dogs was supplemented with approximately 20 grams of wild blueberries per day for two months and were exercised for a distance of seven miles on two consecutive days. Although performance was not affected, supplementation did cause an elevation in plasma total antioxidant potential, which is a measure of the body's antioxidant status.

Choosing well—comparing performance foods

While there are a variety of performance foods available to dog owners today, not all companies produce a food for highly active dogs. By contrast, almost every brand of dog food includes at least one "less active" or "weight control" product. This difference almost certainly reflects the fact that overweight conditions are almost pathologically common among American dogs, while dogs who work for a living or are trained at a level that warrants a change in food are much less common. Still, we know an awful lot about how to feed working dogs (and personally, I think this is pretty cool information), so let's look at how this knowledge has been put into practice in the marketplace. We will follow with an examination of the opposite end of the spectrum—the less active or "lite" products that are sold today.

Figure 6.4 provides select nutrient/ingredient information for a group of twelve different performance dog foods. All of these are dry, extruded products, which allow comparison of nutrient levels without the need for adjusting for differences in water content. (Plus, I found no canned foods marketed for performance dogs.) As we have discussed, the principal nutrients to pay attention to in these foods are fat, protein and calories. Most but not all foods that are marketed for active dogs have increased fat levels (i.e., 16 % by weight or greater). Protein should be increased proportionately, both to supply the extra protein that is needed and because (I cannot reiterate this often enough), a more calorically dense food *must* have proportionately increased nutrients when reported on a percentage basis. In this line-up, there are several helpful examples. I think most instructional is the approach that is taken by Native Foods, the performance brand of a company called Kent Pet Foods. Their line of four foods (foods # 6, 7, 8 and 9) are formulated for graduated increases in exercise intensity and duration. Level 1 (food #6), designed for the lowest level of intensity, contains 24 % protein, 14 % fat and has a caloric density that is considered appropriate for dogs who are normally active (~380 kcal/cup). The company markets this food for dogs who maintain weight easily (what I like to call the "air ferns" of the dog world…plants that seem to require just air to thrive). It is also suitable for dogs with normal or low levels of activity. This bumps up a bit at Level 2, with a 26:16 ratio of protein to fat and about 400 kcal per cup. The company targets dogs who are trained vigorously two or three times a week but otherwise have a normal level of activity with their Level 2 product. For this group, I think of folks who train their dogs in obedience (open/utility), flyball, agility, nosework or other highly active dog sports a few times a week, and at other times enjoy lots of couch-time with their dogs. This group is probably the largest of dog sporting folks, so this food provides a nice example of an appropriate dietary matrix for these dogs. Levels 3 and 4 bump up nutrient and calorie density even further, and are appropriate for dogs who are working hard almost daily or exposed to highly stressful work settings. A hunting dog during peak season may thrive on Level 3, while Level 4 is probably best for those few dogs who work daily at intense levels or experience high environmental stress such as weather extremes or work in natural disaster areas. I like this sequence, as it provides a great example of evidence-based nutrition in practice. The ingredients lists of these products also reflect these incremental changes. While Level 1 includes more carbohydrate-containing ingredients (which are lower in calories than fat-containing ingredients), Level 4 shows that chicken fat is the second ingredient (i.e., second highest in quantity).

#	Brand	Protein (%)	Fat (%)	Kcal/ cup	First 4 ingredients
1	Acana Sport & Agility	30	24	475	Chicken meal, steel-cut oats, chicken fat, deboned chicken
2	Annamaet Ultra	32	20	480	Chicken meal, chicken, brown rice, chicken fat
3	Black Gold Ultimate Performance	31	21	437	Chicken meal, corn meal, fish meal, poultry fat
4	Eukanuba Active Performance	28	18	388	Chicken, chicken by-product meal, corn meal, ground sorghum
5	Eukanuba Premium Performance	30	20	385	Chicken, chicken by-product meal, corn meal, brewer's rice
6	Native Performance—Level 1	24	14	382	Lamb meal, ground rice, ground oats, ground barley
7	Native Performance—Level 2	26	16	404	Chicken meal, ground rice, chicken fat, ground oats
8	Native Performance—Level 3	30	20	438	Chicken meal, chicken fat, ground rice, ground oats
9	Native Performance—Level 4	35	25	481	Chicken meal, chicken fat, ground rice, ground oats
10	Pedigree Active Nutrition	26	12	*NR	Ground whole corn, corn gluten meal, poultry by-product meal, meat and bone meal
11	Pro Plan Sport Performance	30	20	475	Chicken, corn gluten meal, brewers rice, animal fat
12	Wysong Optimal Performance	40	18	*NR	Organic chicken, chicken giblets, poultry meal, ground brown rice

*NR = Not Reported

Figure 6.4 Comparing performance foods (dry).

We can learn a few other things from this sample of foods. Food #10 is promoted by the manufacturer as a food that is appropriate for highly active dogs. However, it contains only 12 % fat, a level that is found in many maintenance foods. Its ingredients list shows the first ingredient to be a carbohydrate source (ground corn), followed by a plant-based protein source (corn gluten meal) and a by-product (poultry by-product meal). We will address ingredient quality in Chapter 10, but for our purposes here, suffice it to say that these are less than stellar ingredients for one to see on any pet food label and certainly are undesirable on a label of a food that is intended for an active dog. In addition, the company that produces this brand chooses not to report its caloric density (kcal/cup) on the label or their website. (Emailing the company for this information was not fruitful.)

There also is a food that has increased protein but only modestly increased fat (food #12). Like food #10, this company declined to provide caloric content of the food, so it is difficult to fully evaluate this product. While the food's ingredients list is acceptable, its energy content may not support hard work and the high protein levels could result in dietary protein being unnecessarily used (burned) for energy during exercise. While not necessarily a health issue, this is less metabolically efficient (and more expensive) than using dietary fat to fuel working muscles.

Another feature to be aware of is the weight density of foods and how this influences our assessment of a dry product. This is important for all dog foods, but is illustrated nicely by two products in this particular example, foods #4 and #5. Like the Native products, these products are designed for dogs with different activity levels. Food #4 is formulated and marketed for moderately active dogs while food #5 is marketed to hard-working dogs such as hunting dogs. However, there is something rather odd going on. Although food #5 contains higher fat than food #4 (20% versus 18%), and is marketed as being suitable for harder-working dogs, the caloric density of food #5 is actually *lower* than that of food #4 (385 versus 388 kcal/cup). How can this be? Although neither of these foods is particularly high in calories for a performance food, the lower density of #5 versus #4 is confusing, considering the foods' nutrient profiles. The explanation of this incongruity lies in the differing weight densities of the two foods. Specifically, food #5, although higher in fat, is less dense by weight than food #4, which means that a particular volume of food (cup) of food #5 actual contains less food that the more dense food (food #4).

Here is how this works. All foods contain varying amounts of air. Extruded foods in particular vary considerably in how much air they contain or how "puffed" they are. The amount of expansion (airiness) of a formulation is affected by the food's ingredients and by a variety of extrusion (cooking) parameters. One of my professors in graduate school had a neat way of explaining this effect. He used the analogy of popcorn versus corn meal. Envision yourself filling two measuring cups, one with freshly popped corn (air popped, no fair adding butter) and then filling a second cup with corn meal. Hold one cup in your left hand and the other in your right hand. Which is heavier? Why? They are the same food, correct? But popped corn of course is puffed up with air and so measuring this into a cup includes all of the air that is trapped within the pieces. Corn meal (which is really just ground corn) is significantly denser, contains much less air and so is heavier. And, the number of calories that the popped corn would provide if you consumed it is much *lower* than the number of calories contained in the cup of corn meal (if you really wanted to consume it), simply because you are eating less air and more corn with the latter.

In the case of dog foods, this becomes an important issue because the degree to which a kibble piece is "puffed up" substantially affects how much food you feed. In the case of the two foods in our example, the difference is corrected when we look at the number of calories by weight (rather than by volume) of the two foods. According to the manufacturer, food #4 contains 4379 kcals per kilogram of food (or, if converted to pounds, 1990 kcal/lb) and as expected, food #5 is higher (albeit not by very much) at 4452 kcal per kilogram (2024 kcal/lb) of food. These numbers are consistent with the nutrient profiles of these foods, even though when we look at the food on a per cup basis, food #4 has more calories. What does this mean in terms of feeding a dog?

Well, in this case, paradoxically, an owner will find himself feeding about the same volume of food (i.e., cups per day) of food #5 as food #4 to provide an equivalent number of calories, even though food #5 is actually more energy dense. Confusing, I know. This example illustrates why it is always important to look at both the calories per volume (cups) of food and the calories on a weight basis. In general, it is most helpful to pay attention to the kcal/cup information that is provided, because the majority of owners measure their food in cups (volume) rather than weighing it in ounces or pounds (weight) when feeding.

A final point must be made, and this is something that we will revisit repeatedly in the remainder of this book. There is an enormous range of commercial dog foods that are marketed to different life stages and lifestyles (activity levels) of dogs. Some of these products have sound science behind them, others do not. Unfortunately, other than the required and AAFCO-defined division between growth/reproduction foods and adult maintenance foods, there exist no nutrient standards for other life stages or conditions to which pet food manufacturers must comply. Nor are manufacturers required to scientifically prove a need for these niche foods (we will examine this particular issue in detail in Chapter 10). Using our current example, although we know a great deal about the nutritional needs of hard-working dogs and can put this information into practice in pet foods, *there is absolutely no regulatory mandate for pet food manufacturers to do so*. There are no nutrient profiles that recommend fat or protein content of performance diets and pet food companies are under no obligation to produce products that reflect current scientific understanding of performance nutrition. A pet food company can market a food as formulated for highly active dogs, yet (as we have seen) that food may have the exact same nutrient profile as a food that is formulated and sold for adult maintenance. In addition, there is no "standard range" or recommended nutrient profiles for this category of foods—it is virtually an open playing field. This is a classic "buyer beware" situation, in which dog owners and particularly dog professionals (whose clients ask them to recommend foods) are obligated to read labels, look at fat levels, hunt down calorie counts and ask questions of manufacturers.

Despite what you see on the food label, when thinking about a performance food for your dog, consider several things. First and most important is whether your dog is working hard enough to need a change in diet (most do not). If you believe he is and are choosing a performance diet, pay attention to fat level (it should be 16 % or greater), calories per cup (they should be 400 kcal per cup or higher) and protein content (it should increase slightly with fat). The food should also contain ingredients that are highly digestible (see Chapter 10 for a complete discussion) to prevent you from having to feed a large volume of food and cause digestive upset. Most importantly, the food should support your dog's energy level, body condition and endurance for the sport of choice. Let's now move on to look at a few foods that are marketed to the other end of the dog activity spectrum—our canine couch potatoes. What types of products are available for the less active dog, and should you feed this type of food?

The meaning of lite

All of the data and new knowledge that research studies of the nutritional needs of racing Greyhounds, sled dogs and working hunting dogs can be put to good use when we consider how we can best feed dogs who are involved in the many dog sports whose popularity has exploded during the last ten years. Yet, paradoxically, at the same time we know that the vast majority of pet dogs face nutritional imbalances of the opposite extreme—they are couch potatoes and they are too fat. Knowing this, the pet food industry has responded by creating a product category whose numbers exceed performance foods by several fold. Almost every pet food brand on the market includes at least one product, often several, that is formulated to be "lite," "low fat" or for "less active" dogs. Indeed, simply perusing the number of different terms that are used to signify these foods can be overwhelming and confusing. Similar to human food products, we see references to the amount of fat in the food and to caloric content (low, reduced, etc.). Other foods use the name to describe the food's intended purpose (weight control, healthy weight) and yet still there is an entire selection of descriptors that identify the dogs who may benefit from these foods (less active, mature adult).

Interestingly, only a small collection of these terms is regulated. These are the same terms that are used in human foods and fall into three general categories. The first include terms applying to calories. If a pet food company uses the term "lite," "light" or "low calorie," AAFCO requires that the food is formulated to provide *no more* than 3100 kcal per kilogram of food (for dry products). By comparison, normal adult foods typically provide between 3500 and 4500 kcal/kg. So, this is a significant requirement that should result in a level of consistency in foods carrying the lite label claim. The second group of terms is those that make a claim regarding fat content. Specifically, if a food carries a statement such as low fat or lean, AAFCO requires that the product (dry foods) contains no more than 9 % fat. Since most adult foods contain between 12 and 16 % fat, this is a substantial reduction and one that can be meaningful to dog owners seeking to slim down Sally. Additionally, just as in human food products, if a company makes a comparison claim, such as "reduced calories" or "less fat," they must also include the name of the product that they are comparing to and the percentage of the decrease.

Unfortunately, the potentially helpful impact of this set of regulated terms is obscured by a larger number of descriptors that imply that a food has reduced calories and fat but that are not regulated. These include phrases such as "weight control," "healthy weight," "weight management," "less active" and "reduced activity" None of these terms are defined or regulated by AAFCO, making them essentially meaningless to consumers. Indeed, and not surprisingly, these monikers are more commonly used than are the few label terms that AAFCO pays attention to. Because these latter terms are not regulated, dog foods that use them vary incredibly in calories and nutrient content. Using just the small sample size included in Figure 6.5, we see that food #2 and food #8, marketed as "healthy weight" and "weight management" foods respectively, provide more calories per cup than many adult maintenance products. Indeed, food #2 contains more calories per cup (415) than some of the performance foods that we have reviewed in this chapter! Interestingly, the food is actually low in fat at 6 %, suggesting that this food is highly dense, an attribute that is very common in low carbohydrate foods. In contrast, food # 8 may contain as much as 12 % fat, a level that is found in many adult maintenance products and which is well above the level set by AAFCO for low fat foods at 9 %. This makes it hard to understand how such a food would be able to manage a dog's body weight.

Several foods in the list do provide lower calories than most typical adult foods. A general rule of thumb when selecting an over-the-counter weight control food is that it should provide less than 360 kcal per cup. Foods #1, #3, #5, #9 and #11 all fit this bill. However, reducing fat content is not the only way in which companies reduce the caloric density of a food. Another approach, and one that has limited scientific data supporting it, is to increase a type of fiber, called non-fermentable fiber, to dilute calories and to add bulk, which is presumed (but not demonstrated) to make dogs who are eating the food feel more sated (full). The first effect is valid. Increasing fiber does dilute calories—a food that includes increased amounts of non-fermentable fiber will provide fewer calories per cup of food than a food with a normal fiber level. However, what has not been proven is the claim that dogs feel fuller and less hungry when fed a low calorie, high fiber food. What we do know for certain is that increasing fiber beyond normal levels can reduce a food's overall digestibility and leads to increased volume of feces and increased defecation frequency (larger poops and more of them). Because of these undesirable side effects and because there is no evidence that the satiety effect is effective, this is an approach that is not recommended. In general, a dry food that reports a crude fiber content that is higher than 5 or 6 % has added fiber. The crude fiber column in the table shows us that food #11 has very high fiber (and relatively high fat), but low calories. A review of the first four ingredients explains this. The ingredient that is second highest in quantity is soybean mill run, a source of non-fermentable fiber. Its presence second in line on the ingredients list signifies a food that reduced energy density by diluting the food with fiber. Food #5 takes a similar approach, but in this case has both increased fiber and reduced fat. While calories are nicely reduced in this food, my guess is that some dogs may refuse to eat it, given that fat promotes palatability (and fiber definitely does not).

What all of this suggests to the well-meaning owner whose middle-aged Lab has put on a few pounds and who decides to switch to a "low cal" food is, once again, buyer beware. Just as most dogs who are exercising do not need to consume a performance food that is designed for hard working dogs, most dogs who are a bit overweight do not need to be switched to a food that is marketed for the "less active" dogs. A healthier approach is to reduce treats, slightly reduce the amount of the food that you are feeding (provided you are happy with it), and increase your dog's daily exercise. If you do decide to select a food with a lower energy density, keep in mind that a company showing a trim and fit dog running across an open field on its packaging and labeled for weight control is under no regulatory obligation to deliver either the fit dog or the controlled weight. So, read labels, compare calories and ingredients, and avoid products that have exorbitantly high fiber or calorie values that look too good to be true (they probably are). Most importantly, if Sally gains rather than loses weight on that weight management food that you selected, time to head back to the pet supply store and try again. Better yet, pick up Sally's leash, put on your walking shoes and head out for a brisk walk together in your local park. Make this a daily habit and you may not need to consider changing foods after all!

#	Brand	Fat (%)	Fiber (%)	Kcal per cup	First 4 ingredients
1	Avoderm Lite Chicken Formula	8 to 9	5	298	Ground whole brown rice, oatmeal, rice bran, chicken meal
2	Blue Buffalo Life Formula Healthy Weight	6	7	415	Deboned chicken, whole ground brown rice, whole ground barley, oatmeal
3	California Natural Low Fat Formula	7 to 9	2	317	Brown rice, lamb meal, rice, sunflower oil
4	Del Monte Kibbles and Bits Weight Maintenance	7	4	NR	Corn, soybean meal, meat & bone meal, ground wheat
5	Diamond Naturals Lamb & Rice Lite	6	9	275	Lamb meal, ground rice, cracked pearled barley, oatmeal
6	Eagle Pack Reduced Fat	10 to 11	4.5	354	Ground yellow corn, ground brown rice, pork meal, oatmeal
7	Innova Low Fat Adult	7 to 11	8	386	Turkey, chicken, whole grain barley, whole grain brown rice
8	Nutrisource Weight Management	9 to 12	5	385	Chicken, chicken meal, brown rice, white rice
9	Nutro Natural Choice Lite Adult	7	10	254	Chicken, whole brown rice, rice bran, chicken meal
10	Organix Weight Management Adult Dog	10	5.5	371	Organic chicken, chicken meal, organic brown rice, organic millet
11	Science Diet Adult Lite	8.6	11.5	295	Whole grain corn, soybean mill run, chicken by-product meal, corn gluten meal
12	Wellness Super-5Mix Healthy Weight	6 to 10	8	325	Deboned chicken, ground barley, rice bran, chicken meal

Figure 6.5 Comparing less active or lite foods (dry).

7

The New Age of Dog Food

(And How it is Influencing Our Choices)

Last year, I needed a new computer. I knew the time had come when my old PC started freezing up whenever I loaded too much data or tried to run several programs at the same time. While I was excited at the prospect of having a faster machine, I was also very apprehensive about the actual selection process. Perhaps these feelings had something to do with my reputation for being somewhat of a Luddite (my friends will tell you more than *somewhat)*. So, shopping for a piece of technology that impacts my professional and personal life so massively was expected to be a bit stressful. (Truth be told, I had a melt-down in Best Buy.) Luckily, I live with someone who makes his living working with computers, so my husband Mike stepped in and chose my brand spanking new computer for me. (I sat out in the car and read.)

We brought the new laptop home, set it up in my office and turned it on. I intended to immediately sit down and get back to work. No such luck. More selections were in store for me. The new computer arrived with an apparently unlimited number of configuration options. Decisions were needed for security systems, internet hookups, networking options, desktop wing-dings, screen resolutions, printer types, cueing sounds, keyboard specs and on and on. Not only were there seemingly hundreds of choices to consider, there were choices *within* choices! I solved the problem in the tried and true fashion. I handed the task over to my husband with the detailed instructions "Here, fix this for me." He did, and I now love my new computer. I have kept almost all of the selections that Mike chose and have spent virtually no time thinking about them. Life is good.

Is more always better?

It is generally accepted in our culture that having options and the freedom to choose contributes immeasurably to our happiness. Certainly, being denied basic freedoms and having *no* choice is not a desirable way to live for anyone. Extreme examples are seen in totalitarian regimes and prison. Indeed, our culture recognizes autonomy and the freedom to choose as being critical for, if not central to, our well-being. Freedom to choose is also important for non-human animals. Good dog trainers build confidence and empower their dogs by allowing them to *choose* desired behaviors and to learn through the consequences (both positive and negative) which of these behaviors they should repeat for more payout. Without question, having some choice, especially in things that are important to us, contributes to our happiness.

Having opportunities to select from a wide variety of consumer products is also viewed as a measure of affluence and innovation in a society. However, does it necessarily follow that having unlimited choices will produce more freedom and more happiness? From the time we get up in the morning until we turn off the last electronic gadget at the end of the day, we are inundated with options to consider and decisions to make. These typically begin with selecting the size, caffeine content, percentage fat, syrup flavor, foam level and brand of the coffee we purchase on the way to work, and end with the 847 cable stations and 342 news feeds from which we must choose to fall asleep to at night. Studies are now telling us that being presented each day with a multitude of choices can become overwhelming and, when taken to excess, can even make us feel miserable. Certainly, I did not find my computer selection experience to be either enjoyable or empowering. Rather the incessant demands and excessive neediness of my new computer led to frustration and thwarted my efforts to get work done.

Dog folks are definitely not immune to this phenomenon. When I first presented the lectures that later became the incentive for this book, I asked attendees, typically trainers and other pet professionals, what questions they were asked most frequently by their clients about dog nutrition. The almost unanimous answer was "What should I feed my dog? How do I choose among all of the different pet foods that I see in the store?" The trainers, pet-sitters and dog day care owners in attendance shared that they too often feel overwhelmed by the sheer number of different brands and categories of dog foods that are available today. Even having a bit of knowledge about dog nutrition does not seem to be of much help when trying to navigate among products and slick marketing campaigns. Unfortunately, this confusion and frustration can lead either to hasty choices that over-simplify or ignore important information or to **choice paralysis**, avoiding a decision altogether and simply staying with the status quo.

Choice paralysis

Dr. Barry Schwartz, a psychologist at Swarthmore College in Pennsylvania, specializes in human decision making and studies the effects of excess choice upon behavior. His popular book *Paradox of Choice* introduces the concept of choice paralysis. Schwartz explains that in today's world it is not unusual for people to react to being presented with too many options by procrastinating or by "choosing not to choose." He reviews a number of research studies that illustrate this phenomenon. One of the most interesting was an analysis of employee enrollment rates in voluntary retirement plans. The researchers gathered data from over one million workers at approximately 2000 different companies who were asked to select a retirement plan from their company's set of options. They examined a variety of influencing factors that might influence a person's decision, including the total number of different investment plans that were available to each worker. A surprising and unexpected result was that, as the number of different retirement plans offered by a company *increased*, the number of workers who elected to participate in the company's retirement program significantly *decreased*. This correlation was so strong and consistent that a 2 % reduction in participation was observed for every ten extra retirement plans that a company offered. In other words, a company that offered 50 different plans had 10 % less participation by their workers than did a company that offered just a few plans. The truly astounding fact of this study was that many of the plan choices included matching funds provided by the employer, so deciding to enroll was definitely financially beneficial (i.e., was strongly reinforced!).

Along with the authors of the study, Schwartz suggested that being faced with too many choices seems to backfire, leading to an avoidance of choosing altogether or relying on a "default" option. For example, a follow-up to the retirement plan study showed that when a participating company added a default option that would automatically select an investment portfolio, employee enrollment dramatically increased from 9 % to 34 %. While procrastinating is not an option for our dogs (they all have to eat), we do witness dog owners who simply throw up their hands in frustration and choose "default." This is most typically the food that their family has always fed (or the store clerk recommends), the brand that is most popular or most convenient, or the food that has a picture on the cover that looks most like their dog. Examples of relying upon the default alternative abound in our world today and they are sometimes the best way to go when attempting to save time and maximize efficiency. However, for our dogs' health, default is rarely a good option.

In addition to being overwhelmed by too much choice, there is a second, perhaps more insidious outcome of having too many options. An overabundance of choice leads invariably to raised (and potentially unrealistic) expectations. Researcher Alex Michalos of the University of Northern British Columbia studies issues of life quality. He suggests that the increased work that is involved with choosing among too many options leads to heightened expectations regarding exactly what the chosen item can deliver in terms of benefits (and happiness). He explains that choosing one option among many requires that we compare it to other options that are available. As the number and complexity of comparisons that must be made increases, we become more committed to the choice that we eventually make. In other words, you may think to yourself "Well, it took me almost fifteen minutes and a lot of study to choose exactly the right degree of crunchiness, saltiness and flavor in these snack crackers—they darn well better taste great!"

Similarly, in this day and age, pet owners must work harder than ever to choose a dog food. And, to boot, we feel the additional pressure of our dog's health and happiness weighing heavily upon us. Not so long ago, owners had a very limited selection of dog foods available. Most were formulated for "all life stages." Ingredient varieties and activity level differences were non-existent. Moreover, the advertising and label claims used by pet food companies were almost laughably simplistic by today's standards. *"Feed our food and your dog will love you"* was the single and universal message that marketers delivered. Today, things are a bit more complicated, aren't they? Our expectations of a food's benefits are raised by the work that we must engage in to choose the food, as well as by the multitude of benefits and health claims that pet food companies make in their advertising campaigns. Together these changes contribute to higher, and in my view, unrealistic and potentially risky expectations of what a dog food is even capable of delivering. It is one thing to expect a food to promote a proper weight, robust condition, lustrous coat and healthy skin. It is quite another to expect the food that one selects to cure arthritis, stop dental disease in its tracks or prevent cancer.

Neither choice paralysis nor unrealistic expectations are a good deal for our dogs. But, there is good news. The way out of the pet food quagmire is to understand the very real pitfalls of being faced with too many options and to understand where true choices exist and where contrived comparisons are mere marketing hyperbole. Although it is difficult, choice paralysis and unrealistic expectations that are a natural consequence of having too many options can be controlled by following the science, avoiding cognitive errors and accepting only claims that represent evidence-based nutrition. Preceding chapters have given you the science, nutrition and critical thinking tools that you need for smart decision making. Let's now turn to the state of pet food choice today (and how we got here), followed by a detailed case example that will engage your critical thinking skills, review the current science and allow you to practice avoiding those pesky cognitive biases and logical fallacies. Let's start with a look at where we are today in terms of available dog foods—and why.

Pet food paradigm shifts

When I was in graduate school, a fellow student recommended a book called *The Structure of Scientific Revolutions* by Thomas Kuhn. Published in 1962, it was already considered a classic in the philosophy of science by the 1980s. Kuhn is responsible for defining and popularizing the concept of **paradigm shifts**. He explains that historically, scientific advancement has occurred as a series of relatively uneventful periods punctuated by intellectually abrupt revolutions. These are discoveries that are so new and unexpected that they change the entire way in which we do science, think about a topic or even live our lives. Once accepted, these new concepts completely replace those that preceded them. A paradigm shift is a change from one way of thinking to another: a new way of looking at an old problem. These shifts do not just happen, but rather are driven by people of great minds or by events of great import. For example, the development of agriculture changed humans from nomadic hunter-gatherers to sedentary community builders, and for better or for worse, allowed us to populate and dominate the entire planet. Similarly, Darwin's theory of evolution changed not only how we looked at all other species on the planet, but (with some continuing resistance) how we look upon being human itself. Paradigm shifts also can be caused by new inventions. The invention of the printing press in the 1400s led to the unprecedented preservation and distribution of knowledge and had a major role in the scientific revolution. In our own time, the introduction of the personal computer and the internet has had cultural ramifications that have impacted our personal and professional lives in ways that could never have been anticipated. These transformations all involve a replacement of old belief systems or way of doing things with an entirely new paradigm.

At the risk of over-dramatization, it appears that we are in the middle of a paradigm shift today that affects how we think about commercial pet foods and how best to feed our dogs. Although not a life-changing event for most people, or even perhaps not for most dog people, the changes that we are seeing in the pet food industry and among owner attitudes during the last seven years are unprecedented and certainly worth examining. If you remember, the pet food industry was literally born in the latter 1950s as a consequence of the development of the extrusion process. Producing dry foods that provided complete nutrition, stored easily and that were convenient allowed dog owners to feed their dogs a single product for a relatively low price and to feel good while doing it. Starting in the mid-1980s, research that studied the nutrient needs of dogs increased dramatically, both at universities and within the private sector (pet food companies). This expansion occurred in large part because of the increasing importance that dogs had to our lives and the creation of an entire pet industry around that relationship. The advances in our understanding of canine nutrient needs and feeding behavior led to improvements in the quality of many foods as well as an explosion in the number of brands and products that were available to dog owners.

By the new millennium, more than 90 % of Americans were feeding a commercial dry (extruded) dog food to their dogs and the explosion of life stage and lifestyle foods has occurred almost exclusively within the extruded dry product segment. In addition to puppy and adult foods, we saw the development of products that target different adult sizes, activity levels, breeds and health conditions. The variety of ingredients included in foods has similarly expanded, with the inclusion of new protein sources, grains (or no grains), types of fat and "functional" nutrients. On the business side of things, the 1990s and early 2000s witnessed unprecedented growth in sales, followed by an epidemic of pet food company mergers and acquisitions. Small, privately owned pet food companies and their brands were gobbled up by a small handful of multi-national corporations. Over time, a single company became the owner not only of multiple brands of food but also numerous product lines within brands. By the early 2000s, the majority of pet food brands sold in the United States were owned by the five giants of the pet food industry: Mars Petcare; Nestle-Purina PetCare; Colgate-Palmolive (owner of Hills); Procter and Gamble (P&G) Pet Care; and Del Monte Foods (more about these in Chapter 8).

The pet food paradigm shift that began in the early 2000s accelerated tremendously in the spring of 2007. Sadly, this change came about not in response to a new discovery or an innovative type of pet food. Rather, it was set off by a massive pet food recall of unprecedented proportion that was caused by the intentional adulteration of a common food ingredient. I will discuss details and the full extent of the recall in Chapter 11, but it is important for this discussion to understand the effects that this catastrophe had upon pet owners' confidence in pet foods and in the companies that produce them. The problem began when numerous dogs and cats started to become suddenly ill with renal failure, many never recovering. Although we now know that the company that was responsible, Menu Foods, had started to investigate the problem by early March, it took weeks of consumer complaints before a voluntary recall was initiated.

I remember that time well. My mom and I were attending a Canine Freestyle seminar together in St. Louis, Missouri. My mother, a trainer also, had been a board member of NADOI, and this seminar was held in conjunction with the organization's annual meeting. During a seminar break, a long-time friend of my mother's came and sat with us. She tearfully related that she had lost her beloved young German Shepherd earlier that week to renal disease, brought on by the tainted food. The most heartwrenching detail that I remember from that conversation was the distraught woman telling us of her continued attempts to entice her sick dog to eat the tainted food prior to knowing that it was the food that was actually *causing* her dog's illness and eventual death. She spoke of warming the food and adding little tidbits to it, in an attempt to nurture her boy back to health. For me, and also for my mom and others in the room, this put a highly personal face on the daily statistics of pet illness and loss that we were reading about in the media. It is an understatement to say that losing a dog in such a way is every dog lover's worst nightmare.

Over the following months and into early summer, the extent of the problem became appallingly evident. According to Dr. Stephen Sundlof, who was the head of the FDA's Center of Veterinary Medicine at the time, the root cause of the contamination came from a switch in ingredient supplier. Buyers at Menu Foods had recently changed to a new supplier of wheat gluten, an ingredient that is included in canned foods as a thickening and binding agent. They had switched to an Arizona-based company called ChemNutra that was importing the ingredient from China. ChemNutra offered wheat gluten at a price that was about 30 % lower than the cost of making (not selling) the ingredient in the US. It eventually became known that the Chinese suppliers were intentionally adding two non-food compounds, melamine and cyanuric acid, to wheat flour in order to make the flour appear to be the more expensive ingredient, wheat gluten. The adulteration had the effect of raising apparent protein levels of the ingredient in a deceptive manner, thus allowing the company to charge a higher price for what was actually a very low quality product. When present together in a pet food, we now know that melamine and cyanuric acid crystalize into a complex that accumulates in the kidney, leading to kidney damage and death. By the end of the disaster, it was estimated that over 5,000 pet food products had been tainted and were recalled, and thousands of cats and dogs were sickened or killed.

This event, along with several subsequent pet food recalls for salmonella and aflatoxin (a toxin produced as a result of mold contamination to corn or wheat ingredients), led to changes in dog owners' understanding of how pet food was made in the United States and to a dramatic shift in overall perceptions of the pet food industry. Perhaps the biggest shock to dog owners was the revelation that a single manufacturer, in this case Menu Foods Limited, was responsible for the production of dozens of brands of pet food that were owned by a wide variety of pet food companies, including the big five companies discussed earlier. As a result, different brands of foods were often produced using the same ingredients that originated from a common supplier. Perhaps even more significant was the realization that many pet food ingredients were sourced from outside of the United States, often in countries such as China, that had few or insufficient regulatory standards. Collectively, the truths that were revealed in the wake of the largest and most devastating pet food recall in history led to a rapid loss of consumer confidence and to increased skepticism toward pet food companies and their products.

While pet food recalls are dramatic and highly salient examples, several other cultural changes have also contributed to the pet food paradigm shift. It is common knowledge among people who work in the pet food industry that trends occurring in the human food industry quite reliably predict what we can expect to see occurring a few years later in the pet food industry. A recent example of this is the increased popularity of grain-free dog foods. These foods have their origins in the gluten-free and eventually grain-free movement in human diets. Grain-free brands of dog food were virtually non-existent before the year 2000. Today, almost every pet food company includes a dedicated grain-free brand or product line and some companies sell nothing but grain-free products. Similarly, as interest has grown about where and how our own food is produced, so too has there been increased interest in knowing more about the origin of the foods that we feed to our dogs and cats. Owners are increasingly sophisticated in their knowledge of foods and are more willing than ever before to scrutinize ingredients and label claims. Market segments that were once considered small and "niche" are now mainstream. Some owners wish to choose only foods that include organic ingredients, some eschew any foods that may contain genetically modified organisms, and others are switching to raw diets for their dogs. Many are concerned about the source of ingredients that go into foods as well as about who is producing their dog's food. And, some are equally concerned with the environmental or animal welfare issues surrounding their own and their dogs' foods or with consuming only foods that originate locally or regionally.

Not just your grandmother's kibble anymore

So, let's take a look at where exactly the pet food paradigm shift has led us. During the last five years, the pet food industry has witnessed an explosion of innovation and the development of new feeding philosophies and products. If you remember from Chapter 4, the development of extrusion in the early 1960s almost instantaneously revolutionized the pet food industry, in large part because it led to the mass production of foods that were convenient, economical and that could be stored for long periods. Because the extrusion cooking process efficiently cooked starch and resulted in both increased digestibility and enhanced taste, dry foods contained a relatively high proportion of starch, plus various sources of animal- and/or plant-based proteins, animal or plant fats/oils and vitamin/mineral pre-mixes. Convenience has been an attractive feature of extruded dry foods. Not only are these foods easy to store and feed, but they can now be purchased at every supermarket and big box outlet found in America's shopping centers. Owners can purchase dry dog foods at grocery stores and mass market retailers such as Walmart, Target and even Walgreens. Together, these large retail sources are responsible for more than 70 % of dog food sales. The pet superstores are responsible for about one-fifth of sales, followed distantly by small pet supply stores. Generally speaking, the perception of owners is that higher quality (i.e., premium) foods are available at pet supply stores, while the lower quality brands, which are also lower in cost, can be readily purchased at grocery store chains and mass market retailers. And generally speaking, these distinctions are true (more about this in the following chapter).

Notwithstanding the continued popularity of extruded foods (and, as we will see in Chapter 8, more brands and product lines and varieties of extruded products are available today than ever before), let us take a quick look at some of the *new* approaches to producing dog foods that have been developed in recent years as part of this paradigm shift and that provide yet another set of choices to pet owners. Several of these approaches are used primarily to produce safe and storable raw foods, such as dehydration and freeze-drying. Others are a new approach to cooking and storing foods that contain ingredients other than those that are typically included in dry foods. While these food forms still comprise a very small portion of the pet food market, I think they reflect the enhanced innovation and exploration into new possibilities that are coming about during the new age of pet foods. Figure 7.1 summarizes these and provides a few brand examples for you to explore, should you so choose.

Food form	Description	Brand examples
Dehydrated	Dehydration involves removing most of the water from the mixed and ground raw ingredients. Gentle heating during dehydration kills microorganisms and partially cooks the food. Portions are rehydrated with warm water immediately prior to feeding.	The Honest Kitchen, Addiction, ZiWi Peak
Freeze-dried	Ingredients are mixed and then frozen under a vacuum, which allows product moisture to sublimate directly from the solid phase to the gas phase. Portions are rehydrated with warm water.	Stella & Chewy's, Nutrisca, Orijen, SoJo
Refrigerated	Ingredients are gently cooked (not extruded), shaped into tubes or patties and refrigerated.	FreshPet
Frozen (Cooked)	Ingredients are gently cooked (not extruded), then frozen. May be complete and balanced or a pre-mix to which other ingredients are added at home.	Evermore, Bil-Jac, Buddy's Kitchen
Frozen (Raw)	Ingredients are combined, frozen and packaged as rolls, or individual meal-size patties.	Stella & Chewys, Nature's Variety, Bravo!
Pre-mixes	A frozen or freeze-dried mix of either non-meat ingredients (to which the owner adds cooked or raw meat), or of meat ingredients (to which the owner adds vegetables, fruits, grains).	Fresh Oasis, SoJo, Bravo!
Raw Coated	Baked or extruded kibbles coated with freeze-dried (usually raw) ingredients.	Great Life, Instinct (treats)

Figure 7.1 Innovative food types.

In the next chapter we explore choice further and examine the important criteria of who, where, what and why you should care of dog food choice. However, before moving on, it is time to pull together your understanding of clear thinking (avoiding cognitive biases), nutritional science and decision making by using a case example. Remember, it is not the purpose of this example to persuade you in one way or another. Rather, the purpose of the following exercise is to examine the science, avoid cognitive traps and use critical thinking to choose well for your dog.

Case example: using your critical thinking skills

It should be evident by now that my goal with this book is not to tell you what food to feed to your dog or how to specifically advise your clients about their dogs. Rather, my objective is to promote well-reasoned decision making that combines a working knowledge of the scientific method, canine nutrition and critical thinking skills. To practice these skills, let's now turn to an example of a relatively new feeding approach that has received a lot of attention and use it to practice the science sleuthing skills that were presented in earlier chapters. The example is the emotionally-charged and oddly polarizing practice of feeding raw diets to dogs. This example is appropriate for this section because feeding raw diets reflects the innovation that is associated with the paradigm shift that we have witnessed in pet foods, and because feeding raw is considered to be the fastest growing new segment of the industry during the last several years.

First, let's all calm down

No other dog feeding issue in recent years has generated a greater number of heated arguments, flaming emails and vehemently divergent opinions than the subject of feeding raw versus cooked dog food. It is certainly the topic that I receive the largest number of questions (and opinions) about at conferences and through consulting work. Sadly, the practice of feeding raw diets to dogs has become so polarized that otherwise reasonable dog folks are increasingly adopting a seemingly volatile "if you are not with us, you must be against us" mindset. This type of thinking has led to cult-like beliefs and devotion on one side and the banding together of opponents to issue position statements against raw feeding on the other. Let us see if we can dial back the rhetoric a notch and examine what is *believed* about raw diets versus what we actually know about them.

Defining raw

The term "raw diet" can encompass a variety of products, but generally refers to feeding a diet that consists of uncooked muscle meat, bones (either whole or ground), organ meats such as livers and kidneys, possibly raw eggs, and various amounts of vegetables and fruits. Some owners who feed raw prepare the entire diet as homemade, while others purchase a commercial product. Either way, the resulting diet may or may not be formulated to be complete and balanced. Those that are not must be supplemented with additional ingredients by the owner to make a balanced diet. Although raw food sales comprised less than 5 % of the pet food market in 2012, raw pet food products are identified as the fastest growing market segment of pet foods. Today, companies provide raw diets and treats in several forms, most commonly frozen, dehydrated or freeze-dried products. In addition, many owners who feed raw are preparing the food either partially or entirely as a homemade diet.

The claims

Let us first examine what each side of the issue is saying. Proponents of raw meat diets for dogs tell us that raw feeding is better for dogs' health when compared with feeding cooked food, especially when it is compared with feeding extruded dry dog foods. Asserted health benefits of raw feeding include improved digestibility and nutrient availability, enhanced vitality and overall health, increased energy (activity level), decreased body odor, improvements in skin and coat condition, prevention of dental disease, enhanced immune system function and even, in some cases, the prevention of chronic disorders such as arthritis or cancer. The reasoning behind these claims falls into two broad categories. The first is that feeding raw is a more natural (and therefore, better) way to feed dogs. Descriptors such as "prey diet," "predatory model" and "ancestral diet" are used to convey the belief that dogs, like wolves, are carnivores that thrive on meat, especially raw meat (plus the intestinal contents of prey, which typically include plant materials that the prey consumed). The second and often congruent argument is that the nutrients that are provided via raw feeding are more available and useable to dogs, and even, according to some proponents, are unique in some way when compared with the nutrients that are provided by a cooked diet.

On the opposite side, critics of raw feeding focus on the potential for nutrient imbalances and purported increased health risks of feeding raw foods. The most frequently mentioned nutritional concerns are imbalances that occur when excess muscle meat is fed along with insufficient amounts of other foods. The most prevalently cited potential health risks are the potential for microbial contamination of raw meats with pathogens and the risk of transmission of food-borne illnesses to both pets and people. If bones are included, increased risk of gut obstruction or perforation from bone fragments is commonly mentioned. Critics also maintain that many, if not all, of the professed health benefits of raw food diets have not been proven.

The science

What does the science tell us? Let's start with the asserted health benefits. Proponents of raw diets point to owner testimonials and stories as supportive evidence for these claims. Most of these focus on skin and coat health (typically allergies), activity level, dental health and overall vitality and energy. Take a look at Figure 7.2 for a sample of dog owner testimonials, posted as food reviews on a variety of websites. Of the seven reviews that are posted, five identify reduction in allergy symptoms, four rave about coat shininess, three mention weight or body condition improvement and three mention gastrointestinal or stool quality benefits of the food. We must agree that these are all simply anecdotal evidence and, of course, just a minute fraction of the number of testimonials that are available on the internet.

Food	Dog owner testimonial
1	I have a German Shepherd with severe food allergies. When a friend told me about ***, feeding it stopped all of the problems. Rudy's ears don't get infected anymore and he is able to keep weight on!
2	My Chihuahua Addie was miserable from some unknown food allergy; she hated the vet foods, and they did little to relieve her constant itching. Within a week of being on *** her coat has improved immensely, and her sister's coat as well. When we wake up in the morning, they follow me around like crazy until they get their breakfast!
3	Our vet suspected that our Australian Shepherd had allergies due to the constant itching and biting. He recommended switching food but we could not afford the really high end foods. We found *** and our pup is better than ever! Her itching went away almost instantly and we also saw a big improvement in her coat. We have since switched our other dog to *** and have had great success.
4	My dog has been eating *** for almost 2 years now. Could not be happier with the results... He's 1/2 beagle and 1/2 dachshund (3 years old), he's very muscular and lean, his teeth/gums are healthy and his coat is SO shiny. Every time he sees the vet they tell me he's in perfect shape... I'll chalk it up to the food!
5	My 3 year old Shi-Poo, Bella has allergies that make her miserable and cause her to lick her paws constantly. I saw your food at my local pet store and decided to give your turkey recipe a try. Bella started to feel better almost immediately! Her paws are no longer red looking and she has stopped licking and chewing!
6	My dog suffers from skin allergies so it's extremely important to feed him foods with protein, fish oils and basically something that tastes good. I've tried a few different brands, organic, all natural, whatever, we tried it. We finally settled on *** because (1) he ate it and (2) it kept him at a healthy weight. As soon as I switched him to ***, the changes in his coat and appearance were immediate...His coat is shiny, the white part of his fur is super white, the black part of coat is glossy, he's at a healthy weight, his skin is healthy...over all he is gorgeous!
7	Our ten-year-old Shepherd has eaten about everything you can imagine. During that time he had both seizures and IBD (irritable bowel disorder). He was really starting to show his age. About six months ago we switched him to *** and there's been a world of difference. He now runs around with our other two dogs and plays with toys. His poop is FINALLY normal.

Figure 7.2 Dog owner testimonials.

If I were to find 500 more like this (which would be quite easy to do, though time-consuming), would the 500 additional testimonials represent more evidence, perhaps even data? (If you read Chapter 3, you know that this is a trick question.) Multiple anecdotes never become data, they just become more anecdotes. We cannot and should not base decisions upon anecdotes and testimonials because, while they seem compelling and are often completely sincere, anecdotes are stories that people tell to others and to themselves. They are emotionally biased, uncontrolled and lack objectiveness or the balance that an impartial observer and a control group bring to a scientific study. And wait. There is one final catch. Of the seven foods for which testimonials are provided in Figure 7.2, not all are for raw diets. Three of these were posted in praise of a raw food and the other four were posted as reviews for cooked or extruded diets. Can you tell which is which? To find out, look below at Figure 7.3. The testimonials of people who feed a raw diet may reflect their personal experience, but the health claims that are made can be just as easily found in the testimonials of people who feed a variety of extruded (cooked) foods.

Food #	Food brand and type
1	Fresh Pet—cooked
2	Stella and Chewy's—raw
3	Authority—dry, extruded
4	Eukanuba—dry, extruded
5	Stewart Raw Naturals—raw
6	Beneful—dry, extruded
7	Bravo!—raw

Figure 7.3 Dog owner testimonials—products identified.

If we cannot trust personal testimonials to inform us about the alleged health benefits of raw diets, is there any scientific evidence of these benefits? Unfortunately, no. *To date there are no data nor any published studies that either support or refute any of the health claims or digestive benefits that are declared for raw diets.* Although raw foods can certainly be formulated to provide complete and balanced nutrition (many companies already do this and do it very well), there is simply no evidence that a raw diet *promotes superior health or cures disease* in dogs. This does *not* mean that a raw food does not provide benefits, simply that there is no evidence of these benefits and no evidence of their superiority over cooked food. To date, the health claims of proponents of feeding raw diets are not supported by scientific evidence. Sure, there are glowing testimonials and positive reviews of these foods. However, as we just saw, so too are there equally positive reports of cooked and extruded foods. People tend to pay more attention to raw diet claims because those who feed raw hope that the claims are true for their own dog and his allergies (the illusion of control plus confirmation bias in play) and because many raw diet proponents are dedicated to the raw food movement, write a lot of blogs and books, and promote their views quite fervently (the availability heuristic). Some also, just like those who sell extruded products, have a vested interest in selling their own foods. When looking at evidence, the winner cannot simply be the person who shouts the loudest. In a nutshell, the various superior health claims made for raw diets should not be made until/if/when they are substantiated through study and certainly cannot be currently viewed as valid evidence when you are making decisions about what to feed to your dog.

Is natural better?

Does the argument that a raw diet is "natural" for our dogs and therefore is the best approach to feeding hold up under scrutiny? This assertion is a prime example of the naturalistic fallacy that we discussed in Chapter 3. Remember that the general form of this type of flawed argument is that if A is natural, it must be good/right/healthful and is therefore superior to B that is classified as unnatural or less natural. Even if we agree that some things are natural and some are not, it does *not* follow that the thing that is deemed to be more natural is superior/better/more healthful than the thing that is less natural. The first to the second is not a valid deduction. Examples of this fallacy abound. We just tend not to notice contradicting examples because of our inclination to cherry pick only those natural behaviors/foods/physiologies that lend support to our beliefs (confirmation bias). Certainly flea and tick infestations are natural. Yet most responsible dog owners prevent infestations in their dogs. One's approach to flea/tick prevention may vary, but still, most dog owners do not respond to flea season by saying "Well, having fleas is the natural state for my dog, so I choose to encourage flea infestations." Similarly, stating that eating raw meat is natural for dogs may have its basis in truth (at least for their wolf ancestors), but it does not automatically follow that we must feed them raw meat or that raw diets are therefore more healthful. Using "it's natural" is a misleading and false argument and simply does not hold up under the smallest bit of scrutiny.

Domestic dogs versus wolves

Even if one decides to ignore the logical flaws of the naturalistic argument, scientific evidence still refutes the highly romanticized view that dogs, having evolved from a wolf ancestor, are physiologically adapted to eat a raw rather than a cooked diet. Both the archeological and the genetic evidence tell us that the dog has been domesticated for between 12,000 and 15,000 years. Although we cannot know for certain exactly what initiated and drove the dog's domestication, there are two prevailing theories. The first holds that humans intentionally adopted and tamed wolf pups, kept them as pets and gradually began to breed them in captivity. The second and more widely accepted theory, first proposed by Dr. Ray Coppinger, is that the initial stages of domestication were unintentional, with dogs evolving as camp scavengers who con-sumed the waste of the early agriculturalists. Over many generations this communal relationship selected for more scavenging and less pack hunting, and the evolving dog became more and more attached to human habitats and to a human-supplied diet. Regardless of which theoretical camp you are loyal to, by all accounts the dog has been consuming human-supplied food for more than 10,000 years. In that period, as we were evolving as agriculturalists, the foods that we used to feed ourselves (as omnivores) have included cooked meat and fish, grains, vegetables and eventually dairy products. And dogs were fed the scraps—those bits of foods or parts of animals that we found to be unpalatable or inedible or that were simply leftover. (Interestingly, many of these food parts, such as organ meats, bones and connective tissues are the same tissues that are included in the protein meals that are used in current-day pet foods.) So, even if the image of their Toy Poodle as an efficient, pack-hunting predator feasting on the raw flesh of a recently killed caribou appeals to a certain type of dog owner, that image is a fiction that is not supported by scientific evidence.

Recent evidence coming from geneticists further divides the dog's "natural" diet from that of wolves. A paper published in *Nature* in early 2013 identified 36 regions in the dog's genome that are associated with changes that came about during domestication (Axelsson et al, 2013). More than half of these regions were involved with brain function, suggesting that these are responsible for the behavior and social structure differences that we see between dogs and wolves. Ten of the 36 groups of genes have key roles in starch digestion and fat metabolism. The researchers specifically found a set of mutations in the dog genome that cause increased production of the enzyme amylase, which is essential for the digestion of starch. The authors of the study speculate that this adaptation, which is similar to changes in the human genome during the same period, allowed early dogs to consume and more efficiently digest diets that contained higher levels of starch (i.e., from their agriculturalist human friends), and constituted a crucial step in canine domestication.

The gradual changes in living environment, social relationships and diet that went along with domestication led to irrefutable changes in the dog as a species. Modern dogs are not wolves. They do not behave like wolves, interact with humans like wolves or hunt prey like wolves. As hard as it seems to be for some to accept, the science shows us that dogs are dogs, not wolves. They have been consuming cooked foods that were given to them by humans (not hunted) for a very long time. Our job, as the human side of the relationship, is to refrain from the naturalistic fallacy of cherry-picking dog as wolf references to support pet (pun intended) theories about how to care for, train and feed them.

Are raw diets more nutritious?

Does the claim that raw foods are better digested and utilized by dogs associated with supportive evidence? Dr. Ian Billinghurst is an Australian veterinarian who is credited with starting the raw pet food movement in the early 1990s via his BARF (Biologically Appropriate Raw Food or Bones and Raw Food) diet. According to Billinghurst, cooking dog food destroys natural enzymes in raw meat that, in his opinion, have anti-aging properties and contribute to pet health. However, Billinghurst never identifies these nutrients or enzymes specifically, so it is impossible to understand what he is referring to. Additionally, there exists no evidence for "anti-aging activity" of nutrients found in raw meat. Like other proteins, most of the enzymes that are found in raw food will be inactivated in the stomach when exposed to gastric acid and are digested to their constituent amino acids in the small intestine. To date, the existence of unique nutrients that are found in raw meat but not in cooked meat has not been demonstrated.

However, it is true that thermal processing (cooking) of all types leads to some loss of certain nutrients in foods. This is true for all foods, including those that humans consume. Temperature, moisture, use of pressure and duration of cooking are all factors that influence the extent of nutrient loss. Nutrients that are most susceptible to heat-related loss are the water soluble vitamins such as vitamin C (which dogs do not require) and the B-vitamins. Most pet food manufacturers account for these losses by either using heat-stable forms of susceptible nutrients or formulating diets to contain overages that correct for anticipated losses. In addition, some of the nutrient changes caused by cooking are beneficial. Heat treatment destroys the anti-nutritional factors that are found in some raw ingredients. The two that are most important to dogs are the presence of a trypsin inhibitor in raw egg white and the presence of an anti-thiamine factor in certain types of raw fish. The trypsin inhibitor in raw egg white reduces a dog's ability to digest the protein that is in the food, and can lead to weight loss and protein deficiency if large amounts of raw egg are fed. The anti-thiamine factor in raw fish can cause deficiency of the B-vitamin thiamine. Both of these factors are completely destroyed by heat and are not a concern when these foods are cooked. They are, however, an important consideration if raw fish or raw eggs are included in a dog's diet.

A number of ingredients, such as meats and fat sources, are well digested by dogs when fed either raw or cooked. Although few studies have been conducted to compare cooked to raw ingredients in pet foods, recent studies with cats that were published in the *Journal of Animal Sciences* measured the digestibility of beef or poultry diets fed raw versus the same foods fed as part of an extruded diet (Kerr et al; 2012 and 2013). Both the raw and the extruded foods were highly digestible by cats, with no statistically significant differences found. Although a similar study has not been reported for dogs, these data suggest that raw meat and fat are not necessarily better digested than extruded products made with meals from the same sources. It is important to note however, that poor quality protein meals or a poorly controlled extrusion process can lead to heat-damaged protein, which will decrease the digestibility and quality of the entire diet. And, unfortunately, as we will see in the following chapter, it is almost impossible for pet owners to know if a protein meal that is included in a pet food is of high quality or low quality from information provided on labels. So, in this respect, protein digestibility of raw diets (when appropriate meats are fed) can be expected to be equal to or higher than that of cooked foods.

Finally, some ingredients, in particular plant-based ingredients, are better digested and provide more available nutrients when they are cooked than when fed raw. For example, studies with humans and with animals show that cooking certain vegetables such as spinach and carrots increases the availability of antioxidants such as beta-carotene (also a precursor of vitamin A) and lycopene. We have also known for many years that cooking plant starches, in particular using extrusion, greatly enhances the ability of dogs to digest and use starch as a source of dietary energy. Extrusion causes an expansion of the granules that make up starch, allowing digestive enzymes better access to the starch molecules for efficient digestion. (It is important to note that this is true for humans as well as for dogs, and is why we generally do not munch on raw potatoes or uncooked wheat flour). The increased digestibility that occurs with cooking varies with the type of plant starch. While ground grains such as rice, oats or corn are about 60 % digestible when fed raw, cooking these ingredients increases the dog's ability to digest them to more than 95 %. What this means is that if you feed your dog 100 grams of uncooked oats or rice, only 60 grams will make it into his body to nourish him. 40 grams ends up in the large intestine where microbes ferment some of it, and a lot of that 40 grams ends up in your yard, as feces. When cooked, almost the entire 100 grams are digested and absorbed to nourish your dog.

Wishing to delve into the starch issue a bit more, I spoke with Dr. George Fahey, a professor of animal nutrition at the Animal Sciences Department at the University of Illinois. Dr. Fahey is considered one of the leading experts on starch and fiber and their use in companion animal diets. He explained that plant species vary significantly in the type and form of starch granules that they contain and that this affects how well a raw plant ingredient can be digested by dogs. Properties such as granule size and the proportion of amylose (straight chain starch) to amylopectin (branched-chain starch) are genetically determined and vary between plant families. It is also important how finely the starch is ground. Finely ground starches will be better digested, an important factor for raw feeders who wish to maximize digestibility of uncooked plant ingredients. Dr. Fahey provided a few guidelines regarding the types of starch to pay attention to. While finely ground grains such as flax or corn will be moderately digestible prior to cooking, other plant starches such potato, sweet potato and tapioca are virtually indigestible to dogs unless they are cooked. This is important information given the increased popularity of using non-grain carbohydrate sources in pet foods today. While potato or tapioca may be a great source of digestible carbohydrate to include in a cooked dog food, it is definitely not a good choice for a raw diet, even if it is ground well before feeding.

Taken altogether, the science shows us that the nutritional claims made by raw food advocates do not all measure up. Cooking, especially the thermal processing of extrusion, alters ingredients and the nutrients that they supply. No argument there. However, these changes are definitely not *all* negative or harmful, as proponents of raw feeding would have people believe. When reviewing the evidence for nutritional superiority, we must look at all of the science, even if what it tells us does not support our beliefs. In the case of raw versus cooked foods for dogs, the science tells us that cooking causes changes in foods. Some of these changes are inconsequential, some lead to nutrient losses which must be accounted for or, if possible, minimized, and some are beneficial because they improve digestibility, nutrient availability and food safety.

Can raw diets be nutritionally balanced?

This is an easy one. Of course they can be. And many of the raw foods that are marketed and sold today are. The companies who produce them meet the same standard requirements that companies producing extruded and canned products meet to allow the "complete and balanced" label claim. Of course, nutrient imbalances may occur when an inadequate homemade or commercially prepared raw diet is fed. For example, a study published in 2001 analyzed three homemade raw diets and two commercially prepared foods and found nutrient deficiencies and excesses in all five diets. Of importance was the presence of an inverted calcium to phosphorus ratio in four of the five foods, meaning that the foods had very high phosphorus levels and very low calcium levels. This will occur if owners feed a diet that is excessively high in muscle meats (high phosphorus) and lacking in calcium-containing foods. (That age-old myth that "dogs thrive on meat" really, really needs to be put to rest once and for all.) Still, this is an old study, it examined only five foods, and the production of raw diets, and the availability of balanced recipes, has come a long way since then. Making a well-balanced and nutritious raw diet is possible and is accomplished regularly, both by companies that sell raw foods, and by owners who prepare homemade foods that use well-researched and formulated recipes.

Are raw diets safe?

Two safety issues are raised concerning raw diets: risk of microbial contamination and risk of bowel perforations (if large bones are fed). Bacterial contamination of raw meats is a definite concern and has been documented in the literature. The most prevalent issue is the risk of meat contamination with food-borne pathogens and transmission of these pathogens to both pets and to people. Proponents of raw food diets counter these concerns by claiming that bacterial pathogens do not cause illness in dogs because of a unique adaptation of the canine intestinal tract that protects dogs from infection. However, once again, there is no evidence to support this claim. There are also documented cases of fecal shedding of *Salmonella spp.* and of clinical salmonellosis in dogs and cats who were fed raw meat. For example, a study of 138 dogs in 84 homes in Ontario reported that 25 % of the households had at least one dog shedding Salmonella (Lefebvre et al; 2008). Several risk factors for shedding *Salmonella* were identified; the strongest of these was feeding a raw food diet. In addition, several studies have examined the prevalence of microbial contamination in raw pet food diets. In a small pilot study, eight out of ten samples of chicken-based, home-prepared raw diets for dogs were contaminated with *Salmonella spp* (Joff and Schlesinger, 2002). The raw food diets were significantly more likely to be contaminated than were the commercial dry dog foods in the control group. Another published study evaluated 25 commercially available raw pet diets and found coliform bacteria in all 25 foods (Weese et al; 2005). Although chicken is the most common type of meat that is included in home prepared raw diets, the commercial foods in this study contained a wide variety of meats, including chicken, beef, lamb, rabbit, ostrich, venison and salmon. Another study of commercially prepared raw foods collected 240 samples from 20 different commercially prepared raw meat diets for dogs (Strohmeyer et al; 2006). The authors reported that more than 50% of the raw diet samples were contaminated with non-type-specific *Escherichia coli*. Collectively, these studies indicate that homemade and commercially prepared raw meat diets for pets may present a risk to both pets and their owners for exposure to potentially pathogenic bacterial species.

However, it is equally important to note that raw diets do not have a corner on the Salmonella market these days. In one twelve month period, from January of 2011 to the end of December 2012, the FDA reported a total of eleven separate advised recall events due to a finding of Salmonella contamination. In all of these cases, the foods that were recalled included extruded products and/or various types of food treats. None of the recalls involved raw food products. In addition, the Diamond Pet Food recall of 2012 resulted in documented illness in dogs and people as a result of coming into contact with extruded dry foods contaminated with Salmonella. While human illness from raw dog diets has never been documented, this is not the case regarding salmonellosis caused by a commercially produced dry food (more about these risks in Chapter 11).

Choosing well

One of the conclusions that I expect readers to take away from this book is the understanding that there are many ways in which we can (and do) feed our dogs well. The trick to feeding well lies in sorting nutritional fact from fiction and learning to be effective "science sleuths" as we evaluate choices and make evidence-based and well-supported decisions, both for our own dogs and when advising clients. So, where does all of the current evidence lead us regarding whether or not to feed raw? Here is a summary of what we know:

- Raw diets have not yet been shown to provide any unique health benefits to dogs, nor have the claims for these health benefits been disproven via controlled studies.

- There is no evidence supporting the claim that dogs are better fed as wolves. There is evidence that dogs have evolved during the period of domestication to consume a more omnivorous diet that includes starch-containing plant foods.

- Raw diets can be formulated to provide complete and balanced nutrition to dogs. A balanced raw food can either be purchased as a commercial product or made at home using an appropriate recipe.

- Some raw ingredients may have higher digestibility and nutrient availability when compared with extruded versions, especially if the extruded version was poorly processed. Other ingredients are less digestible and certain nutrients are less available to dogs when fed raw. If a raw diet is fed, special attention should be paid to sources of raw fish, the inclusion of raw eggs and the type of plant starches that are fed.

- Raw diets may be contaminated with bacteria such as *Salmonella* and coliform bacteria. This may pose a risk of transmission to dogs and humans in the home. Commercial cooked foods may also pose a risk, as demonstrated by recent pet food recalls. Careful food or ingredient selection, feeding only human grade ingredients and using good hygiene practices can minimize risk if a raw diet is fed.

The bottom line? Feeding raw, just like feeding a homemade diet or choosing a grain-free or low carbohydrate diet, is a preference of some owners. Raw foods can be nutritionally balanced and so can provide a healthful diet to your dog. When handled and prepared (or produced) carefully, they can also be safe. However, raw diets have no proven special benefits or qualities that make them inherently superior to cooked food. Moreover, a claim of "naturalness" (true or not) cannot be used as evidence for the healthfulness or superiority of feeding raw. If you choose to feed raw, select a reputable manufacturer with a good track record for safety and quality ingredients or use a well-developed (and tested) recipe (or preferably, recipes) if you are preparing the food yourself. In all cases, use proper hygiene practices (just as you should when preparing human foods and handling any raw ingredients), and *avoid making claims to others about the way that you feed your dog that are not substantiated by evidence-based scienc*e. Let's now move on to other selection criteria that are important when choosing among dog foods and how we must consider who owns, makes and markets your dog's food.

8

Who Owns Your Dog Food?

And What is in It?

In this age of too many choices, how much do people know about the food that they purchase for their dog? And, what would they like to know, but are having trouble finding out? These are questions that my consulting company, AutumnGold Consulting (www.autumngoldconsulting.com) has been asking for a couple of years, through our online survey research program, The Dog Talk Project (www.dogtalkproject.com). The purpose of Dog Talk is to study numerous facets of our relationships with dogs through direct questioning of dog owners, enthusiasts and professionals. We have several nutrition surveys, one of which includes a pair of open-ended questions asking participants to report the brand name and company name of their dog food. In addition to providing information regarding which pet foods are most popular today, this set of two questions has also provided a surprising result. We find that more than 50 % of dog owners do not distinguish between the *brand* name of a food and the *company* that produces (owns) that brand. This confusion is not the fault of owners, by any means, since it is in the best interest of large companies to keep consumers in the dark regarding exactly how many brands of food they produce and market. The same situation occurs with consumer goods that are sold for human consumption and use. I certainly cannot say off the top of my head who produces the brand of clothing detergent, paper towels, toothpaste, kitchen cleaning solution and batteries that Mike and I buy for our household. (When I checked, I found that it was a single company, P&G.)

In our present-day world of too many products and too many choices, most people, including me, are unable or unwilling to keep track of who owns what, and we become confused by the conflation of company names, brand names and product lines. Although this may not matter much when I am picking out paper towels, it does matter to me, and many dog folks, to know who owns and who makes the food that I select for my dogs. Oddly enough, today these are often not the same entities. And, since we are talking about dog food, not paper towels, the ingredients that go into those foods are also of great importance. In this chapter, I examine the who, what, and where of commercial dog foods and arm you with the facts that will help you to rank these factors in terms of their importance to you and to choose in accordance with what is best for you and for your dog.

Who owns your dog food?

A group of big five pet food manufacturers (Nestle-Purina, Mars, Procter & Gamble, Colgate-Palmolive and Del Monte) have dominated the dog food market in the United States for the last two decades. Their presence has become increasingly ubiquitous due to the continuous acquisition of smaller pet food companies plus the expansion of both the number of brands offered and the number of product lines within existing brands. In the year 2012, Mars ranked number one in global pet food sales, topping out at more than *$16 billion* in annual revenue. When we look within the US market alone, Nestle-Purina ranks number one in dog food sales with $3.5 billion in sales. They are followed by Mars ($1.8 billion), P&G ($1.2 billion), Colgate-Palmolive's Hill's division ($1.2 billion) and Del Monte Foods ($1.0 billion). In the year 2012, these five companies were responsible for producing more than 80 % of the dog food that was sold in the United States.

What I find most interesting about this is that, while the majority of pet owners are purchasing from one of the giants, most are unaware of the name of the company that owns their brand of food (much like me with my laundry detergent). Each of these companies sells at least two different brands of dog food and treats (see Figure 8.1). Nestle-Purina tops the list with *16 different brands*. Second in line is Mars, which has a paltry five brand names. Hill's has just three active brands of foods, one of which is their line of veterinary diets. P&G first entered the pet food market about 15 years ago, when they purchased The Iams Company, developer of two brands of food, Iams and Eukanuba. In 2010, P&G added to their line-up of brands by purchasing Natura, a company with five brands of food (California Naturals, Evo, HealthWise, Innova and Karma) plus a brand of dog biscuits, Mother Nature.

Perhaps the most surprising company in this line-up of corporate players is Del Monte. Personally, when I think of Del Monte, canned pineapple comes to mind, not dog food. While most of us do not associate Del Monte with pet food, they have an enormous presence, in particular within the biscuit and treat segment of pet food sales. Dog trainers who use food treats as reinforcers may discover that they are some of Del Monte's most loyal customers. The company owns five brands of dog food and at least six different brands of biscuits and treats, all of which are sold through grocery stores and some of which are found in specialty stores. The most recent addition to the Del Monte line-up was their acquisition of Natural Balance in May of 2013. Additionally, unlike the other four big companies, which are all multi-national corporations, Del Monte's pet food market, at least currently, is confined to the United States.

Mars Petcare	Nestle Purina PetCare	Colgate Palmolive (Hill's)	P&G Pet Care	Del Monte Foods Co.
Cesar	Active Senior 7+	Science Diet	Eukanuba	Canine Carry Outs*
Greenies*	Alpo	Prescription Diet**	Iams	Gravy Train
Nutro (Natural Choice)	Beggin*	Ideal Balance	Iams Veterinary Formula**	Jerky Treats*
Pedigree	Be Happy		Natura	Kibbles 'n Bits
Royal Canin	Beneful			Meaty Bone*
	Chef Michael			Milk-Bone*
	Dog Chow			Milo's Kitchen
	Fit & Trim			Natural Balance
	Frosty Paws*			Nature's Recipe
	Mighty Dog			Pup-Peroni*
	Moist & Meaty			Snausages*
	ONE			
	ProPlan			
	Puppy Chow			
	Purina Veterinary Diets**			
	T-Bonz*			

*Treats or biscuits.
**These are therapeutic dog foods, sold only under the supervision of a veterinarian.

Figure 8.1 Dog food brands of the big five pet food manufacturers (US brands).

Where is it sold?
The five companies that have come to dominate the pet food industry sell most of the food they produce at the major grocery store and pet supply store chains. As the number of independent grocery stores and pet stores have declined (mirroring what is happening elsewhere in the retail sector), large chains (think WalMart, Kroger, PetSmart) have gained significant shares of the market. Only the largest pet food manufacturers have the ability to supply these large chains, leaving smaller producers to seek outlets elsewhere. Pet foods first made it into grocery stores in the early

133

1900s and despite initial resistance by both store owners and consumers, the increased convenience quickly led to grocery stores becoming the largest outlet for pet foods. Nestle-Purina has held the largest proportion of the grocery market share for many years. In 2010, it was responsible for almost half of all supermarket sales, followed by P&G (which sells its Iams brands in grocery stores) and Mars (whose Pedigree brands are strongly represented in supermarkets in the US). Of the Nestle-Purina brands, the best-selling supermarket product is Beneful, followed by Purina Dog Chow (15.8 and 14.5 % of sales, respectively). Iams and Pedigree brands follow closely, accounting for 14 and 12 % of grocery store sales.

The second major outlet for pet foods, and one that has been growing steadily for the last two decades, is the specialty pet supply store market. Generally speaking, foods that are classified as "premium" or "super-premium" are sold in these outlets (more about these classifications and labels in Chapter 9). Two Mars brands that are sold through these outlets are Nutro's Natural Choice and the somewhat less well known Royal Canin product lines. P&G sells Iams (which was one of the first premium brands), Eukanuba and their five newly acquired Natura brands at specialty outlets. Of the big five manufacturers, Colgate-Palmolive is the only company that sells exclusively through specialty store markets, selling product lines within their Hill's brands in this market. It should be noted that their second brand, Prescription Diet, is sold exclusively through veterinarians. Many veterinarians also carry the non-prescription Hill's brands of foods, which contributes to "veterinary-recommended" sales for that company. And, there is of course some crossover. P&G sells its Iams brand products in both grocery and specialty stores, and Purina does the same with its higher end products, ONE and Pro Plan.

Exploding product lines

Although it appears that P&G, Mars and Colgate-Palmolive lag distantly behind Nestle-Purina and Del Monte Foods in the number of pet food brands that they market, we must look one layer deeper to understand another way in which our choices have expanded to what we experience as out-of-control lengths. This is the proliferation of product lines *within* brands. One trend that is evident is the proliferation in the specific market niches within which each brand is sold. If a company believes that brand loyalty is an important factor in their sales, they are often hesitant to develop an entirely new brand name. Instead, they capitalize on existing brand recognition by developing new product lines targeting specialized market segments within an existing brand. P&G excels at this type of marketing, having many years of success with it in personal care and household cleaning products. Their Iams brand of dry dog food currently includes five separate product lines and their Eukanuba brand has six product lines (Figure 8.2). And, each product line typically has between two and six individual products, formulated for different life stages or lifestyles (no wonder pet owners are confused). Interestingly, although the structure of their company/brand/product line classifications differ, the total number of dry dog food products offered by Colgate-Palmolive, P&G and Mars within their Hill's Science Diet, Eukanuba and Nutro brands, are remarkably similar (35, 31 and 32, respectively).

As their names imply, each of these product lines targets a specific dietary approach and/or pet owner demographic. For example, Hill's Science Diet "Advanced Fitness" products are sold only through specialty pet stores and are promoted in their advertising materials as foods that "provide precisely balanced nutrition for a visible difference." The specific benefits that this product line promote include omega-6 fatty acids to improve skin and coat, high quality proteins and high digestibility. Alternatively, the same company's "Healthy Advantage" product line is sold exclusively through veterinarians, and while these foods are not classified as therapeutic foods, they are promoted by the company to provide specific health benefits such as oral health, weight management and joint support. (Just in case they did not have the oral health covered with this veterinary-exclusive product line, they also have an over-the-counter oral health dog food that is sold in pet stores.) Similarly, both Eukanuba and Royal Canin sell "Breed Specific" product lines. These foods (obviously) target owners of specific breeds who wish to believe that significant (and scientifically proven) differences in nutrient needs exist among dog breeds (they do not). Oddly, the breeds that allegedly differ enough in nutrient requirements to warrant their own dog food are also breeds that are most popular, having the highest AKC registrations during the last several years. Coincidence? Probably not. One has to ask—where is the Nova Scotia Duck Tolling Retriever food?

While it is possible that there may be some benefit to some of the small differences between the many product lines, comparisons of these foods often expose a distinction without a difference. For instance, comparing Eukanuba's Breed Specific Labrador Retriever food to its German Shepherd food reveals almost identical ingredient lists, guaranteed analysis panels and caloric content (306 versus 313 kcal/cup, respectively). Similarly, the only discernible distinction between Royal Canin's adult Cocker Spaniel and Miniature Schnauzer foods is a minor difference in the order of ingredients listed and slightly higher calorie content in the Schnauzer food. Is one really to believe that feeding a Miniature Schnauzer a food that contains the same ingredients and protein/fat/carbohydrate proportions, and is produced by the same company as a food marketed for Cocker Spaniels, will provide health benefits for the Schnauzer's (as claimed on the company's website) teeth, body weight and coat? Suppose an owner purchased the Cocker Spaniel food for his Schnauzer by mistake? Would the Schnauzer's health fail if fed the wrong breed diet? Would the dog lose out on those dental, weight and coat benefits? Would the dog begin to resemble a Cocker Spaniel?

Is there science behind all these niches?
These foods beg the question that pops up throughout this book—where's the evidence? To date, there are no peer-reviewed studies in scientific journals studies showing that Labrador Retrievers have nutrient needs that differ from those of German Shepherds or that feeding a Miniature Schnauzer a food that is designed specifically for that breed is superior to feeding a food that is designed for a Cocker Spaniel. In other words, despite these foods (and their claims) there is no evidence showing that nutrient needs vary significantly among breeds of dogs. We will examine the marketing value that such foods have in Chapter 9 and the regulation (or lack thereof) of claims such as these in Chapter 10, but for the purposes of this chapter, suffice it to say that the pet food industry, like many consumer industries, contains product lines that are designed more for consumer wants than for the true nutritional needs of dogs. While there are certainly many examples of unsupportable differences, other distinctions such as the inclusion of certain ingredients or the exclusion of others may

be important and healthful. We will examine some of these distinctions later in this chapter and also in the following chapter.

Hill's Science Diet	Eukanuba	Nutro Natural Choice
Advanced Fitness (4)	Adult Formulas (7)	Breed Size (6)
Healthy Advantage (3)	Breed Specific Formulas (8)	Grain Free (6)
Healthy Mobility (3)	Custom Care Formulas (3)	High Endurance (1)
High Energy (1)	Naturally Wild Formulas (6)	Limited Ingredient Diet (5)
Ideal Balance (4)	Puppy Formulas (5)	Senior (3)
Large Breed (3)	Senior Formulas (3)	Weight Management (4)
Light (2)		Wholesome Essentials (4)
Mature Adult (4)		
Oral Care (1)		
Puppy Healthy Development (3)		
Puppy Large Breed (3)		
Sensitive (2)		
Small & Toy Breed (2)		
TOTAL: 35	**TOTAL 32**	**TOTAL 31**

Figure 8.2 Examples of product lines within brands (dry foods).

Why you should care

One might ask, why should I care about who owns my brand of dog food and how many different brands and product lines a particular company owns and sells? This is a good question, and for many people, it might be something that they generally do not give a healthy hoot about. However, more and more consumers are aware of and concerned about ongoing mergers and acquisitions that lead to the consolidation of consumer brands for all types of products. For the dog food market (as well as for other goods), the production of multiple brands of food by a single multi-national corporation means that different brands are often produced using common supply chains, ingredients, factories and internal quality control measures. If all of these components pass muster with a consumer and engender trust, all should be fine. However, if a pet owner is purchasing Nutro Natural Choice specifically because he believes it to be of higher quality and to contain superior ingredients over a Royal Canin product, it is of obvious importance that he be aware that these foods are produced by the *same* company. Similarly, if an owner prefers to make most of her purchases from small, privately held companies, and originally selected Evo as a brand owned by Natura, it is important for this owner to know that the company was acquired by P&G and as a result is no longer either small or privately held. The bottom line is that consumers deserve to know who owns the pet foods that they are feeding to their dogs for exactly the same reasons that we are entitled to know who is producing the foods that we eat. Information that allows pet owners to differentiate among brands that are owned by multi-national corporations versus those that are not is information that may be very important to some dog folks, while not important to others. Regardless, this information should be available to all so that informed decisions can be made.

Who *makes* your dog food?

While today many pet professionals are aware that the company that owns and sells the brand they feed may not actually be manufacturing the food, many dog owners do not. A substantial number of companies "co-pack" their foods, which means that the pet food company gives their formulation (recipe) to a manufacturing company that produces, bags, labels and ships their food. The manufacturer mixes ingredients according to the specified formulations and produces a wide variety of pet foods that are sold under different brand names. So while you may think that P&G or Nestle Purina make the food you feed your dog, in some cases the company that actually puts together the final product is a business you have never heard of such as Ohio Pet Food, CJ Foods and Simmons—none of which would qualify as household names.

This process becomes even more convoluted when one considers that, like many consumer goods today, the supply chain of ingredients may be outsourced to several different middleman companies (consider the sequence from the 2007 disaster—Chinese supplier to ChemNutra to Menu to Pet Food Brands). In addition, pet food companies also may contract food production to several different factories, some of which are located in the US, while others are not. One of the reasons that the Menu foods recall was so extensive was that Menu Foods specialized in producing wet (canned) products. While many of the large pet food companies own and operate their own dry food factories, there are only a handful of factories that operate as canneries and produce wet pet food. As a result many companies, including the large corporations, contract the manufacture of their wet foods to another company, typically referred to as a co-packer. Another example is chicken treats, many of which, until the 2012 recall anyway, were completely sourced and produced in China.

In the industry, the co-packing companies that specialize in the manufacture of multiple brands of foods (that are often direct competitors to one another) usually enjoy very little brand recognition themselves. While most own one or more of their own brands, the brand name is typically different from the manufacturer's name. For example, Ohio Pet Food is one of the largest US manufacturers of pet food in the United States but owns a single brand, called Blackwood pet food. Other examples of US co-packers are CJ Foods, Tuffy's Pet Foods, Simmons (canned products only) and Diamond. The end result is that many pet foods are manufactured by a small group of manufacturing plants. To illustrate: every February, the *Whole Dog Journal* compiles and publishes their annual list of "Approved Dry Dog Foods." Several criteria are used to determine which commercial products "make the list" each year and which do not. Once the list is determined, products are presented alphabetically and include information regarding product lines, primary ingredients, name/address/website of the company and identification of the food's producer. In the 2013 list of 56 WDJ-approved dry dog foods, eight were produced by CJ Foods, seven were produced by Ohio Pet Foods, four were produced by Diamond and four were produced by Tuffy's Pet Foods. This means that almost half (42 %) were not produced by the company that owned the brand. Remember that these are all foods that have passed muster with WDJ and that are generally considered to be some of the top choices that are available. Conversely, of these 56 foods, nineteen (33 %) were produced exclusively by the brand's company-owned plants. Examples of these nineteen foods include (alphabetically) Ainsworth, Hill's Science Diet, Fromm, Merrick, Natura, Precise and P&G (Eukanuba and Iams).

Dog owners may be concerned not only with who makes their food, but also with *where* their dog food is produced. In late 2012, after more than a year of pet owner and veterinarian complaints of pet illness to the FDA, a voluntary recall of chicken jerky treats produced in China was advised. Fallout from the 2007 recalls plus increasing distrust of products produced overseas has led many owners to purchase only foods that are manufactured in the United States. For some, this may also extend to ensuring that ingredients included in their dog's food originate only from domestic sources (see below). Having control over the manufacturing process is also of concern regarding adherence to good manufacturing practices. Proper manufacturing practice, control of the supply chain, quality control and adherence to safety and sanitation regulations are essential for preventing bacterial and fungal contamination of products. So, not only should we ask *who* is making our dogs' foods, but we should also be concerned about *where* those foods are made and if proper safety measures are in place (I discuss pet food safety in detail in Chapter 11). If the name and place of manufacture is not included on the dog food company's or brand's website, it should be supplied promptly in response to an owner's email or phone inquiry. Should you encounter resistance (as I did with several such enquiries when researching this chapter), this should serve as a red flag telling you that the company does not wish to divulge that information to its customers. If the question of where and by whom your dog food is produced is important to you, it is time to look elsewhere for your dog's food.

As a final example, let's look at a group of private label foods. More and more pet supply superstores (PetSmart, Petco) and mass merchandisers (Walmart, Walgreens and Costco) are developing and selling their own private label pet food brands. The term "private label" refers to "house brands" that carry the store's name and that are manufactured or provided by one company for offer under another company's brand. Private label goods have traditionally been positioned in the pet food market as lower cost alternatives to national or international brands and often carry labels that mimic the colors, fonts and artwork of the nationally known brands that have high brand recognition. (These are often called "clone" products in the industry.) In recent years, however, private label brands are increasingly being positioned as "premium" brands to compete with the existing "name" brands. For example, PetSmart launched a higher end brand, Simply Nourish, which targets a more involved and discerning pet owner demographic than its Authority brand, and Walmart added a new (supposedly higher quality) brand called Pure Balance. Even Whole Foods has jumped on board, selling a brand called, of course, "Whole Paws." Other private label dog foods include Walgreen's The Pet Shoppe, Sam's Club's Simply Right, Dollar General's EverPet and Costco's Kirkland brands. In all cases, private label dog foods, by definition, will be co-packed, since the firms that are producing these brands are *not* in the business of pet food. Therefore, if you consider such a brand, it is important to always find out what company or co-packer is producing the brand. And, this information may be difficult to obtain. Of all of the brands listed above, only Kirkland and Ol' Roy provide manufacturing information (Diamond and Mars, respectively). Current regulations require only that the pet food label identify the distributor of the food, which in these cases is not the same entity as the manufacturer, and websites for these stores do not provide this information. Moreover, email inquiries for this information were ignored. As stated previously, if a company will not tell you where the food that you are interested in purchasing is produced, time to look elsewhere.

What's *in* your dog food?

The ingredients that make up a dog food are (and should be) of great concern to dog owners and pet professionals. A food's ingredients have the job of providing all of the essential nutrients and energy (calories) to the dog who consumes the food, as well as contributing to the food's flavor, texture and appeal. As a result, when dog owners are selecting and comparing dog foods, the first place that they typically look is the label's ingredient list. We naturally expect this list to tell us what we need to know. Unfortunately, while the Federal Food, Drug and Cosmetic Act requires that pet food labels (like human food labels) are truthfully labeled and must include all of the food sources present in the product, current FDA and AAFCO labeling requirements fall far short of what is needed to allow informed and well considered choices by consumers.

It is not the purpose of this book to provide yet another list of AAFCO ingredient definitions or to describe the differences between various pet food ingredients. Several of the excellent and thoroughly researched books listed in the reference section at the end of this book provide that information. I also have provided a list of commonly used ingredients and their AAFCO definitions in Appendix 4. Rather, since the purpose of this book and this chapter in particular is to provide dog owners and professionals with the skills and knowledge that will support smart decisions, let's start with identifying what exactly you *can* know about the ingredients in a food, what you *can find out* with a bit of sleuthing, and what unfortunately you will never, ever be privy to (if the pet food industry continues its current practices). Let's begin with ingredient information that is readily available to all consumers.

What the ingredient list provides

As with human foods, federal law requires that pet food companies report all included ingredients in decreasing preponderance by weight on their product's label. This means that ingredients that are listed first are present in the highest amount in a given product. However, and here is the catch, the weight of each ingredient includes the moisture (amount of water) present in the ingredient at the time of processing. This makes interpretation a bit tricky because some ingredients contain a lot of water (up to 70 %) while others contain very little water (12 % or less). The result is that an ingredient that is listed first on the list may appear to be the most important component of the food, when in effect it contributed a lot of water and much less in the way of essential nutrients. When evaluating dry dog foods, a general rule of thumb is that the first five ingredients that you see in the list provide 80 % or more of the food's nutrients. This is helpful to remember when comparing foods, as it allows comparisons between the primary sources of protein, carbohydrate and fat among foods. Let's practice with a few examples.

Figure 8.3 on page 142 reports the first twelve ingredients that are listed in a sample of five dry dog foods that are advertised to contain salmon. Indeed, all five foods have the word "Salmon" in their product name and report salmon as the first ingredient in the label's ingredient list. Certainly, on the face of it, this suggests that all five foods are salmon-based foods, right? Well…not necessarily. Salmon (fresh or frozen) contains 65 to 70 % water (moisture). All five of these dog foods are extruded dry products, which contain about 10 % moisture. The water provided by the salmon (or any meat that is added in a fresh/frozen form) is "cooked off" during the extrusion process, leaving the salmon protein and other nutrients in the food. This is generally still a good thing, since whole salmon is considered to be a high quality protein source because it is an animal-source protein and because it was not subjected to the heat processing and drying that are used to create a protein meal. However, because this ingredient has a very high moisture content, it also means that the actual amount of salmon-source protein that remains in the finished product is probably lower than the protein that is provided by other ingredients that are added as meals (dry). Therefore, when a high-moisture ingredient is listed first on the ingredient list of an extruded food, *keep reading* and pay special attention to the protein sources that immediately follow on the list. When a dry protein source (typically a meal) follows the fresh meat, *this* will be the protein source that actually provides the bulk of the protein to the food. Let's return to Figure 8.3 to examine these sources and discuss some of the finer points of brand name regulations.

This word that you keep using…

All five of the foods have the ingredient "salmon" in their brand name. Including an identifying ingredient in the brand name of a pet food is strictly regulated by AAFCO, and with good reason. Reading "Salmon Dinner" brings to mind sitting down to a filet, and seems to imply that the so-labeled food is composed of a lot of, if not mostly, salmon. Most would agree that such a food should contain, well, at least a little salmon. The AAFCO regulation that governs the use of ingredients as brand names can be abbreviated and easily remembered as the 95-25-3 rule. Each of the three numbers signifies a percentage of the ingredient in question. The first number refers to pet foods that are branded using an ingredient name followed by the word "food" and requires that such a food contain *no less than 95 %* of that ingredient. Thus, Happy Paws Salmon Dog Food must contain *at least 95 %* salmon. Wow, that is a lot of salmon. Obviously this in not true of the five examples below, given the number of other ingredients that we see included in their list of ingredients. (And, in reality, we would not want to feed a food that contained 95 % salmon as it would be somewhat difficult to make such a food nutritionally balanced.)

So, what's going on? These foods all seem to be salmon-based, even though none actually use the word "food" in their brand name. Enter the 25 rule. This regulation allows the use of what AAFCO euphemistically refers to as "qualifying terms," which in effect are all synonyms for the word food. Qualifying terms that this regulation allows to be used in conjunction with the major ingredient (in this case, "salmon") include "dinner," "entrée," "recipe" or "formula"; basically anything goes, other than the word "food." This sort of double-speak brings to mind the popular line from the classic movie The Princess Bride, "*you keep using this word; I do not think it means what you think it means…*" Anyway, when one of these words that means food, but does not *really* mean food (according to AAFCO anyway) is used, the named ingredient must comprise at least 25% of the product at the time of processing (i.e., before water is cooked off). This is a very important rule because it leads to great confusion and to (intentionally or not) ambiguous labeling. Personally, when I read "Salmon Dinner" or "Salmon Recipe," I don't naturally jump to thinking "Oh, this product must not have very much salmon in it, seeing that it says dinner and not food in its brand name." Like most folks, I think "Oh, this food must have a lot of salmon in it." By law, all that the product is required to have is 25.1 % salmon, prior to cooking (processing).

The final rule, the 3 % rule, has to do with a seemingly simple and innocent-sounding word: "with." If a pet food label contains that word in its product name, the product is required to have only *3 % of the ingredient* in the formulation at the time of processing. If you measure out 100 pieces of kibble from a food labeled "with salmon" and then remove three pieces of kibble from the pile, those three pieces are equivalent to the amount of salmon that is found in that pile of kibble. Not much. Yet consumers are expected to know, understand and differentiate between the 95 % Salmon Food, the 25 % Salmon Dinner, and the 3 % Adult Dinner *with* Salmon foods. This rule is by design imprecise (from 95 % *down* to 25 % for food versus *dinner*, really?) and in practice misleads (and possibly even deceives) consumers. If you wish to feed a salmon (or chicken or turkey or venison) based food, look for one of AAFCO's qualifying terms (dinner, recipe, formula) and avoid brands with the term "with." Then, keep reading.

What's in a name?

Let's now turn to ingredient names, specifically how protein sources such as salmon are labeled (and what they actually consist of). When we look at the list of ingredients, all five foods identify salmon as the first ingredient. The terms used to describe pet food ingredients are required by law to be consistent. In addition, AAFCO strictly controls the types of ingredient terms that can and cannot be used on pet food labels. Animal-based ingredients are classified as either "fresh" (typically frozen) or "rendered," which means processed (cooked) and dried into a meal. Keep in mind that fresh meats typically used in pet foods are usually not the same as meats that we consider to be dinner for humans. Rather, in addition to including flesh (skeletal muscle), most meats also include skin and discarded animal parts that are not sold for human consumption (tongue, diaphragms, heart, some bone). By law, these "parts" are labeled as "inedible" and are not handled during production, transport and processing in the same manner that "edible" (i.e., foods intended for human consumption) are handled. This does not necessarily mean that these animal parts are not nutritious or digestible or safe for dogs. A wide variety of animal meals have been studied as pet food ingredients. Animal meals that are properly handled and processed are highly digestible and are capable of providing high quality protein and other essential nutrients to dogs.

However, it is also true that the "salmon" (or chicken or turkey) on the pet food ingredient list is *not* the same meat or fish cuts that you purchase at your local grocery store. (Teach yourself to ignore the attractive photographs on the label.) Rather, most (but not all) pet food companies purchase animal-source ingredients that are not intended for human consumption and which may contain animal parts that we do not generally consider edible. Additionally, once a food item has been labeled "not for human consumption" (inedible), it enters a completely different supply chain than that of human food, which means that many of the ingredients that end up in dog food are subject to a separate set of regulations that govern their handling, transport and processing (more about this in Chapter 10 and 11). So, if you see salmon, or chicken or turkey first on the ingredient list, followed by salmon or chicken or turkey *meal*, do not assume that the first ingredient is of higher quality than the meal. The "fresh" meat is often the same product that was used to produce the meal and could even be of lesser nutritional value. (If ingredients are human grade, and they can be, you can bet this will be on the food's label and all of the company's advertising materials. This is a good thing, but is still relatively rare in commercial dog foods. We will address the issue of quality in detail in Chapter 10.)

Finally, if the meat or poultry meal was produced from a single animal source, chicken, beef, lamb, etc., the ingredient will carry that name (chicken meal, salmon meal, etc.). Alternatively, the more generic terms of meat meal, poultry meal or fish meal originate from a combination of animal species within that group. Generally speaking, these generically labeled meals will be of lower ingredient quality as protein sources than named animal meals.

#	Brand name	First 12 ingredients
1	Blue Buffalo Wilderness Adult Salmon Recipe	**Deboned salmon, chicken meal, menhaden fish meal, peas, tapioca starch,** chicken fat, flaxseed, natural chicken flavor, tomato pomace, potatoes, alfalfa meal, potato starch
2	Halo Spot's Stew Wild Salmon Recipe	**Salmon, eggs, pea protein, oats, vegetable broth,** pearled barley, chicken fat, whole peas, chicken liver, chicken, flax seed, salmon oil
3	Innova Salmon & Herring Formula	**Salmon, herring, menhaden meal, whole grain brown rice, whole grain barley,** peas, chicken fat, flaxseed, pea fiber, calcium carbonate, natural flavors, potassium chloride
4	Taste of the Wild Pacific Stream Formula with Wild Salmon	**Salmon, ocean fish meal, sweet potatoes, potatoes, canola oil,** salmon meal, smoked salmon, potato fiber, natural flavor, salt, choline chloride
5	Wellness Simple Salmon & Potato Formula	**Salmon, salmon meal, potatoes, peas, dried ground potatoes,** tomato pomace, ground flaxseed, canola oil (preserved with mixed tocopherols), dicalcium phosphate, natural fish flavor, chicory root extract, vitamins

Figure 8.3 Sample of five dog foods advertised as containing salmon.

Comparing the five foods

So, armed with an understanding of labeling rules and ingredient terms, how does our list of five salmon-containing foods measure up? First, note that none of the five products use the word "food" in their brand name. This is not an unexpected finding since feeding a dog 95 % of anything will not provide a balanced diet; therefore a dry food that is formulated to provide complete and balanced nutrition will always contain a variety of ingredients. (The few products that fall within the 95 %-rule category are canned pet foods that are intended for supplemental feeding or treats used as training aid that are usually not formulated to be nutritionally balanced.)

The qualifying terms used in the brand names are important to take note of—**recipe** is used in two of the names (#1 and #2) and **formula** is used in two others (#3 and #5). This immediately tells us that these four foods fall within the 25 % rule category and that each must contain at least 25 % salmon. Because salmon is expensive and is probably the most costly ingredient in these foods, it is safe to assume that actual percentages (prior to processing) are hovering considerably close to the 25 % minimum. Remember, and this is important, that fresh salmon contains at least 65 % water. This water is cooked off during the processing of dry foods. Therefore, 25 % of a high moisture ingredient added at the time of processing results in a much smaller contribution to the end product. For example if salmon made up 27 % of the food, and the finished product was 10 % moisture, the proportion of the finished food comprised of salmon would be in the range of just 9 to 12 %!

Of additional interest is food #4. Here you see the 3 % rule in the brand name in practice, "**** *with* Wild Salmon." Only 3 % of this food needs to be actual salmon. Because ocean fish meal is the second ingredient, followed by sweet potatoes and potatoes, this food would be more honestly labeled as an ocean fish and potato food, rather than as it is. Although we see salmon meal and smoked salmon on the ingredient list these are found in the sixth and seventh positions, respectively, following canola oil. This tells us that a very small amount of these ingredients make up this product.

So, can these ingredient lists help an owner to distinguish among these five products? Well, sort of. First, the careful consumer should always move to the second protein source listed after seeing a fresh/frozen animal-source ingredient listed first on a dry dog food. In almost all cases for dry dog foods, the first protein source that is dry (i.e., a meal) will be the principal protein source in the food. In our list of foods, an examination of second-in-line protein sources shows that salmon actually provides the primary source of protein in just one food, #5, in the form of salmon meal. On the other hand, food #1 is a chicken meal and menhaden fish diet, the protein in food #3 comes principally from menhaden fish, and the protein in food #4 comes from an unnamed "ocean fish" source. Of special interest is food #2, whose primary protein source is of plant origin, in the form of pea protein. (Like salmon, eggs contain more than 60 % water and so comprise a low proportion of the actual food.) In general, animal-source proteins (meals and fresh/frozen sources) are considered to be higher quality than plant-source proteins, although this is not always the case. Unfortunately, as we will see, it is virtually impossible for the consumer to differentiate between high and low quality protein sources in pet foods of any type.

The ingredients list also allows dog owners to choose among the many various carbohydrate (starch) and fat sources that are included in foods. In recent years, carbohydrate selection has become important to owners who are avoiding grains (often for their own diet as well as that of their dog). Some owners specifically avoid gluten-containing grains; these are wheat, barley and rye (rye is not a common pet food ingredient). Commonly used grains that are found in dog foods include wheat, rice, barley and sorghum. Although corn is not technically classified as a grain plant, many consumers lump it in with this group as well. Non-grain sources of carbohydrate (starch) in foods include tapioca, flaxseed, potatoes, sweet potatoes, oats and pea starch. In our group of sample foods, three of the listed products are grain-free (#1, #4 and #5). Food #2 contains barley and food #3 includes brown rice. Because cooking (extrusion) completely cooks starch and increases its digestibility to more than 95 % (depending on the plant source), almost all of the plant starches that are included in dry dog foods will provide a good energy source. Owners may select one particular source or avoid another based upon real or perceived sensitivities in their dog or simply a desire to avoid certain types of starch.

The inclusion of a starch-providing ingredient high on the ingredient list can also provide a rough idea to the consumer regarding the food's total carbohydrate content. Food #4 shows two carbohydrate sources immediately following the ocean fish meal and potatoes are third in line in the ingredient list of food #5, which indicates a relatively high starch content in these products. Conversely, if an owner prefers to feed a "low carb" food, the first starch-containing ingredient is expected to fall later in the list, typically in the fourth position or later.

Fat sources may be animal or plant-based and like protein sources, may be a named animal (or plant) source or a generic term. Commonly used animal fats include chicken fat (a source of linoleic acid) and menhaden oil (a source of omega-3 fatty acids). Plant sources include canola oil and, less commonly, corn oil. Because increasing intake of the long-chain omega-3 fatty acids is a goal for some pet owners today, selecting a food that includes fish oil is often desirable.

Finally, the ingredient list provides adequate information to owners that allow them to choose foods with or without artificial preservatives. Artificial antioxidants include BHA and BHT, and less commonly today, ethoxyquin (see Appendix 4 for descriptions of these). Naturally-derived antioxidants include the mixed tocopherols (forms of vitamin E), vitamin C and rosemary extract. Because naturally-derived preservatives do not preserve foods as long as artificial preservatives, the shelf life of naturally-preserved dog foods is often shorter than that of products that are preserved with artificial compounds.

What's missing?

Unfortunately, quite a bit. Although the ingredient list ranks a food's ingredients in order by weight in the product, it does not provide information regarding the actual percentages of the ingredients listed. While this information is prohibited on the pet food label, there is no regulation that prevents companies from providing it to consumers through their websites or marketing materials. In other words, if they wanted to provide this information, they could. Most, however, do not do this. In fact, many companies refuse to divulge this information when it is requested because it is considered to be proprietary information about their formulations. This is certainly a valid argument, if consumers were asking for the actual formulation (recipe) of the food. However, all percentages are not needed, nor is the food's recipe. What is needed is accurate reporting of the proportions of ingredients that are included in the product's brand name (*Salmon* Dinner) or that feature prominently in the food's promotion and marketing materials. This is needed because, in practice, the 95-25-3 rule leads to misleading labeling, especially when ingredients that contain a high proportion of water are used in the formulation of a dry food (and are featured prominently on the package's artwork).

Some may argue here that as consumers we also are not privy to the exact ingredient percentages included in the processed foods that we put into our own mouths. The difference is that, as humans, we consume a wide variety of food items, which may or may not be highly processed, but none of which is expected to singularly provide all of our daily nutrient and energy needs throughout our lives. By contrast, the prevailing paradigm of pet feeding today is that we should select a single food and that food is expected to provide "complete and balanced" nutrition to our dogs for years or even for the dog's entire life. If we hold dog foods to such high expectations, then it follows that the bar should be equally high regarding the ingredients that go into them, both in terms of quality and label reporting. There is some movement in this direction in recent years. Today, a small number of companies are providing detailed ingredient quantity information on their websites. For example, Pet Chef Express, a company that specializes in home delivery, provides exact ingredient percentages for all of their foods on their website. However, the vast majority of companies do not provide this information through marketing materials and will not provide it upon request. Perhaps this will change as consumer pressure for transparency increases. Time will tell.

The second type of information that is missing from the pet food ingredient list, and indeed is missing from the label, and from website and marketing materials, and from anything to do with commercial dog foods, is any reference to ingredient quality. While pet food regulations require that the food's ingredients conform to those listed on the label, they expressly prohibit terms that refer to the *quality* of the ingredients that are used to make the food. The quality of an ingredient includes how digestible it is to the animal that consumes it, the level of essential nutrients that the ingredient contains, and how available those nutrients are to the animal. Availability refers to the amount and biochemical form of nutrients in an ingredient. For example, if an essential nutrient is bound to compounds that impair its absorption into the body or influence the body's ability to use it once absorbed, the ingredient is not a quality source of that nutrient, even though it might contain large amounts. The most commonly used example is damaged protein. While rendered animal meals can be of high quality, if they are poorly processed or handled, protein can be damaged, making that meal a poor source of essential amino acids for dogs. The problem is that there is no way for a consumer to tell from a product's label if the meal that is included is of high, moderate or low quality. Because meals make up the bulk of protein that is fed to dogs in dry products, information about their quality (and ability to nourish our dogs) is basically the most important consideration that we should be concerned with when we look at an ingredient list. Yet there is no simple way to determine ingredient quality. Without a doubt, all "chicken meals" are not created equal. The problem is, we have no way of knowing which chicken meals are "more equal" than others. We will return to the question of quality again in Chapter 10. Before leaving our discussion of ingredients, let's examine an ingredient issue that has been getting a lot of attention recently—the "by-products or no by-products" issue.

Beaks, feet and guts: the by-product controversy

A wide range of animal- and plant-source protein ingredients are used in commercial dry (extruded) dog foods, and these ingredients vary tremendously in digestibility and quality. This variability is greatest among animal-source proteins, which paradoxically is a moot point since consumers are provided with little information that allows discrimination among ingredient quality. Therefore, it is not all that surprising that one of the few available quality designators, the distinction between meals and by-product meals, has acquired an inflated level of importance among consumers. And, some pet food manufacturers (their marketing departments, actually) further exploit these perceptions by stating "No By-Products" on their label and proclaiming the many (supposed) failings of by-products. So what is the truth? Are by-product meals lower in quality by definition when compared with meals? Should the critical consumer avoid by-product meal-containing foods like the plague? Well, it depends. And once again, it seems to depend upon items of information that consumers are not always privy to.

Let's begin by examining the exact difference between these two types of meals, as legally defined by AAFCO and put into practice by the pet food industry. Let's use a specific and common example: chicken meal versus chicken by-product meal. AAFCO provides the definitions for feed ingredients that pet food manufacturers are allowed to include in their foods and to list on their product labels (more about AAFCO in Chapter 11). For chicken and poultry ingredients, the term "meal" refers to the *"dry, rendered product from a combination of clean flesh and skin with or without accompanying bone, derived from the parts of whole carcasses of [chicken], exclusive of feathers, heads, feet and entrails"* (AAFCO, 2013). In other words, meals come from parts of chicken that we typically think of as the parts that we eat ourselves. (This is not completely true however, as these parts often come from "chicken frames," the part of the chicken that is left over *after* the chicken meat for human consumption has been removed or from chickens that have been removed from the human food supply for other reasons.) AAFCO tells us that chicken by-product meal on the other hand may contain varying amounts of clean flesh and skin (as found in meals), *plus* chicken heads, chicken feet and chicken guts (viscera). In other words, the difference between a chicken (or poultry) meal and its respective by-product meal is the inclusion of beaks (okay, heads), feet and guts in the latter and the exclusion of those body parts from the former. Seems like an obvious quality distinction, does it not? After all, any product that has heads, feet and entrails in it not only sounds yucky, but certainly must also be of poor quality, right? Well, maybe. While certainly the general (and understandable) perception is that, given this definition, meals will be of higher quality than by-product meals, that distinction does not always hold up under scientific study. Meals have been compared with by-product meals as protein sources for dog foods in a number of research studies and feeding trials. The published results usually show that meals are slightly more digestible and contain slightly more available essential amino acids than do their associated by-product meals, but that these differences are neither dramatic nor worthy of the hysteria that seems to accompany the "BP word" among dog folks today.

In truth, the inclusion of other body parts in the creation of by-product meals may either reduce, maintain or improve the quality of an animal protein meal. In a small pilot study that was presented at a professional meeting in 1998, two researchers individually measured the digestibility (quality) of the three types of "chicken parts" that are included in chicken by-product meals—heads, feet and entrails (Aldrich and Daristotle, 1998). And what did they find? Well, first that viscera (internal organs and intestinal contents) were similar in protein quality to the chicken flesh components included in very high quality chicken meals. In other words, including organ meats and intestinal contents in a by-product meal does not negatively affect protein quality (and may even improve it in a poor or average quality meal). Conversely they also found that chicken heads were slightly lower in quality and feet were much lower in quality when compared with chicken meat. This may be more detail than you want or need, but chicken heads were considered *in-between* because they added both bone from skulls (not good) as well as the brains (good) to the mix. Feet, on the other hand, were simply bad and had quality values similar to feeding connective tissue or bone residue. Their results suggested that the respective amounts of additional body parts (heads, feet or guts) in a given chicken by-product meal can affect the resultant meal's protein quality either positively or negatively, depending upon the proportion of the three different body parts that were included. Support for these researchers' results came from another study, conducted several years later, that measured the protein quality of over 400 different poultry by-product meal samples from multiple manufacturers and sources (Locatelli and Howhler, 2003). They reported a wide range of protein quality values; values that overlapped (i.e., were higher than) with those of some poultry and chicken meals. And to add a final and rather bizarre twist to the by-product story, the proportion of chicken feet found in pet food grade by-product meals has reportedly decreased precipitously in recent years due to increased export of chicken feet to Asian countries to supply a source of "chicken paws" sold as human food items in Asian markets. Reduced feet in chicken by-product meal should improve the ingredient's protein quality.

Knowing these things, there are two important points to be made. First, the differences in ingredient quality that are reported in studies have not been very large; usually just a few percentage points in digestibility are seen between meals and by-product meals when fed to dogs. So, we could say that while a particular meal may have been found to have excellent digestibility, its by-product counterpart had moderate or good quality (and this quality may still be better than or equal to plant-protein sources). So, the marketing hyperbole and excessive "patting oneself on the back" by companies that include meals but not by-product meals should be received with a hefty dose of skepticism. True, there is a difference in many cases, but probably not enough of a quality difference to warrant all of the inflammatory language and excessive claims that are being made by companies that are jumping on the by-product free bandwagon. I would argue that this exaggeration of difference has occurred because there are so few available ways to truly assess the quality of pet food ingredients in meaningful ways. As a result, the single AAFCO-defined difference (meals versus by-product meals) has caught on like a house on fire, with marketing folks flinging additional gasoline to fuel the flames and causing the issue to garner more importance than it warrants, given the evidence that we have.

Bottom line? Meals are in most cases of moderately higher quality than by-product meals (less so if the by-product is missing its feet). However, the consumer has no way of knowing if the meal that is used in the food is of good or poor quality, of the extent of the difference between a given meal and by-product meal, or if this difference has any significance at all from a feeding or health standpoint. So we are back to square one—meaningful ways in which dog owners can assess ingredient and product quality and discriminate among products are sorely lacking, despite what manufacturers of "by-product-free" foods are proclaiming to you.

Choosing well

Is there any way to discern ingredient quality for the careful consumer? Well, there are a couple of approaches to this. The first is to look for an animal-source protein ingredient within the first three ingredients on a dry food's ingredient list. Remember, if a named animal meat that is not in meal form is reported first, this may not mean much because that meat contains a lot of water. Look for the meal (of the same animal) immediately following or third in order. This tells you that animal-source protein makes up the bulk of that food. In the example that we use in Figure 8.3, food #5 meets this criteria. While food #1 also includes a named animal meal early in the list, it loses some credibility because that named animal meal (chicken) does not match the brand name's protein source (salmon). Similarly, named fat sources (chicken fat, menhaden oil) are considered to be of higher quality than generic fat sources (animal fat, fish oil).

A further step that careful consumers can take, but which takes a bit more time and effort, is to learn about the source of origin and other quality measures of ingredients and the finished product. Focus on criteria that you personally determine to be important for you and for your dog. For example, some consumers are increasingly concerned with the way in which livestock are raised and treated. There are pet food companies that state that they only purchase animal source ingredients that originate from animals that were humanely and or locally/regionally raised. Others assure consumers that their products are all organically certified or that production animals were pasture raised without hormone or antibiotic feed additives. An increasing number of consumers also seek foods that include only ingredients that originate within the United States or North America or that expressly exclude ingredients from China. All of these criteria are gaining importance, and some companies have responded to pet owner demands. Check websites and email or call companies to find out as much as possible about your food's ingredient quality and origins.

A growing number of pet owners seek foods that use human grade ingredients (as opposed to feed-grade). This topic is worthy of additional attention because it is a tricky issue in terms of the way in which pet foods and human foods are differentiated within the food manufacturing business and particularly in the way in which the term "human grade" is regulated with pet foods. Current regulations only allow use of the phrase "human grade" on pet food packaging if every ingredient in the product and every processing method meets FDA and USDA requirements for producing, processing and transporting foods suitable for consumption by humans. This also means that every producer of the ingredients is licensed to perform those tasks. In other words, this label is only allowed if the finished product is classified as human grade; just purchasing human grade ingredients and then producing the food in a pet food factory is not sufficient. Because only a small number of pet food companies can meet these very stringent criteria, the inclusion of "human grade" on the food's label itself is relatively rare. However, companies that are purchasing only human grade ingredients but that do not meet the criteria of producing their food in a USDA-inspected human food facility, can (and do) include this information on their websites and via their marketing materials. If feeding a food that includes human grade ingredients is important to you as a selection criterion, read labels and check websites to find this information.

Although human grade ingredients and finished products that can be labeled as such are generally considered to be of higher quality, this does not mean that foods that do *not* contain this claim are necessarily of poor quality. Published results of digestibility trials that study the use of animal-source meals in pet foods demonstrate that meals vary greatly in their digestibility and quality, and secondly, that high quality meals are a good protein source for pet foods. The problem is that the consumer has no way to discern the difference between a good and a poor quality meal, other than by asking the company directly about the source of their ingredients. We should not be forced to do this. Because the 95-25-3 rule muddles consumers' understanding of what is in their dog's food (and how much), because ingredient quality and source vary tremendously, and because current regulations expressly prohibit mention of quality measures on pet food labels, change is needed. Just as owners are entitled to know who makes their dog food and where it is produced, so too should we be privy to more complete information regarding what is in our dog's food.

9

Pet Food Marketing

(Where Science Goes to Die)

"Americans' deepening identification with their pets creates a big opportunity for brands; trends show that pets are one of the most meaningful ways to engage consumers."

"Pets Are Serious Business for Marketers,"
Rebecca Armstrong, Forbes Magazine, April 2013

Like every person who picks up this book, I am a consumer. And like you, though loath to admit it, I am influenced by the advertising and marketing campaigns of products that interest me. Sometimes, despite myself (and especially during the Super Bowl), I am even affected by commercials for products that I have no interest in at all. Oddly, this seems to be most likely to occur if the Super Bowl commercial features a dog. And like many others, I am certain that I am not unduly influenced by the sea of marketing or advertising that surrounds us. When I am being courted, cajoled and wheedled by advertising gurus, I am highly conscious of this and so can still make my purchasing decisions in a clear and rational manner. Yeah, right.

Living in today's world, it is inevitable that our choices are influenced by marketing tricks and ploys. This influence is especially insidious when it pertains to things that are important to us, such as our dogs' health and welfare. We tell ourselves that we pay attention to ads and promotions for dog foods because we want to learn more about the nutrition and health benefits of the food and to determine if it meets the criteria that we determine to be essential for our dog's activity level and life stage. And pet food companies make it easy for us because advertisements are, well, everywhere. While you may need to work a bit to find a book (such as this one) or nutrition research article or an article in a dog magazine, you don't have to do anything at all except turn on your computer and open a browser to be inundated with advertisements for dog foods. Walking through your local pet supply store includes multiple display panels and sales campaigns promoting different (and new) brands and product lines. We read, we digest and we often act. And the action that pet food companies are bargaining on is a purchase of their products. Here's an example (true confession time).

Mike and I currently live with four dogs and one cat. We have lived with and loved primarily Golden Retrievers since we were in our early 20s. Several years ago we began to expand our horizons a bit. We added Vinny, our beloved and quirky Brittany to our family. Following him, Chip, our gentle, funny and rather loud Toller (if you know Tollers you are certainly familiar with their "voices") joined the Case clan. Chip has been a true ambassador for the breed both at our training school and within our community. He is a gentle and sweet soul who loves to swim, run, train and has excelled at learning all sorts of silly tricks. He is the first dog that I trained to ride a skateboard, something that he actively seeks to do whenever we walk into our training building. Suffice it to say that we adore Chippy and have loved learning about the Toller breed through him and his breeder, Dan Rode, who has become a good friend. Because Tollers are also still relatively unknown, and because we are identified in town as the training school couple who "has Goldens," people in our community naturally assume that Chip is either a Golden or a Golden mix. Responding (again) to their queries with *"No, he is a Nova Scotia Duck Tolling Retriever,"* often leads to facial expressions that suggest we are pulling some dog-related joke on them, since a breed with such a funny name cannot possibly exist.

Against this backdrop, consider our delight during a weekend grocery shopping trip when we entered the dog food aisle to see that trademark happy smile, gold face and white blaze—a Toller on the front of a popular dog biscuit box! Holey Bat Cave, Batman, the Toller has made it to the big leagues! We were of course thrilled that others too could now enjoy the smiling happy face of a Toller and perhaps learn about this wonderful breed. We were also all too happy to purchase a box ourselves. Never mind that we never feed that brand of biscuit or that we pride ourselves on purchasing all of our dog products at a locally owned pet supply store. We capitulated without even the semblance of a cognitive struggle. And, for the next six-month period or so that the box continued to carry this beautiful dog on its cover, we continued to look for it during every shopping trip, as well as to purchase the occasional box. Until, that is, they switched the photograph to a picture of a Chinese Crested. The first time that we noticed the breed on the box had been changed I thought, "Now, for goodness sake, where is the Toller, and who in the world will buy *that* box?"

Who's the customer?

The presence in my kitchen cupboard of multiple boxes of dog biscuits, all displaying a smiling Toller on the front panel, bears testimony to the fact that it is the *owner*, not the dog, who is targeted by pet food company marketing campaigns. But then, we all know this, right? Sure we do. Years ago, when marketing psychology was still in its infancy, pet food companies clearly directed their message to dog owners through two very simple messages. These were "your dog will love this food" and its natural extension "your dog will love you for giving him this food." I remember watching Gravy Train commercials as a kid in which the family dog happily, if not a bit maniacally, chases a miniature [gravy] train into the kitchen where Johnny and Mommy are dishing out a can of the goopy stuff. Rover dives in, Johnny smiles, Mom pats Johnny on the head and everyone is happy. This approach worked well for a long time and continues to be a cornerstone of many dog food advertising campaigns today. We all want to feed a food that our dogs relish and enjoy. Additionally, as we saw in Chapter 1, the love and caretaking that is part and parcel of feeding our dogs is a cherished daily ritual that we share with our dogs.

However today, more than ever before, many dog owners are highly committed to providing a food that supports their dog's health and vitality and comprises wholesome and safe ingredients. Moreover, a growing proportion of dog folks are likely to be highly discerning and critical consumers. For example, pet industry growth predictions for 2013 identified these issues to be of increasing importance to pet parents: food safety; ingredient quality and source of origin; and access to wholesome and healthful foods. Pet food companies recognize not only how strong the bond with dogs has become, but also how important our dog's health and wellness is to us. For example, Leslie May, owner of Pawsible Marketing, a marketing firm that exclusively serves the pet industry, wrote in early 2013: "The past few years we've seen a growing trend in healthier, grain free and organic options for feeding pets as consumers demand a healthier life for their pet. Any pet food that doesn't meet these requirements of healthier options for pets will struggle in finding ground for the most prolific pet product buying consumer." The days of saying "Your dog will love this food and will love you for giving it to him" are past. As we saw in earlier chapters, the criteria that matter to critical consumers rightfully include their dog's stage of life, body size and activity level, and the food's nutrient content, ingredient quality and for some, sources of ingredients and place of production. While these are all distinctions and criteria that have the science behind them to matter, there are a host of other product differentiators that exist solely as marketing hype designed to sell food. The trick is differentiating between the two. Where does the science end and the marketing hype begin?

Some marketing campaigns are easy to dissect, and many discerning consumers are not duped (though some are, or else the campaign would not continue). One of the most common examples occurs when photographs or illustrations on the pet food label do not match what is actually "in the bag." When you see photographs of fresh produce, trout leaping out of streams or savory roasted chicken, take a moment to check if these photographs actually match with the ingredient list. You may be unpleasantly surprised. Here's an example. The current bag of a Nestle-Purina Beneful product called "Healthy Fiesta" includes colorful illustrations of fresh vegetables, chunks of meat and avocado displayed enticingly on the package's principal display panel. The product vignette shows kibbles of varied shapes (and colors), presumably representing the carrots, tomatoes, chicken and avocado included in the food. However, the ingredients list of the food tells a different story. The first eight ingredients are as follows: ground yellow corn, chicken by-product meal, corn gluten meal, whole wheat flour, animal fat, chicken, soy flour, rice flour, water, propylene glycol. So, where are the carrots? They are identified as "Dried carrots" and are listed *eighteenth* following both salt and propylene glycol (a preservative). Remember, ingredients lists are ordered in preponderance by weight, with the most abundant ingredients listed first. Tomato shows up in the twentieth position and avocado at the twenty first position, behind water, sugar and animal digest. While technically the label is not false advertising, it certainly could be construed as misleading since the bulk of this food consists of ground corn, chicken by-product meal and corn gluten meal, not the whole, fresh vegetables and chunks of meat that are pictured on the label.

Hopefully, after reading the first sections of this book, you are not easily fooled by marketing ploys that obscure differences between what is *on* the bag and what is *in* the bag. However, as we will see, not all advertising tactics are quite so obvious. The creation of niche markets, whether or not supported by scientific evidence, makes it difficult to separate marketing from science. In this chapter, we will examine techniques that marketing and advertising companies use to influence our purchasing decisions along with advice regarding how to recognize these tactics and avoid your own purchase of "the Toller biscuit box." Let's begin with an examination of the most prevalent buzz-word and marketing campaign to have hit the pet food industry in a long time.

Humanization—seriously?

The first time I heard the term "humanization" as it relates to dog food was during a presentation at a pet food industry conference several years ago. The lecture was given by a prominent marketing executive who was expounding upon this newly identified marketing concept. Taken in the best light, the term humanization simply means thinking of dogs as members of our family (as, in my opinion and that of pretty much anyone who lives with a dog, they certainly should be). However, if taken to an extreme, it can also mean treating one's dog as if he or she is a little fur-covered human. Marketing concepts that are centered upon this term were subsequently developed by a group of market researchers who discovered a series of published studies showing that human relationships with dogs have become increasingly important during the last 50 years. Not surprising to anyone who lives with animals, these studies found that the majority of people consider their dogs and other pets to be family members and that most people benefit tremendously from the companionship that their dog brings to their life. So, this is big news? It seems that it was to the marketing people, even though much of the research showing the importance of our bond with dogs and the health benefits that dog ownership brings to our lives has been around for more than twenty five years.

What is new, however, is the mercantile attitude toward the human-animal bond. It seems that once marketing agencies discovered this research and started to add their own marketing studies to the mix, the next natural step (for marketing companies, anyway) was to identify ways to exploit the bond between people and their dogs so as to increase market shares and profit for dog-related products. Since dog food is far and away the largest money maker within the pet industry, this is where the term humanization landed and took root. Make no mistake—when marketing people talk about humanization, they are not so much extolling the joys and positive benefits of sharing one's life with a dog. Rather they are seeing dollar signs. Packaged Facts is a global marketing research and analysis firm that produces marketing outlook reports for the pet industry. A recent blog article by one of their analysts includes this statement as its introduction: "Pet industry statistics make it no secret that the more affection pet owners feel for a pet, the higher their levels of spending. The pet stores that welcome dogs inside, offering biscuits at the checkout are genuinely being pet-friendly—but it's no coincidence that those pet products are located at the cash register, the better to engage exactly the kind of pet owner who brings their pet to the store." (Frei, 2013.) Because their interest centers upon how much money we spend on our dogs, marketers have examined the spending differences between people who consider their dog to be part of the family and those who do not. And what they found was that the truly big spenders are, naturally, the dog folks who consider their dogs to be part of the family. Figure 9.1 reports several results from these studies. Not surprisingly, people who consider their dogs to be family members purchase higher end foods, do not skimp on veterinary care and spend more of their expendable income on their dogs.

However, what is important for the critical consumer to understand is exactly how this information is being used by marketing agencies and in advertising campaigns. Packaged Facts identifies several important areas of pet feeding and nutrition that they consider to be potential winners for the next few years. These include pet foods that contain functional ingredients such as omega-3 fatty acids (krill oil, fish oil), chondroitin sulfate and glucosamine (joint health supplements), supplements that support intestinal health such as prebiotics and probiotics, and dental health foods or chews. Similar to the human foods market, interest in natural and organic pet foods has been increasing steadily over the last five years, particularly since the 2007 pet food recalls. Additional segmentation of life stages and lifestyles of dogs has also been identified as a lucrative market. None of these trends are necessarily undesirable, of course, provided the new foods and trends evolve from evidence-based nutrition. For example, we have good evidence supporting the inclusion of omega-3 fatty acids in foods, some evidence for probiotics/prebiotics, but not much evidence for clinical benefits of chondroitin sulfate and glucosamine. When benefit can be shown, formulating foods with functional ingredients and charging consumers more for them is just fine and dandy. However, if these trends are used only as marketing strategies to target a particular type of dog owner and make claims that lack evidence, then dog owners are being misled by slick advertising campaigns that may be of no real benefit to their dog's health and life quality. This is precisely where nutritional science and marketing part company.

Dog spending behaviors:	Dog is family	Dog not family
Purchase the lowest priced dog foods	6%	33%
Reduced spending on dog because of the difficult economy	12%	30%
Skipped routine veterinary care during last twelve months because of the economy	19%	67%
Spent less than $30 in the last 30 days on your dog	22%	40%

Source: Packaged Facts, 2013

Figure 9.1 Pets are family versus pets are not family.

It's a chick thing

According to the American Pet Products Association (APPA), women are the primary pet shoppers, accounting for more than 80 % of dog-related spending. The APPA explains that, because women are still often the primary caregivers and nurturers in the family, they are also usually the primary caregivers for the dog in most households. Alan Siskind, publisher of the magazine *Dog News Daily*, offered an additional reason that dogs may be more of a "chick thing" (my phrase, not his), saying that today more women are choosing to stay single and to not have children and so "dogs are the four-legged child." He goes on to state that we are "pampering dogs like never before." While the facts of what the APPA and Siskind state are true, their interpretations require some critical examination. First and foremost, I may be going out on a limb here and certainly do not profess to speak for the entire female sex. However, I would suggest that most women are quite aware that our dogs are not human, nor are they our children. Dogs without question provide us (both women and men) with an outlet for love and nurturing and care, not to mention the joy and fun and richness that they bring to our lives. However, the way in which this care is interpreted by the marketing and advertising arm of the pet food industry is as a completely one-sided relationship, as if we are caring for a car or a new video system or a stuffed animal. Here's a clue to you marketing MBAs: dogs give back to us much more than we give to them. It is the best deal ever. And knowing this is one of the most precious and universal joys of sharing our lives with dogs, and it is something that you will hear over and over and over again from dog people (if you would just start to listen without the constant clanging of a cash register in your ears). Dogs are not just "something that we purchase stuff for," nor are they "child substitutes." For example, research conducted and published during the 1980s found that the relationships that people have with dogs are distinct and different from our relationships with other humans, and that these relationships add to rather than substitute for our relationships with other humans. Finally, to classify the attitude that caring well for a dog who is a living, breathing, loving family member as *"pampering"* is both patronizing, and well, just plain insulting. Why ever should good care for a friend and family member be designated as "pampering"?

True, there is a small (albeit highly publicized—remember the availability heuristic) segment of dog owners who dress their dogs in designer clothing, cart them around in baby carriages, feed them foods that, while considered delicacies by humans, are not a balanced diet for dogs, and espouse all sorts of silly theories about why Muffin urinated on their bed or tore up their favorite pair of Gucci shoes when the nanny was not watching her. In her 2010 book *It's a Dog's World*, Wendy Diamond apparently thinks that this sort of dog person is representative of all dog owners. However, I would argue that such extremes make up a very small proportion of dog owners. (And, hey, if Muffin does not mind getting dressed up and is well cared for and loved, why judge?) My point is that focusing on dogs being loved (by women) only as a potential source of more of the market share of pet products, including food, is an ill-conceived path. Yes, a lot of women are involved with dogs. The vast majority of trainers, behaviorists and small animal veterinarians are female, as are most breeders, kennel owners, day care owners, shelter professionals and pet sitters. These well-educated and dog-savvy people adore dogs, understand and respect them as dogs, and also know that they are dogs and not furry children. To trot out yet another over-used marketing buzzword, these women are "influencers." They are the people who *other* dog owners turn to for advice about nutrition and feeding and diet selection. And, if they see a pet food label showing floating fresh produce and chunks of whole meat and then read an ingredient list that is dominated by by-product meal and corn gluten meal, chances are they will not be duped into recommending that food (nor will they be among that 80 % of *pet purchasers* who marketing companies apparently think they are targeting). And, as a dog owner or professional (or female!), don't allow yourself to be fooled by such tactics.

Advertising appeals (and how they influence us)

The pet food market is both enormously crowded and highly competitive. As we have seen in previous chapters, the number of brands and product lines that are available to choose from continues to increase annually, with no signs of leveling off. In addition, the marketing and advertising campaigns that are used to promote pet foods have become increasingly sophisticated. For example, market research companies under the hire of the large pet food companies regularly poll pet owners, conduct survey research and monitor focus groups to learn more about how dog owners are "segmented," marketing jargon for identifying groups of consumers who share certain demographic characteristics and attitudes. For example, Ipsos-Reid, a Canadian market research firm, conducted a telephone survey study of over 50,000 pet-owning households in Canada. Their results were published in a report entitled *Paws and Claws: A Syndicated Study of Canadian Pet Ownership*. The data that they collected led them to identify four major categories of pet owner. They labeled these segments as follows: pet humanists; conscientious pet lovers; pet pleasers; and pet traditionalists. What I found intriguing (but not surprising) about this report was how the information that it contained was intended to be used. For each of the four pet owner categories, Ipsos-Reid included a set of marketing strategies that were specifically designed to sell more product (dog food) to that particular segment of pet owner. Similarly, a recent study conducted by an academic researcher, Dr. Annie Chen at the University of Westminster, studied the buying patterns and degree of pet attachment in almost 600 pet owners. Her paper, published in the *Journal of Targeting, Measurement and Analysis for Marketing*, identified three major dog owner market segments that she called: (1) anthropomorphic owners who value quality; (2) attached, quality-seeking owners; and (3) owners seeking economic value. Again, just like the Ipsos-Reid study, a principal objective of this study was to use the results to identify new opportunities for marketing strategies that lead to increased sales.

Marketing appeals

Marketers and advertisers use appeals and claims to sell products. Appeals are exactly what they sound like—advertising campaigns that appeal to the way consumers view themselves and to ways in which certain products can be beneficial to their needs, lifestyle or worldview. Claims, on the other hand, are statements that refer directly to a product's benefits, characteristics and/or performance that prove its superiority over other similar products. Unlike appeals, pet food claims are subject to some scrutiny and regulatory oversight, which is intended to help protect consumers from unsubstantiated assertions about a product. (We will examine specific pet food claims and their regulation in detail in Chapter 10.) Together, the messages conveyed through advertising appeals and claims are intended to influence purchasing decisions. Appeals and claims may or may not have a basis in scientific truth, and the degree of agreement with science is largely dependent upon regulatory oversight. Because claims are more regulated than appeals, we see a departure from science most dramatically when we examine the effects of advertising appeals. While on one hand it is argued that marketing research and the advertising campaigns that come from it help pet food manufacturers to meet the changing needs of pet owners and their dogs, it is also true that this information is used to *create* new needs and to manipulate our choices in accordance with what marketers learn about us as dog owners. The bottom line: *buyer be aware*.

While many advertising appeals are obvious (smiling Tollers on biscuit boxes), others are subtle or so common in our consumer world that we easily miss them. Let's look at several examples of the appeals that are commonly used by pet food marketers and how we can train ourselves to recognize and critically evaluate them.

New puppy effect

In his book *The Power of Habit: Why We Do What We Do in Life and Business*, Charles Duhigg examines how and why people develop routines and habits that lead us to make automatic (and often uniformed) choices in our lives. A chapter that is portentously entitled "How Target knows what you want before you do" explains something that market researchers have known for many years: consumers are generally very predictable creatures who thrive on routine and habit but who are likely to alter their routines and habits (and buy new products) during major life events or upheavals. The most important of these from a marketer's point of view are marriage and divorce, relocation to a new city or home and the birth of a baby. In all of these cases, an individual's normal daily routines will be changing to a small or large degree, and so too (the theory goes) will their purchasing habits. Because these life events are associated with a new set of needs (grocery shopping for two people instead of for one, purchasing new furniture for the new house, and all of that baby-related stuff), people undergoing such changes are exceptionally vulnerable to advertising campaigns that attract their attention and offer them information about the new products that they need.

An example of this phenomenon at a highly sophisticated level is the megastore Target's campaign to attract and sell to pregnant women. According to Duhigg, marketing analysts for Target have determined that among all of the major life events that we may experience, the one that causes the most dramatic change in consumer behavior is the birth of a child. This happens because many of a new parent's previously established daily routines completely evaporate overnight to be replaced by new responsibilities and habits that involve caring for a child. So, a woman who previously spent a lot of her time perusing Target's women's clothing or shoe department is suddenly spending time in the baby care aisles and comparing prices on strollers. The sophisticated part comes from Target's ability to collect, analyze and ultimately use information about their shoppers' (they like to use the word "guests") purchasing habits. Target uses credit card data, frequent-buyer and discount coupons, surveys and mail-in refund cards to collect mountains of information about consumer behavior. They use this information to build complex statistical models that are capable of identifying specific aspects of an individual shopper's demographics, interests and needs, based simply upon what happens to be in their shopping cart on a given Saturday afternoon. (In case you were wondering, we have met Big Brother and he is a mega superstore.) Because Target also knows that having a baby is a time that moms- and dads-to-be are unusually vulnerable to advertising and are going to be buying lots of baby stuff, they have directed their considerable efforts towards identifying women who are pregnant. Duhigg explains how this is done in considerable detail, but suffice it to say that the Target statisticians are so good at this that they are able to not only predict whether or not a woman is pregnant, but can also identify which trimester she is in and assign a predicted due date! Once a pregnant woman is recognized, the advertising department gets to work. Suddenly (and seemingly out of the blue) she begins to receive dozens of advertisement flyers and discount coupons for maternity clothing, diapers, lotions, cribs, both via postal mail and through internet browsers and email. If you can ignore the intrusive nature and outright creepiness of all of this, it is rather impressive.

During interviews, a senior statistician for Target told Duhigg (before he was ordered to stop talking) that *"new parents are a retailer's holy grail."* For pet food companies, it is new puppy owners, hence the term the **new puppy effect**. Pet food companies understand this and use similar approaches to Target's pregnancy campaign, albeit perhaps not quite (yet) at the same level of sophistication. Like Target and parents, pet food companies know that a momentous life event for people who love dogs is when we are adopting a new puppy or dog (especially if it is our first dog), and that it is during this period that our pet food purchasing habits are most easily influenced. They exploit this period with several types of marketing approaches. Some market their foods directly to breeders, who then promote their food to puppy buyers. Breeders not only have direct access to us when we are at our most vulnerable—selecting and bringing home our newest canine family member—but they are also a clear authority figure to many new dog owners (see the "argument from authority" concept that follows). A second approach is using shelter campaigns. All of the multi-national pet food companies have extensive shelter programs that include free food giveaways, educational programs, grant support and new puppy packets for adopters. And of course, these packets include coupons for discounted food. These programs are a real win-win for companies because they provide needed support to non-profit shelters and rescue organizations and at the same time influence new owners when they are considering what food may be best for their new dog, right when their habits are inclined to change. Another clear benefit of this type of campaign is that the company appears to be promoting a cause (adoption, pet rescue) rather than hawking its food. And of course, this is not a bad thing—pet food companies provide a great deal of welcome support to shelters and animal advocacy groups across the country. Just keep your critical consumer hat firmly in place, especially if you work in rescue or are a shelter professional, because keeping your dogs healthy is not generally the underlying motivation of pet food marketers who develop these campaigns.

If you think this is not the case, let me provide an example of how marketers who work in pet food sales think. Following President Obama's first election in 2008, the president mentioned that he wanted his daughters to have a dog with them in the White House. Within days, Pedigree (Mars) went into action, using a newspaper ad to encourage Obama to adopt a dog from a shelter or rescue organization. When asked about this approach, John Anton, Pedigree's director of marketing at the time said this of the cause-marketing approach: "It's the right message to send out at this time. More dogs are going to end up in shelters because of home foreclosures. And, every time we run this [type of] campaign, we see increased [pet food] sales." So, accept the donations, the food samples and the puppy start-up packets with thanks, but remember to evaluate the food based upon its nutritional merits, not upon the new puppy marketing strategy that is without question going to be influencing you during your new puppy days.

Appeal to authority

A second and related type of advertising strategy is the **appeal to authority**. This approach is related to the new puppy effect because the authorities that are enlisted by pet food companies include breeders, veterinarians, shelter staff and trainers—all professionals who we tend to visit when we are adding a dog to our family. Pet food companies use an appeal to authority to improve trust in their brand and to enhance their food's image of healthfulness. By itself, such an appeal is neither misleading nor false, since most of the authorities that are used in these campaigns actually *do* have expertise in canine health or nutrition. However, where this type of campaign can get us into trouble as consumers is when it encourages us to blindly accept claims that are not based upon the true merits of the food but rather only upon perceptions of an authority's opinion. Arguments from authority work well in today's world of information overload because they provide a convenient shortcut around having to do the work of researching and learning about a product ourselves.

Several different authorities are commonly used in pet food advertising campaigns. Veterinarians, of course, immediately come to mind. The Ipsos-Reid study reported that 73 % of dog owners identified their dog's veterinarian as their primary source for information about nutrition and feeding. For pet food companies, this means that veterinarians are essential authorities whose recommendations of a particular brand can lead to many new and loyal customers. Veterinarians are naturally viewed as being in the role of pet expert, given their training and their role in animal health. In addition, visits to the veterinarian provide a natural opportunity to ask about nutrition and feeding. Pet food advertising campaigns also use breeders as authority figures. Pedigree was one of the first brands to use this approach. I remember watching their commercials as a kid. Each ad included a specific breed along with footage of gorgeous, meticulously groomed dogs, brimming with health, as the breeder's voiceover narrative extolled the many benefits of feeding Pedigree to her champion dogs. In fact, the Pedigree slogan for many years was the simple but powerful *"Recommended by Top Breeders."* This worked well for a long time and was replaced only in 2007 by their current slogan, *"Dogs Rule"* (whatever that means). Finally, some pet food companies use the appeal to authority through the selection of a brand name. Examples of these include Breeders' Choice, Dr. Gary's Best Breeds and Showbound Naturals (the last of which interestingly captures two key appeals—the appeal to authority and the appeal to nature).

As a critical consumer, should entertaining commercials that include veterinarian or breeder recommendations, the use of phrases such as *"Veterinarian Recommended"* or *"Chosen by Breeders,"* or the inclusion of such recommendations in the food's brand name influence your decisions? Nope and double nope. These are all marketing strategies intended to trigger your brain's appeal to authority bias and that have no scientific backing because—here is the important part—such appeals have absolutely no standardized meaning or regulatory oversight. Pet food manufacturers are not required to substantiate these types of appeals, in any way, shape or form. According to the FDA's Center for Veterinary Medicine, which oversees health-related claims on pet foods, there exists no minimum number of veterinarians who are required for a company to be able to state its product is recommended by veterinarians. Likewise, no data showing that X number of breeders prefer Pedigree were needed. (Conversely, if the company made such a claim *against* another company, such as X % of breeders prefer Pedigree over Purina, the company is required to back up such a statement with data.) The bottom line? Don't let empty appeals that attempt to convince you that veterinarians, breeders or Joe down the street who knows a lot about dogs all recommend the food that you are considering. There is no science behind these appeals; science has left the building. Be aware that appeals to authority capitalize on our bias toward listening to authority figures and dutifully following their recommendations. Be strong, be a rebel, read labels and ask questions—learn for yourself.

Appeal to celebrity

Let me begin this section by saying that I really like Ellen DeGeneres. I think she is witty, charming, generous and smart. Her first TV sitcom, *Ellen*, was not only entertaining and funny, but tremendously courageous when in 1997 she because the first major Hollywood actress to come out publicly as a lesbian. And really, anyone who did not adore Ellen as the voice of Dory in *Finding Nemo* simply must not own a functioning heart. Finally, many dog folks also love Ellen DeGeneres because she is an animal lover who promotes shelter adoption and lives with several dogs and cats of her own. All of this said and agreed upon, I have to add that I have no reason to believe that Ellen DeGeneres, while a great comedian, talk show host and animal lover, is also an expert in canine nutrition. She may know a bit, she may feed her pets well, but her ownership and endorsement of a particular dog food brand should hold about as much credibility as I would have attempting to be funny on national television. Ditto for Paul Newman (Newman's Organics), Dick van Patten (Natural Balance [until May of 2013]), Rachel Ray (Nutrish) and Johnny Depp (Benny & Joon Dog Food). Okay, I made that last one up.

These foods all fall under the marketing strategy that is aptly labeled **appeal to celebrity**, a tactic that is so widespread that we hardly even stop to wonder why in the world Dick van Patten, the beloved dad from the *Eight is Enough* TV show, is selling dog food (Figure 9.2). Is there anything inherently wrong or misleading about this form of marketing? Well, maybe. There are two important decision biases to be aware of whenever you come across a celebrity-endorsed (or owned) dog food. The first, and most obvious, is that most celebrities who are endorsing products are actors or sports stars; they are seldom experts on the products that they endorse. Of course, sports celebrities often endorse athletic shoes and other equipment, and it is at least plausible that they have expertise with those products. Similarly, we would all agree that Rachel Ray does know *something* about food, at least about human food, and Ellen, well, she does love her dogs (and she is really funny). However, teaching people to cook pasta on national television and celebrating one's love of dogs on a popular daytime talk show do not equate to knowing how to formulate a high quality dog food. Celebrities are rarely doctors, veterinarians, scientists or canine nutritionists (although they may play one on TV…). While this should be obvious, it is a fact that typically gets lost in the hype and can affect our choices.

The second problem with celebrity appeals has to do with **economic bias**. The celebrities who endorse products are either owner or part-owner of the company, or are paid (handsomely) to endorse that particular product. Thus, such an endorsement cannot be viewed as an unbiased and objective point of view. Remember our discussion about website testimonials? We should consider the appeal to celebrity to be just an unusually powerful form of testimony, one that should carry no more weight in your decision about whether or not a food is good for your dog than does Joe down the street who happens to know a lot about dogs.

One last example should be included in this section, if only for its sheer marketing audacity. It seems that sometimes, the celebrity that is used to sell the dog food is not *really* a celebrity. Or more correctly, the celebrity is not *real*. Enter Chef Michael, Nestle-Purina's fictitious celebrity. On the face of it, one would assume that Mike is a famous chef, sautéing and basting his days away in a fancy, high-priced restaurant in downtown LA or New York City, or perhaps self-promoting as a flamboyant character who entertains foodies from around the world on his own cooking channel. Nope. Trying to find him, anywhere, is a futile exercise because he does not exist. Rather, he is an invented character created by marketing professionals with the goal of selling Purina foods to a niche market of foodie dog owners who love celebrity chefs. I spent some time trying to hunt down Chef Michael, to no avail. I finally came upon an article in the *Wall Street Journal* relating the same problem (Where's Michael?). When contacted and asked directly about where this celebrity lived and what he was up to cooking, Nestle-Purina eventually, after much prodding, responded *"Please know that Chef Michael is not a real person, but a reflection of the many people inspired to make mealtime special for their dogs."* Huh? Wow. A fictitious celebrity. So, Chef Michael is not, in truth, as the brand's Facebook page claims *"our executive chef."* So much for truth in advertising. And, in case you are wondering if Chef Michael makes a decent food, following chicken (remember, that's 65 % water), the leading ingredients of Purina's Chef Michael "Oven Roasted Chicken Flavor" food are soybean meal, soy flour, animal fat, brewers rice, soy protein concentrate, corn gluten meal and ground yellow corn. Go figure. Chef Michael appears to be in need of canine culinary school.

Celebrity	Dog food brand	Product claims
Ellen DeGeneres	Halo, Purely for Pets	*"If you're going to have pets you should treat them like you'd treat yourself."*
Paul Newman	Paul Newman Organics	Company is managed by Nell Newman (daughter); foods are 95 % organic
Rachael Ray	Nutrish	*"Like you, Rachael Ray wants the best for furry family members, like her Isaboo."*
Dick van Patten	Natural Balance	*"We wanted a pet food based on sound scientific principles and truth about cat and dog nutrition needs, not marketing hype."*
Chef Michael (fictional character)	Chef Michael's (Purina)	*"It's not just dog food. It's Chef Michael's. Crafted with great care, attention to detail and inspiration from our executive chef."*

Figure 9.2 Examples of "celebrity" dog foods.

Anchoring effects

Marketers know that not only are consumers interested in the quality of the products that they choose, many are also concerned with price. A number of strategies are used to influence our purchasing decisions when a consumer is considering price and economy. One of the most widespread of these techniques is called the **anchoring effect**, also referred to in psychology circles as the relativity trap. In general terms, anchoring occurs when people become attached to a certain concept and retain that bias when making future decisions. Price anchoring occurs when we reflexively use a price point that we are initially presented with, or that we are accustomed to, to make all subsequent decisions about products within the same category. The initial information sets an anchor to which we compare all other numbers, in this case, prices. Once an anchor is set in our minds, our subsequent judgments are made by adjusting from that anchor, and we become naturally biased toward interpreting other information around the anchor rather than by objectively assessing the product's actual value. Two common examples in today's world are the initial price tag on a car and the asking price for a house. Each of these prices set a standard for negotiations, so that prices lower than the initial price seem more reasonable even if they are still higher than what the car or house is actually worth.

One of the most curious characteristics of the anchoring effect is how arbitrary it can be. A completely irrelevant number can influence our decisions without our conscious awareness. In his book *Predictably Irrational*, Dan Ariely describes a set of research studies in which participants attend a party that includes a silent auction for a wide range of appealing consumer goods such as chocolates, wine and computer or electronic gadgets. He developed several clever and entertaining ways to include an anchor in each event. In one study, Ariely asked participants to write the last two digits of their social security number on their auction bid form, prior to placing and submitting their bids for a variety of items. The results showed that the attendees who had high numbers (i.e., greater than 51) submitted bids that were up to 120 % higher than those with the lower social security numbers (50 or less). Completely outside of conscious awareness, simply writing down a number between 1 and 99 had a significant anchoring effect on subsequent assessments of what was thought to be a reasonable price to bid on a bunch of different and unrelated consumer goods.

Similarly, an early study of this effect, conducted by Daniel Kahneman (author of *Thinking Fast and Slow*) had participants spin a wheel painted with numbers from 0 to 100 (think Wheel of Fortune game). After the wheel stopped, they were asked if they believed that the percentage of countries in Africa that were members of the United Nations was higher or lower than the number that the wheel landed on. Unbeknownst to the study participants, the wheel was rigged to land on either the number 10 or on the number 65. The anchoring effects of these two numbers were dramatic. People whose wheels fell on the number 10 guessed, on average, that 25 % of African countries were in the UN. In contrast, those whose wheel fell on the number 65 guessed, on average, that 45 % of African countries are in the UN. This difference was caused simply by locking a number (10 or 65) into the participants consciousness (or perhaps more correctly, their sub-consciousness) prior to asking them to make an estimate of a number that was completely unrelated to the whims of a roulette wheel. (In case you were wondering, the answer was 100 %; all of the African nations are members of the UN.)

Our brains use anchoring every day as a sort of mental footing that helps us to estimate how much time something will take, how much money something should cost or even how many nations are part of the UN. And, like many cognitive errors, anchoring has great value, in that much of the time it helps us to consider options and make decisions rapidly. Because anchoring operates below the level of conscious awareness, it effects are very difficult to avoid. For example, in one study students were given anchors that were obviously wrong. They were asked whether Mahatma Gandhi died before or after age 9 years, or before or after age 140. Clearly neither of these anchors could be correct, yet the 9-year group guessed an average that was significantly lower than the age guessed by the 140-year anchored group. This study also showed that anchoring can be either higher (as in the housing market prices prior to 2008) or lower than the true value of the item being considered. In the pet food realm, I would argue that our anchor has been set (and remains) too low, especially considering the value that many of us are seeking in dog food.

Our current-day perspective of what is a reasonable price to pay for dog food has been strongly and arbitrarily anchored to what is actually a very low number—a number that was set many years ago when our relationships with dogs were quite different than they are today and at a time when we did not demand high quality foods for our canine best friends. Remember that early dog foods were developed principally to feed working hunting dogs, during a period of time that most dogs lived outdoors, were used for hunting or protection and for the most part did not enjoy as close a relationship with their owners, at least when compared with what we consider to be the norm today. When early foods were developed and introduced, they all contained grain by-products, animal slaughter by-products and very little else. They were also very, very cheap to produce and to purchase.

Fast forward to today. Dogs are considered family members by the vast majority of pet owners. Together with our dogs we enjoy a wide variety of dog-related activities and sports, we spend time walking, training, exercising and traveling with our dogs, and an entire industry of day cares, training centers, specialty stores and parks has sprung up to support all that we celebrate as dog. We love our dogs as never before and many of us aspire to provide them with the very best of care. We also want to feed them well, and a growing number of people recognize the importance of paying attention to what actually goes into the food that we choose to feed to our canine family members. Yet, herein lies a significant disconnect—psychologists might even call it an example of cognitive dissonance. We declare that we love our dogs and want to do the very best for them, while at the same time believing that we should not have to pay much for their foods, in fact, thinking that we should have to pay very little, even for the very best products. In my view, our perception of what is reasonable and normal to pay to feed our dogs was anchored to a very low number many years ago, when feeding dogs was a completely different experience than it is today. Unfortunately, our price anchor for food has not shifted along with our attitudes towards dogs. Let me illustrate this anchoring effect with a set of comparisons.

Figure 9.3 provides the price per bag and unit price (price per pound) for a sample of ten dog foods. I obtained these prices in the spring of 2013, from a single, large, online pet supply website. To allow for accurate comparisons, each of these foods is a dry (extruded) product that is formulated and marketed for normally active adult dogs. When a specific protein source or flavor was available, I always chose chicken. I also chose the smallest package size that was available for each food. Several differences are immediately apparent when you review this list. First, notice that, when compared by price per pound of food, there is more than an eight-fold difference between the most expensive food (Wellness Core Grain-Free) which costs about $4 per pound, compared with Dad's Economets food, which was priced at 50 cents per pound. What is more important than the price per pound of a given food, however, is the price that it costs to feed the food. I used a hypothetical 45-pound, normally active adult dog for this part of my experiment. A dog of this size should require approximately 1000 calories of food energy per day to maintain an optimal body condition (see Appendix 3 if you would like to know how to calculate this estimate). Using the caloric values (kcal/cup) that were provided on each brand's website, I was able to calculate the price that it would cost to feed this dog each day, for each of the ten foods. (Oops—nine foods. The Dad's product did not provide caloric content in any of their materials so I could not calculate a cost/day for that food.)

When we compare these prices, keep in mind that by using the smallest container size for each food, I chose the most expensive product size for that brand, since typically we see a decreasing unit price as the size of the container increases. I also searched for a wide range of product prices, so the high end of this list provides a good representation of the most expensive dry dog foods that are available to adult dogs and the low end provides a representation of the least expensive foods that are available. The most expensive food, Wellness, would cost *less than two dollars and fifty cents per day,* to feed our best friend. The cheapest? You can feed your companion, your family member, your pal, for a paltry *47 cents a day* should you choose the most "economical" product on this list, Ol' Roy. Most of us will probably agree that we are certainly willing to spend more than half a buck per day to feed our dog. However, the most expensive food, Wellness, still costs less than a cup of coffee at Starbucks to completely nurture our best friend for an entire day.

At risk of further upsetting those of you who are huffing and puffing right now that "I spend a lot of money on my dogs, thank you very much," I offer this. Many dog people, myself included, believe that our dogs deserve, and that we should demand, a selection of dog foods that are produced from high quality ingredients (not by-products of the human foods industry), that these foods should be wholesome, safe and well regulated and that they should keep our dogs healthy and well nourished. Agreed? Okay then, we need to step up and be willing to pay a bit more for such foods. If we want higher quality and safer foods, then we need to remove the antiquated dog food price anchor from around our necks and become accustomed to paying a bit more for quality dog foods. Even if we doubled the price of the most expensive dry food that I could find to say, 5 dollars a day to feed a medium size dog, is this really so outrageous? Data from The Dog Talk Project show us, in survey after survey, that owners believe feeding a proper diet to be one of the most important factors (for many, it is the most important factor) for their dog's health and well-being. If we believe this, and want quality foods, then we have to be willing to pay more than one or two bucks a day to nourish our best friend.

Brand	Price (size of package)	$ per lb	Calories (kcal/lb)	$ to feed 45 lb dog/day
Wellness Core Grain-Free	15.99 (4 lb)	4.00	1663	$ 2.40
Eukanuba Naturally Wild	13.99 (4 lb)	3.49	1460	$ 2.39
Royal Canin Boxer	19.99 (6 lb)	3.33	1872	$ 1.78
Fromm Four Star	12.99 (5 lb)	2.60	1780	$ 1.46
Avoderm Adult	9.99 (4.4 lb)	2.27	1568	$ 1.45
Diamond Naturals Grain-Free	9.99 (5 lb)	1.99	1627	$ 1.22
Purina Beneful	10.99 (7 lb)	1.57	1675	$ 0.93
Authority Adult	12.49 (8 lb)	1.56	1652	$ 0.94
Ol' Roy Healthy Mix Original	11.98 (15.5 lb)	0.77	1620	$ 0.47
Dad's Economets	8.87 (17.6 lb)	0.50	NP	-----

Calculated using a moderately active, 45-pound adult dog requiring approximately 1000 kcal/day

Figure 9.3 Prices of ten dry (extruded) dog foods for adult dogs.

Appeal to emotion

We cannot discuss pet food marketing without examining tactics that **appeal to emotions**—most specifically to the love that we feel for all dogs in general and for our own dog(s) in particular. Emotional appeals are ubiquitous in the advertising campaigns of all types of products and are especially influential when it comes to dogs. In fact, the challenge lies more in finding a dog food advertisement that does *not* have an emotional component than identifying those that do. The most obvious forms of emotional appeal are those commercials and advertisements that depict happy dogs spending time with loving owners. Depending on the target audience, these ads may show active owners hiking or playing on the beach with their dogs, a child snuggling in to sleep at night with her puppy or a family picnicking and throwing a ball for their dog.

Similar to the appeal to authority, marketing campaigns that are based upon emotions are not inherently misleading or false. However, when an advertising campaign relies *only* on the emotions that it elicits to convince us that the product is healthful for our dogs (and superior to its competitor), they neglect to provide the actual evidence for why we should believe this to be true. And, of course, your emotional reaction to the advertisement does not necessarily have any bearing on the truth or falsity of the nutritional claims that are being made for that food. Marketing strategies that rely principally upon evoking the "Awwww" response are hoping that consumers are so overcome with soppiness that we neglect to examine the actual merits of the food. As we saw in Chapter 2, most of us are not consciously aware of how strongly our emotions affect our decisions. This can leave us vulnerable to being manipulated by clever, emotionally-appealing ad campaigns (like, say, Tollers on biscuit boxes).

Emotional appeals are not limited to just the love that we feel for dogs. Other emotional responses can also sell dog food. Sympathy and empathy are evoked when pet food companies include shelter or rescue pets in their advertising campaigns. A brilliant example of this was used by Pedigree in a series of shelter dog commercials that aired in 2010. Each opened with a close-up shot of a sweet-looking dog sitting in a kennel at an animal shelter. People visiting the shelter walked by his kennel without speaking to or interacting with the dog. The narrator then states that for every bag of Pedigree purchased they will donate a portion of the proceeds to their adoption fund, which will lead to more dogs (like Muffin, in this commercial) being adopted into loving homes. Again, there is nothing inherently wrong with appealing to emotion, and certainly not with a company's charitable fund to help homeless dogs. Still, should one's logical brain happen to kick in, it would remind you that you can directly donate to shelter groups and rescue organizations of your choice (i.e., without buying this particular food), thus freeing you to purchase a bag of food based upon its nutritional value rather than upon an appeal to your sympathies. Another emotional appeal that is used, albeit less commonly, is pride (also called the appeal to snobbery). This is evoked by campaigns that flatter us by telling us how smart, cool, attractive and superior as pet owners we will be (like the people in the commercial) if we feed their food. The bottom line is that almost all effective advertisements appeal to our emotions in some fashion or another. Just be aware that this is occurring, that it intentional and designed to sell food to you, and often has no bearing whatsoever upon the quality of the dog food that is being promoted.

Appeal to nature

The "natural foods" market in pet foods has been increasing more than any other category of food for the last several years. The marketing research firm Packaged Facts reports that natural pet products are projected to grow by more than 30 % in the year 2013, an increase that is almost unprecedented within any consumer category. Almost three-quarters of dog foods that are marketed as being "natural" are sold through specialty channels, which means that we find them most frequently in small, independent pet supply stores rather than in the grocery store aisle or through mass pet supply retailers such as PetSmart or Petco. The same report identified Nutro and Blue Buffalo as the two biggest players in the natural pet foods market, together capturing 40 % of sales. Other companies that focus on selling natural pet foods include WellPet, Natural Balance, Merrick and Natura.

So, with all of this growth and increased interest, it begs the question—what exactly IS a "natural" dog food? Herein lies the rub. Like many label terms, the word "natural" is regulated by the American Association of Feed Control Officials (AAFCO). AAFCO defines "natural" as follows: "a feed or ingredient derived solely from plant, animal or mined sources, either in its unprocessed state or having been subjected to physical processing, heat processing, rendering, purification extraction, hydrolysis, enzymolysis or fermentation, but not having been produced by or subject to a chemically synthetic process and not containing any additives or processing aids that are chemically synthetic except in amounts as might occur unavoidably in good manufacturing practices." Wow. This broad definition means that any ingredient or nutrient other than those that are wholly synthetic (produced artificially) are allowed and may be labeled as "natural."

For example, if an ingredient that is being processed (rendered, fermented, digested, etc.) is treated with a synthetic additive that is considered to be part of standard manufacturing practice that is acceptable. If a food contains only such ingredients, it may carry the term "natural" as a descriptor on its label. Using this definition, it is difficult to even think of an ingredient that would *not* be considered natural! Those that do are typically vitamin "pre-mixes," taurine (typically added to cat foods and some dog foods) and certain purified amino acids. Many pet food companies use synthetic vitamin pre-mixes because they are the most economical and efficient way to balance a food's vitamin content. According to AAFCO rules, when vitamins are added to a product for which all other ingredients fit the natural definition, it may be labeled as: *"Natural with added vitamins"* and they are good to go. Whether or not these artificial vitamins are better or worse than naturally derived nutrients, at the very least this type of labeling misleads consumers to think that the product has attributes (i.e., naturalness) that it may not truly have. When it comes down to it, all that the "natural" label means in dog foods today is that artificial preservatives such as BHA, BHT or ethoxyquin have not been added by the pet food manufacturer. Typically, vitamin E and other naturally-occurring antioxidants such as rosemary and citric acid, are used to preserve these foods.

Interestingly, this is an area in which the state of human food regulation is no better. Current federal labeling laws for human foods do not provide a precise definition for "natural" either. The FDA and USDA loosely define it as meaning ingredients and foods that are minimally processed and contain no artificial additives, and that companies are prohibited from using statements that are misleading. This laxity has led to problems in the human food industry similar to what we see among dog foods— the ubiquitous and almost meaningless use of the term natural. Finally, there is yet another caveat. The AAFCO definition above applies only to pet food ingredients. When the term "natural" or "nature" is used as part of the brand name, the rule is generally believed to not apply (or at least it is not regulated in the same way). A quick search for pet foods that include one of these terms in their brand name brought quite a flood of responses—fifteen brand names that used the word natural and ten that used the word nature (Figure 9.4). A review of who owns and makes these foods, what ingredients they include (and where ingredients are sourced) and the targeted life stage/activity level for each food reflect such a wide range of foods as to make the word natural virtually meaningless when attempting to use it when making decisions.

In trying to understand this phenomenon, let's revisit the naturalistic fallacy concept that we discussed in Chapter 4. In that discussion we were examining the evolutionary history of the dog and attempting to determine where the dog (not the wolf) actually falls in terms of the somewhat artificial carnivore versus omnivore controversy. If you remember, the naturalistic fallacy holds that just because something is identified/classified as being "natural," it does not logically follow that it is good for us, better than something else or superior in any way, based solely on its state of naturalness. As we saw, there are plenty of things existing in nature that will, if not kill us, make us feel pretty darn sick should we eat them. Similarly, while we all intuitively believe (and possibly are correct) that eating something that is less processed and does not include artificial additives should be more healthful for us (and for our dogs) than eating something that is more processed and contains artificial additives, to date, there is no evidence showing us that this is indeed the case. (It does not mean that naturally-derived foods are not better for our dogs, just that they have not yet been shown to be better for them.) So, if you prefer to eat less processed foods yourself, and also prefer to feed them to your dogs, your best bet (as of today, anyway), is to read labels, contact companies and keep in mind that the word "natural" found on the food's label or in its brand name is marketing hype and not scientific evidence. As such, it should not be used in your decision-making process.

Natural	Nature
American **Natural** Premium	By **Nature**
Avoderm **Natural**	Kirkland Signature **Nature's** Domain
Castor & Pollux **Natural** Ultramix	**Natura**
Darwin's **Natural** Selections	**Nature's** Logic
Eukanuba **Natural** Lamb & Rice	**Nature's** Recipe
Iams Simple and **Natural**	**Nature's** Select
K9 **Natural** Freeze Dried Raw	**Nature's** Variety
Lassie **Natural** Way	Science Diet **Nature's** Best
Natural Balance	Three Dog Bakery Bake to **Nature**
Natural Life	
Natural UltraMix	
Nutro **Natural** Choice	
Natural Planet Organics	
Only **Natural** Pet MaxMeat	
Perfectly **Natural**	
Simply **Natural**	
Timberwolf Wild and **Natural**	
Tuscan Simple and **Natural**	

Figure 9.4 Pet foods that include natural or nature in their brand name.

Amalgamation of appeals

The next time that you find yourself standing in the pet food aisle, staring wistfully at the bag of food that shows (put your dog's breed or breed-mix here) running happily through a field, ears flapping, face smiling, tells you that it is "veterinarian recommended," has the word "natural" any place on the label (or in the name), uses a font type that has been shown to appeal to women, includes shelter/rescue group promotions, and is endorsed by Betty White...put down the biscuit box, step away and look for the nutritional science information. Chances are it is hidden, minimal or non-existent. Go home, find the brand's website and look at its ingredients, its caloric content, who owns it and who makes it, and what life stage it is formulated for. If, on the other hand, you come across a biscuit box that includes a photograph of Johnny Depp plus a smiling Toller, please buy a case and send it to me.

10

Label Claims—Testing Your Critical Reading Skills

"Touting health benefits leads to market success."

A.E. Sloan, May 2013 issue of Food Technology

Like many people, I have a favorite breakfast cereal. I have been buying it for about six years and eat a bowl several times a week. After initially selecting the brand I confess that I have not paid much attention to the box's label claims. This morning, I took the cereal box from the pantry and read the health statements on its front panel. Wow. There are some pretty hefty and impressive assertions here, all of which are crammed onto the premier advertising section called "front of package" (or simply FOP). My cereal professes the following: First, it tells me that it is made with whole grain and provides a good source of fiber (not surprising—it is cereal after all). Further down on the panel, and in a large and very attractive font, are the words "Heart Healthy" with a little cartoonish-looking depiction of a heart. Below the heart are the words "Antioxidant Vitamins C & E, Including Beta Carotene." Here is where it gets interesting. The FOP also includes three statements about how exactly this cereal is going to benefit my heart: It helps to reduce cholesterol (because it contains oats); it supports healthy arteries (because of those antioxidants and vitamins); and it manages hypertension (because it is low in sodium).

I turn the box over, expecting to see ingredient and nutrient information displayed prominently, since after all, the claims on the front of the bag tell me that this is a nutritious food that will save my heart from doom. Instead, I find photographs of a currently popular female athlete and her endorsement as (I am not making this up), a "Breakfast Believer." I also learn that this athlete is a recent mother and that, as a mom, she makes sure that her family starts off each day with a good breakfast. For readers of the male persuasion, I should also mention that our female athlete is wearing pretty skimpy and quite revealing (athletic) clothing. Pretty slick, really. Three marketing appeals in one display: appeal from celebrity, appeal to emotion (the mom factor) and for the men, an appeal from sex (we did not cover that appeal when discussing dog foods, for obvious reasons). Reminding myself not to succumb to these blatant marketing ploys, I keep looking for ingredient and nutrient information. Ahhh, there it is, on the side panel. Here I find the **Nutrition Facts** box, and below that, the ingredients list.

Looking at this panel, I find that a serving of my cereal provides me with 3 grams of fiber, which is only 12 % of my daily dietary fiber needs. Hmmm…does this really constitute a *good* source of fiber? By comparison, a fresh pear provides almost twice this amount of fiber (5.5 grams), a cup of raspberries provides almost three times this amount (8 grams) and a cup of beans contains five times this amount (15 grams). While I am personally not inclined to eat black bean soup for breakfast, the point is that the statement "good source of dietary fiber" could be construed as misleading, since there are many other foods to choose that provide significantly more grams of fiber per serving. And, not to put too fine a point on this, if I compare this claim with other breakfast cereals, it really falls apart. All Bran cereal provides 15 grams of fiber (more than 50 % of the daily allowance) per serving.

What about the antioxidants that are so prominently displayed on the front panel? Well, the Nutrition Facts panel tells me that, indeed, one serving of my cereal provides all of the vitamin E and all of the B-vitamins that I need in a day—100 % of my requirement. It also provides 25 % of the vitamin C, and 30 % of the vitamin A that I need. What the label fails to tell me is that the cereal provides these things *not* because it contains whole grains, but rather because it is fortified with added vitamins and minerals. (Note: just as these nutrients are added to processed dog foods.) And last, what about the "healthy heart" claims regarding cholesterol, hypertension and keeping my arteries healthy? At the bottom of the cereal box, in very small print, is the statement "While many factors affect heart disease, diets low in saturated fat and cholesterol may help to reduce the risk of heart disease." This cereal is both low in saturated fat and, as a plant product, of course, contains no cholesterol at all.

If you have read the previous chapters of this book, you should now be asking about evidence. Is there actually scientific evidence that eating *this cereal* specifically will reduce my blood pressure, reduce my cholesterol, protect my arteries and keep my heart healthy? The answer is no. The disclaimer at the bottom of the box is intended to convey this to the shopper (should they have their reading glasses or a magnifying glass handy). Rather, a diet comprised of foods like this cereal that contain (or exclude) certain ingredients or nutrients, when consumed regularly as part of a balanced diet, may help to protect me from heart disease. For breakfast cereals, health claims generally focus upon heart health and weight control. Other human food products promote immune benefits (yogurt), bone health (dairy products), weight management (low fat products), reduced risk of dental caries (sugar-free products) and even cancer prevention (low fat foods, antioxidant-containing foods). Here is the tie-in: Just as health-related claims on human food labels have proliferated (exploded, really), in recent years, so too have such claims increased on dog food packages. And, like the claims on the yogurt, cereal and dried fruit snacks that you choose for yourself, the claims that are made on our dog foods influence our perceptions of the product and our purchasing decisions.

What are "claims"? And why should you care about them?

In both human and animal foods, a **claim** refers to statements included on product labels (packages) and supporting materials that promote specific attributes of the product or imply a relationship between the product and a desired result in the person (or dog) who consumes the product. Claims that are used on food labels are generally classified into four broad categories: romance/marketing, nutrient content, structure/function and health (Figure 10.1). We see all four of these categories frequently on commercial dog food packages. Pet foods may also carry a small set of statements called "descriptive claims" that are defined and regulated by AAFCO. We discussed these in Chapter 6, and they define exactly how reduced fat and calorie claims can (and cannot) be made on pet foods. Without a doubt, all of the four types of label claims identified above have proliferated on pet food labels in recent years, right along with those being made on my cereal box and on other human foods. Can these claims be helpful in assessing nutrient content and comparing foods? Do they convey factual and relevant information or can they be misleading and confusing, functioning primarily as marketing ploys designed to increase sales? A bit of history can help to sort this out.

Claim type	Definition	Dog food label examples	Proof needed?
Romance/ Marketing	Catchy phrases and product attributes that "romance" the consumer into identifying with and purchasing the product.	• Healthy and great tasting • Outstanding flavor and taste • Love them like family; feed them like family	NO
Nutrient content	Identifies a specific nutrient or ingredient and makes a claim about its inclusion or exclusion in the food.	• Source of EPA and DHA • Contains high quality proteins • Grain-free; gluten-free	NO
Structure/ function	Describes the role of either a nutrient or an ingredient in terms of how it affects normal structure/function.	• Contains calcium for strong bones • Promotes active lifestyle	NO
Health	Statements that describe a relationship between a nutrient, ingredient or food and the risk of a disease.	• Antioxidant nutrients for a strong immune system • Promotes joint health • Supports healthy digestion	NO

Figure 10.1 Types of claims.

Label claims—how did we get here?

To understand where we are today, we need a bit of history of how it is that health claims first came to be found on food labels. As with so many things in the pet food industry, the trends that we are witnessing with label claims on pet foods closely

171

follow trends that are occurring in the human food arena. This current trend is quite recent indeed. Prior to 1990, the FDA specifically prohibited food manufacturers from including any type of label (package) claim that implied that their food could prevent, relieve or treat a particular disease or condition. The Nutrition Labeling and Education Act (NLEA), passed in 1990, recognized the important link between diet and health, and was intended to provide consumers with nutritional information that would aid them in making more informed and healthful food choices. One of the strongest components of the act was to require the inclusion of the Nutrition Facts panels on most processed foods. These panels identify the number of calories, fat, types of fat, cholesterol, dietary fiber and several important vitamins and minerals on a per serving basis. Most of us have become accustomed to these panels and regularly use them to select and compare foods.

A second component of the NLEA allowed the use of label claims about health with the stipulation that all claims would be reviewed and authorized by the FDA to ensure that statements were truthful and not misleading to consumers. This provision was intended to prevent overzealous claims from suddenly appearing on food labels. And quite prescient it was, seeing what ensued during the following years. Almost immediately, companies began to complain that the required Nutrition Facts panels made their foods "look bad" (hmmm…how many grams of fat are in a serving of your potato chips, anyway?). Because they could not do anything about the required panels, their solution was to begin to pressure the FDA to allow more expansive health claims on the FOP to counterbalance the negative messages conveyed by the nutrition facts panels. Some companies even resorted to the all-American way of solving disputes: they brought lawsuits against the FDA whenever the agency denied a claim, using the argument that prohibiting label claims infringed upon the company's free speech.

It became even more difficult for the FDA to stem the tide of health claims on human food labels when the Dietary Supplement Health and Education Act (DSHEA) was passed in 1994. This new law severely curtailed the FDA's regulatory oversight of dietary supplements (not foods), which included no requirements for producers to prove either effectiveness or safety of their supplements. Take note of this if you are a fan of dietary supplements. In much the same way that you would expect a small child to throw a temper tantrum upon seeing his brother given a piece of candy that he himself was denied, food companies immediately began to demand the same freedom for their health claims that the supplement producers were enjoying. By the late 1990s, following passage of the 1997 FDA Modernization Act which eliminated the requirement for the FDA's pre-market approval of packaging claims, the FDA's regulatory powers over food label claims was considerably weakened and the number of nutrient, structure/function and health claims on food labels continued to expand. The reason for this is that marketing researchers had quickly learned that health claims on food labels led to immediate and dramatic increases in sales. Indeed, the use of health claims on foods opened up an entirely new and unprecedented marketing and advertising niche, one that has continued to expand to this day. For example, a recent article in the journal *Food Technology* reported that the average number of claims that are included on food labels has increased from 4.2 in 2002 to 6.2 in 2012. This may not sound like a lot on the face of it, but consider—*six claims per label?* This is on average—some have more than this. These claims are for our hearts, our immune systems, our gastrointestinal function, our bones, our teeth and even our waistlines.

Goodness gracious, next thing you know my food will be claiming that it can clean my house and mow my yard.

Which brings us to pet food. Just as the nutrient and health claims made for human foods have increased dramatically since passing of the NLEA and DSHEA, so too have those that we see on pet food labels. While my first dog Judy's box of Purina claimed to "taste great; dogs love it!" today such a simple claim would be completely overshadowed by assertions about the healthfulness of the food's ingredients, nutrients and the many benefits that the food is going to provide to my dog. So how are these pet food product claims regulated? Well, when all things are said and done, none of the acts that are identified above have jurisdiction over pet foods. *In fact, other than the FDA's strict prohibition against pet food label claims that might be construed to be "drug claims," there are currently no laws that specifically cover the many nutrient and health claims that we are finding on pet food labels.* Even AAFCO has little to say about claims other than their clearly defined set of descriptive claims, identified earlier. AAFCO also has no procedures for (or authority over) pet food companies to receive approval for or against all other types of claims that they place on their label and websites. While all US states adhere to the basic regulatory rule that pet food claims must be truthful and must not be misleading to the consumer, there is an awful lot of latitude on the "misleading" part of the regulation. For example, a label showing whole carrots, avocados, tomatoes and fruits is only required to have these products listed somewhere on their ingredient panel, even if the amounts comprise a mere 1 or 2 % of the product.

As it stands today, pet food companies may include nutrient, structure/function and general health claims on their labels. Moreover, scientific substantiation in the form of randomized, controlled studies is *not* required for these claims. Pre-market substantiation is never required for food label claims and is only required for drugs. The pet food manufacturer is responsible for ensuring the accuracy of its claims and does not need pre-approval by the FDA (or any other regulatory group) for the inclusion of these claims on the label. It is only when a pet food company makes a claim that might be construed as a drug claim that action is taken. A drug claim is any statement that implies that a food (or an ingredient or nutrient in the food) can treat, manage, prevent or reduce risk of a disease. If an AAFCO official or the FDA's Center for Veterinary Medicine (CVM) interprets a dog food label claim as potentially a drug claim, it will be subsequently investigated by the CVM. If CVM decides that the claim is in violation (i.e., is a drug claim), the company is required to remove the statement from its label or become subject to regulatory action that may require scientific substantiation.

Do label claims influence our choices?

In addition to concerns about evidence-based claims on labels, we must consider how pet owners are influenced by these claims and whether they are truly helping people to select healthful products for their dogs. It is difficult to measure how influential these claims are since the effect of this information upon pet owner understanding and decision making has not been studied. It has, however, been studied with human foods, in response to concerns about the proliferation of increasingly expansive (and sometimes outrageous) claims found on food labels. The general intent of NLEA was to enhance consumer understanding about nutrition and the components of a healthful diet and to encourage healthful food choices. It proposed to do this both through the use of the Nutrition Facts boxes and via the use of FDA-authorized health claims. However, when food companies learned how effectively these claims function to increase sales, the numbers of claims exploded and FDA oversight was challenged and weakened. These unanticipated consequences have led to questions about how much good these claims were actually doing in today's marketplace.

Yale University's Rudd Center for Food Policy and Childhood Obesity is at the forefront of research addressing these questions. Studies conducted at the center have examined the effects that front-of-package health claims have on consumer perceptions of a food's healthfulness. Not surprisingly, they have found that the health and nutrient claims that are displayed prominently on the front of packages significantly increase consumer perceptions of the healthfulness of the product and their willingness to purchase the product. This result occurs regardless of whether or not the product's actual ingredients and nutrient content support the label claims. Additionally, studies have shown that FOP displays reduce consumer use of the Nutrition Facts panel (often hidden on the side panel, as on my cereal box) and ingredients list, and may generate inaccurate inferences about the product. These effects were clearly evident in the results of a study from the center revealing that breakfast cereals that were high in sugar and low in essential nutrients and fiber nonetheless carried an average of three to four health claims on their FOP panels (Roberto et al; 2012). Moreover, the same study showed that these claims were interpreted by parents to mean that the cereal was nutritious and might provide specific health benefits for their children, leading to increased willingness to purchase the cereals. It is not a big jump at all to expect a similar response from dog owners who pay attention to the label claims that they see on pet food labels.

Although similar studies have not been conducted with pet foods (and probably will not be, given that pet food companies are the primary researchers and funding groups and they have little incentive to look into this issue), it is probable that the existing label claims that we see today on dog foods are more effective in boosting sales than in educating pet owners. Consider Figure 10.2 below. The column on the left includes a set of nutrient, structure/function and general health claims that are allowed and that are regularly found on many dog food brands today. The corresponding rows in the right-hand column report similar label claims that are prohibited by the CVM because they represent a drug claim and so are not allowed. In many cases, the difference between the two is a simple word or phrase. I suspect that the average dog person does not stop to consider or even is aware of the subtle differences between the allowed statements on the left and the prohibited claims on the right. For instance, does the owner of an eleven-year-old Lab who has been showing some pain after long walks read a senior dog food label that states: "Helps to maintain healthy joints and mobility" and think to himself, "Well, it does not say that it reduces the pain of arthritis, so I do not really know if it will help my boy or not"? No, most likely he thinks, "Well, they say this helps dogs' joints, [and I assume they have to prove that to get it on the label], so I will give it a try." Ka-ching. Another sale is made; no substantiation needed.

Allowed	Prohibited (drug claim)
• Supports healthy skin and shiny coat • Promotes a glossy coat	• Reduces skin flaking and itchiness • Prevents skin problems • Hypoallergenic
• Helps maintain healthy joints and mobility • Glucosamine and chondroitin help maintain joint and cartilage health	• Reduces signs of arthritis and pain • Prevents progression of joint disease • Reduces joint inflammation and repairs damaged cartilage
• Source of omega-3 fatty acids for skin and coat • Includes fish oil, a natural source of omega-3 fatty acids	• Omega-3 fatty acids to reduce skin inflammation • EPA to manage allergic disease
• Supports a healthy immune system • Contains antioxidants for immune system health	• Improves immune response • Prevents infection through support of your dog's immune system
• Promotes oral (dental) health • Helps to keep your dog's teeth clean • Controls tartar build-up on teeth	• Prevents dental problems such as gingivitis and periodontal disease • Treats gum disease
• Supports a healthy gastrointestinal tract • Promotes efficient digestion	• Prevents digestive problems • Improves digestion in sensitive dogs
• Helps reduce risk of food sensitivities • Developed for sensitive dogs	• Hypoallergenic for the treatment of food allergies • Manages/treats food allergies
• Veterinarian recommended • Veterinarian formulated • Veterinarian developed	• Veterinary Approved (the illegal term is "approved" because veterinarians do not officially approve labels or products)

Figure 10.2 General health claim or drug claim—can you tell the difference?

Health claims are great for sales. After all, who does not wish their dog's food to support or promote healthy skin, shiny coat, strong bones and joints, a healthy immune system, and efficient digestion? Certainly we all look for this and really, shouldn't a healthy diet provide these things by design? In my opinion, the problem lies in the intent. Even though the same food is prohibited from claiming that it actually prevents (or treats) a particular health problem, the use of verbs such as "promotes," "supports," or "helps" certainly implies exactly that to the consumer. The use of these terms is especially concerning given the fact that pet food companies are not required to provide any scientific substantiation to any regulatory body for these claims (just as human food companies are not). While it is certainly in their best interest to have that proof (and in all fairness, most of the large companies that have active R&D departments do regularly research their products), companies are only subject to oversight if there are complaints (or lawsuits from other companies) or if any of their claims are deemed to be a drug claim. So, let's examine the types of dog food label claims that we frequently see today and provide a few guidelines for adhering to our mantra of using evidence-based nutrition to make food choices for our dogs.

Meaningless label claims

In a perfect world, the claims printed on human foods and pet foods would function to educate us about healthful eating for ourselves and healthy feeding practices for our dogs, and would aid, rather than hinder, our quest to make smart food choices. But, alas, we do not live in a perfect world. We live in a world that includes marketing and advertising agencies. And the role of marketing and advertising agencies is to sell stuff, and, if that stuff is already selling, their role is to sell more of it. They are really, really good at this. So, we must all train ourselves to read labels with a cynical and discerning eye.

Currently popular, but meaningless, label claims that we see on dog foods can be grouped into several types that have been shown have appeal to consumers. As you read through the next several pages think about how these claims might impact your own buying decisions. And, it should not be surprising to you at this point to learn that most of these claims have their origins in human foods, so think about your own food consumption as well as what you feed your dog. (Remember—pet food trends follow human food trends almost unfailingly.)

Natural, holistic and organic claims

If any word has been overused, misused and abused on human and pet food labels, it is the word natural. We have already discussed its use as a marketing strategy in Chapter 9, so to recap, suffice it to say that use of the word natural to imply natural as healthy, is meaningless at best and misleading at worst. Remember that the FDA does not define the term at all and the definition that AAFCO endorses is so broad that it encompasses everything other than artificial preservatives, flavors and coloring agents and synthetically produced vitamins and amino acids. And even when these latter two ingredients are used, the label can read "Natural with added vitamins and amino acids" and still be in compliance.

The term "holistic" also appears on dog food labels, web materials and even as part of a food's name. This term is used most commonly as an adjective, i.e., holistic medicine or holistic lifestyle, and presumably refers to more of a philosophy of life than a specific type of food or diet. Humans who profess to live a holistic lifestyle tell us that it refers to the totality of an individual's physical, mental and emotional health and well-being, with each aspect of life being in balance with the others. There's certainly nothing at all wrong with that. However, how exactly calling a dog food "holistic" can attain this balance has yet to be demonstrated. Those brands that promote themselves using a holistic claim have not been shown to contain any different ingredients or have any unique properties that set them apart from other foods. Consider "holistic" to be a marketing strategy, rather than a claim that can be used when choosing wisely.

There is an important distinction between the terms natural (or holistic) and organic. According to the USDA's National Organic Standards Board, the group that oversees organic labeling for human foods, a food can be labeled organic if the plant ingredients that are included were grown without pesticides, artificial or sewage sludge fertilizers, or irradiation and exclude genetically modified organisms (GMOs). Animal-source ingredients must come from animals that were raised exclusively on organic feed, were not treated with hormones or antibiotics, and were housed/fed according to an agreed upon animal welfare standard. However, because several vital differences exist between foods that are certified with the USDA organic seal and pet foods that contain organic ingredients, pet foods are not (yet) allowed to carry the USDA seal. As it currently stands, AAFCO recommends that pet food companies *attempt* to follow the organic food regulations for human foods in their labeling practices. However, they are not required to do so. In other words, whether or not pet food companies comply with this recommendation is completely optional. If the company chooses to follow the guidelines of the National Organic Program (NOP), you should be able to tell by reading their claim, followed by the ingredients list. If the label states 100 % organic, every single ingredient must be organic. (It is almost impossible for a processed dog food to meet this standard and none that I have found do so.) The second best standard is foods that are labeled simply "Organic." These foods must be comprised of at least 95 % organically produced ingredients. Below this level is the label claim "Made with Organic Ingredients," for which at least 70 % of the product's ingredients are organic. As an interesting aside, the NOP standard for using the word "*with*" requires a whopping 70 % of the ingredient in question. Compare this regulation to the AAFCO "*with*" requirement for pet food labeling, which comes in at…3 %.

Regardless, when you see the "organic" claim on a dog food, first pay attention to how it is worded and second, look at the ingredients list. If the first five ingredients are all prefaced with the word "organic," you can be assured that the manufacturer is following AAFCO recommendations for organic claims. Conversely, keep in mind that, should a company choose to ignore AAFCO recommendations, they can say whatever they wish about their food's organic nature, regardless of whether or not it contains a single organic ingredient. (Though, in such a case, it would be hoped that a State Feed Official would notice this and deem such a label as "misleading" and out of compliance.) A final caution: Remember that currently there is no evidence that foods produced organically provide relatively more nutrition or health benefits to those who consume them. There is, however, evidence that organic production methods have less harmful impacts on the environment than do industrial production methods. Therefore, the organic designation does have some demonstrated value for consumers who desire to feed a product that contains at least some organically produced ingredients to their dogs. What you cannot and should not do however, is claim health benefits for these foods that have not yet been proven.

Meaningless quality claims

One of the most meaningful measures of a food's quality, if not *the* most meaningful for consumers, is the food's digestibility. However, the actual measure of a food's digestibility is *never* reported on dog food labels and is rarely, if ever, reported in a food's web or supporting materials. While many pet food manufacturers make label claims that their foods are "highly digestible" or "easily digested," such descriptors are absolutely meaningless unless backed with actual (measured) digestibility values. Companies typically provide materials stating that good stool quality and regular (and not too many) defecations are reliable indicators of a food's digestibility and that dog owners should use these criteria as guides when selecting a good food. This is good advice. Generally, a highly digestible food will lead to the production of firm (but not too firm) feces and just two or three defecations per day. However, companies mislead by omission. The very best indicator of digestibility is a *direct measure of the food's digestibility*, which they do not provide to their consumers. So, unless you see an actual number in percentage points (i.e., 85 % digestible—more details about this later), consider quality claims for digestibility to be useless.

In addition, there are several common quality claims that sound impressive but in actuality tell you nothing and cannot help you to differentiate among products. Quality terms that have no standardized or regulated meaning and which should be ignored include the words premium, super-premium, ultra-premium and gourmet. During the 1980s and into the 1990s, the term *premium* was associated with a small group of pet food manufacturers who stood apart (and above) other manufacturers by their inclusion of higher quality ingredients, dedication to life stage feeding and evidence-based nutrition, and emphasis upon food quality and pet health. These foods were sold only through pet supply stores or veterinarians, could not be found in grocery stores and generally were more expensive (on a weight basis) than brands that were broadly classified as grocery store or private label brands. However, beginning in the late 1990s and continuing until present day, large corporations began to acquire many of these companies. As markets expanded, quality distinctions between *premium* brands and grocery store brands became increasingly blurred. Today, while some of these brands continue to self-identify as premium (or super-premium), these changes have resulted in a distinction that is essentially meaningless and is of no help to consumers. There is no official measure or regulatory definition to which pet foods must comply to use these quality terms, even though you will find them on many labels and brand websites. Nor are the foods carrying these terms required to meet higher safety or nutrition standards than do other brands.

Last, a recent addition to the quality claims arena is the "no fillers" claim. We discussed the problem with using this phrase in Chapter 4, so it should be clear why such a claim is misleading and not helpful when choosing a dog food. Since there is no particular ingredient that is identified or defined as "filler," a company is free to define this in any way that they like. Second and as importantly, the term implies that the ingredient that is labeled in this way provides nothing to the diet, which is literally impossible (even non-fermentable fiber provides fecal bulk and affects transit time). Consider the "no fillers" claim to be another marketing term that is designed to promote sales but has no real meaning and so one that should be ignored.

First ingredient claims

A claim that a named meat (chicken, lamb, etc.) is the first (#1) ingredient has been the fastest growing popular claim on dry foods in the last five years. As we know, ingredients are listed on the label by weight, and whole meats (chicken, turkey, salmon, etc.) contain more than 50 % water. Therefore, on a dry basis, it is the meal (chicken meal, poultry meal, salmon meal) that provides the bulk of the protein in the food.

This is not necessarily a bad thing—properly produced meals (and even some by-product meals, as we discussed in Chapter 9) can provide quality protein that is highly digestible. The problem lies in the misleading nature of this claim. Because most of the water that is found in the fresh meat is cooked off during processing, the actual amount of protein that the fresh form of the meat provides to the end product is very small. The "first ingredient" claim is an effective marketing gimmick, so popular that you will find it in almost every brand of food, which makes it meaningless when attempting to differentiate among products.

Skin, coat and other general health claims

There are a set of general "health and well-being" claims that are considered to be "hot topics" in the pet food industry today. Many of these were included in Figure 10.2 on page 175 and include skin and coat, joint, gastrointestinal, dental and immune health. There are two specific arguments to make against the usefulness of these general health claims. The first has to do with nutrition and the second has to do with the types of claims that are permitted on labels. The nutrition argument is in the form of a logical fallacy called the **appeal to hypocrisy** (also called the argument from inconsistency). One of the longstanding and widely promulgated doctrines of the pet food industry is that commercial dog foods are formulated to be "complete and balanced," which means that the foods that carry this statement are proven to provide all of the nutrients that your dog requires and in the correct amounts needed to support his health and well-being (throughout his life, no less). I do not generally disagree with this assertion, but like most nutritionists, recognize that it is a pretty ambitious claim that we must hold pet food companies accountable to. And indeed, AAFCO does hold them accountable, making pet food companies substantiate their labels' "complete and balanced" claims through either feeding trials or by meeting the AAFCO nutrient profiles through analysis (see Figure 10.4 and discussion below). Although there are certainly some limitations with these standards, the point is that a claim of complete and balanced nutrition for dogs is regulated, which is certainly superior to the level of substantiation that is required for most label claims.

So, if this is in fact true and we are to trust companies to produce foods that provide "complete and balanced nutrition for all stages of life" for our dogs, then should not these foods, when fed to a healthy dog with no known medical problems, *by definition* result in a shiny coat (appropriate for the dog's breed or breed type, of course), healthy skin, a normal and protective immune system and an efficiently functioning digestive system? A good diet is *expected* to support health. So why do we need all of the extra claims? Sure, there is some evidence that omega-3 fatty acids are helpful in reducing the inflammatory response in dogs who have atopic disease, that probiotics can reduce the severity of stress-related diarrhea, that glucosamine and chondroitin sulfate may reduce joint pain during the early stages of arthritis, and maybe (just maybe—the research is pretty thin on this one), antioxidants and/or probiotics can improve immune response in animals exposed to antigens (infectious agents). However, and I will say this again, a *healthful food, fed to a healthy animal, should by definition continue to support health*. Therefore, there is something hypocritical about pet food manufacturers' insistence of worshiping at the "complete and balanced" alter while at the same time attaching what are in essence health claims to the labels of the very same "complete and balanced" foods. If the food is complete and balanced and made from high quality ingredients, why is there any need at all to promote "extra" health claims like these? (Hint: Because health claims sell product.) 'Nuff said. Off my soapbox.

The second argument is regulatory in nature and has to do with the absence of a requirement for the substantiation of claims. Structure/function claims (which in effect are really general health claims), are permitted by both the FDA and AAFCO. It is only when a claim drifts into wording that connotes a drug claim (the right hand column of Figure 10.2) that a company may get its hand slapped and will be instructed to remove the claim from their label or change its wording to stay within compliance. Research proof (substantiation) is not required for any of these claims. Therefore, *all* of the claims that you see on the left-hand column can be placed on a pet food label without a requirement for any evidence. To be fair, many pet food companies, especially the large corporations that have very active research and development departments, conduct research and many also regularly publish in academic journals and present their research at professional conferences. However, the point remains for the consumer that general claims such as these do not need to be supported by research evidence. If Food A's claim about joint health has research supporting it, while Food B's identical claim does not, it is irrelevant because the consumer has no way to differentiate between the two claims based only upon what she reads on the label. This regulatory loophole makes these claims virtually useless. The bottom line is that all foods use these claims (shiny coat, healthy skin, functioning GI tract, an immune system that does its job), and none are required to substantiate them. By now, the answer should be obvious to you—if you are genuinely interested in learning about omega-3 fatty acids, chondroprotective agents, probiotics, antioxidants or any other nutrient that may influence your dog's health, get online, look for the published research and get your information from science, not from the label on your dog's food package.

Some dental health claims

Dental health statements are classified as either romance claims (i.e., for pleasant breath or white teeth) or as structure/function claims (i.e., helps to clean teeth or promotes dental health). Therefore, they are not regulated, do not require research to prove effectiveness, and are generally allowed on any label that wishes to use them. This is a definite problem for dog owners because the texture of some dry foods and biscuits has long been purported to improve dental health in dogs, which can magnify the potential for such claims to be misleading. Interestingly, several research studies of the actual effectiveness of dry food in reducing plaque and calculus (tartar) formation have reported little to no benefit. This is probably because physical abrasion is needed to remove plaque from teeth and most dogs do not engage in much grinding/chewing of dry foods, even if they are crunchy and hard. The very best way to provide this dental abrasion is through regular teeth brushing, of course. However, pet food companies are aware, as are veterinarians, that many owners do not brush their dogs' teeth.

There is some evidence that certain compounds, when included in the food or as a coating on biscuits, can help to reduce calculus formation. For example, a compound called sodium hexametaphosphate has been shown to reduce plaque and calculus formation by keeping calcium that is present in saliva from being deposited onto plaque. Currently, the CVM allows claims such as "helps control plaque" and "helps control tartar" to some foods and strongly encourages companies to provide research substantiation for these claims. However, the CVM cannot force companies to submit these materials to them and can only act when there is a label claim violation. Claims that a food treats or prevents gingivitis (inflamed gums) or periodontal disease (gum disease) are specifically prohibited because they are considered to be drug claims.

However, there is some good news. Unlike any other general health claim on pet foods, there exists a third-party oversight for dental claims on pet foods. The Veterinary Oral Health Council (VOHC) consists of a group of veterinary dentists that reviews dental and oral health claims along with published and company-supplied research materials that substantiate claims. They provide a "VOHC Seal" to foods, treats and chews that pass muster in terms of effectiveness. If dental health is an important criterion for you, look for this seal on the food that has a dental claim. (However, remember that regular brushing is more effective than any food or treat can be in keeping our dogs' mouths and teeth healthy and free of periodontal disease.)

Downright silly claims
To end this section with a bit of levity, let's look at label and website claims that, well, to be honest, are downright nonsensical. A random selection of claims that tell us nothing (other than that marketing people have some pretty wild imaginations), but those that provide a chuckle are included in Figure 10.3.

Brand	Claim	Really?
Nutro Ultra	• *Superfood* blend with proteins from chicken, lamb & salmon • *Powerful* antioxidants	• *Superfood?* Is this what Superman's dog eats? • Powerful! None of those weak antioxidants in this food!
Wellness Core	• *Natural, protein-focused,* grain free formula	• As opposed to *unnatural* and protein-*ignoring?*
Eukanuba	• Promotes *optimal health* for adult dogs • *Natural* fish oil	• Shouldn't all complete and balanced foods support health, by definition? • Any such thing as "unnatural" or synthetic fish oil? (No)
Beneful	• *Real* chicken and soy • Accented with vitamin-rich vegetables	• None of that fake chicken or synthetic soy in this food! • *Accented?* Really now.
Blue Buffalo	• *Active* nutrients for your dog's health and well-being • *Healthy* fruits and vegetables • Contains *Life Source Bits*	• It is unclear how exactly a nutrient can be "*active*" • No *sickly* fruits or vegetables included • Life Source Bits? Really?
Castor & Pollux	• *Natural* chicken is the first ingredient • *Natural* formula with added vitamins, minerals and trace nutrients	• Is there any such thing as "unnatural" chicken? • Natural *with*… Remember what this means.
Halo	• *Farm-raised* fruits and vegetables • *Butcher-quality* chicken	• All fruits and vegetables are "raised" on farms • "*Butcher-quality*" is a meaningless term

Figure 10.3 Meaningless (and often silly) label claims.

Label claims you can actually use (if they are provided)
Now that we have looked at claims on the pet food label that cannot help you to select a good food for your dog, let's turn to items found on pet food labels and packages that may be of some help. We will begin with a review of the claims that can help you to differentiate among brands as you review labels and evaluate foods. We will also examine label information that, at least in my humble opinion, *should* be included but rarely is (a girl can dream, can't she?).

AAFCO label requirements (not claims)

The AAFCO has a set of pet food label requirements that all pet food manufacturers must include on their products labels to stay in compliance (see Chapter 11 for a complete discussion of how AAFCO regulates pet foods). These are listed and explained in Figure 10.4. Some of these items are important and helpful when distinguishing among dog foods—others not so much. In addition to these seven required items, the food must state the species for which it is formulated (dog food), and reportedly starting sometime in 2014, must also include a calorie statement, reported by weight (kcal/kg) and by measuring volume (kcal/cup).

Required	What this tells the consumer
Product Name	• Essential for "brand recognition," important from a marketing perspective. • Because marketers know that the inclusion of certain ingredients is important to many dog owners, many companies incorporate the name of a "popular" ingredient into the product name. • Percentages of named ingredients in the total product are regulated (remember the 95-25-3% rule).
Ingredient statement	• Ingredients are listed in order of predominance by weight. • Weights are determined *as added* to the formulation, which includes water, an important consideration when ingredients of different moisture contents are included. • Provides no information regarding ingredient *quality*.
Guaranteed (Nutrient) Analysis	• Reports the food's minimum crude protein, minimum crude fat, maximum moisture and maximum crude fiber (%). (The term "crude" refers to the type of laboratory methods used to analyze these nutrients.) • Helpful only when comparing major nutrients among similar products.
Nutritional adequacy statement	• All "complete and balanced" claims must identify the life stage or stages (all life stages, adult maintenance or puppy). • The "complete and balanced" claim must also be substantiated (proven) either through the completion of AAFCO-sanctioned feeding trials or by formulating nutrient content to meet standard nutrient profiles.
Feeding directions	• All dog foods that carry a "complete and balanced nutrition" claim must include feeding guidelines. • Reported as an estimated volume (cups) to feed based upon body weight. Amount should be adjusted up or down in response to an individual pet's response to feeding.

Required	What this tells the consumer
Manufacturer	• A *"manufactured by"* statement identifies the company that produced the food and is responsible for its quality and safety. • A *"manufactured for"* statement signifies that the listed company contracts its food production with an outside manufacturer (co-packed).
Net quantity statement	• Reports the weight of the product in the package. • FDA regulations dictate the format, size and placement of the net quantity statement.

Figure 10.4 AAFCO label requirements for pet foods.

Life stages and life styles claims

When it comes to AAFCO requirements, remember that there are really only two life stage categories for which foods must meet nutrient standards for labeling: growth (and reproduction) or adult maintenance. We examined the science that is behind life stages feeding for dogs in detail in Chapter 5 (Age Matters). To recap here, remember that for large and giant breed puppies, feeding for controlled growth rate by restricting caloric density and slightly reducing calcium are scientifically sound approaches. Conversely, different needs for growth are not as dramatic for small and medium breeds, but foods that are formulated with slightly higher protein, are highly digestible (see below) and are designed to be consumed by smaller mouths (and go into small stomachs) are also probably warranted (i.e., pay attention to these claims on labels).

Our nutritional concerns for healthy adult dogs are primarily about energy balance, specifically not providing too many calories. For this, use the food's actual energy density (calories per cup) to be your guide rather than catchy phrases such as "less active," "healthy weight" or "mature adult," all of which are non-regulated, meaningless terms. And for the seniors—look for slightly reduced calories for lower activity levels, chondroprotective agents that *may* help with joint issues (though the jury is still out since the laboratory evidence does not seem to be translating well into actual clinical evidence with dogs) and possibly enhanced antioxidants, for which there may be some benefit, in moderation. (But again, not to put too much of fine point on this: A well-balanced food should already be replete in antioxidants, so why do we need an extra claim?) Lifestyle differences are mostly about energy needs, a few alterations in protein level, and maybe (just maybe) about a few functional ingredients that can confer benefit (though, again, evidence is not tremendously strong for most of these). Bottom line: Active dogs need more calories (and more nutrient dense foods); inactive dogs need less. Feed to good body condition and avoid obesity. When we look at lifestyle, highly active dogs need performance foods that are formulated to get a lot of calories and a lot of nutrients into a volume of food that does not stress the dog's gastrointestinal tract. As far as label claims go, dogs do not, on the other hand, need separate foods for agility versus hunting versus flyball versus search and rescue. (Such claims are not found on dog food labels…yet.)

Inclusion claims

Inclusion claims are declarations on a food's label that the food contains a desirable ingredient or nutrient. If you are selecting a dog food based upon an interest in a particular set of ingredients, these claims can be helpful, provided your reasons are sound and evidence-based. This is a significant prerequisite, of course, and one that is often ignored by dog owners and pet food companies alike. Unfortunately, a substantial number of the "we have it cuz it's good" and the "we don't have it cuz it's bad" claims are marketing responses to current feeding fads that are designed to sell more food rather than to impart knowledge or support healthful choosing. Inclusion claims that can be helpful to consumers are those that identify specific types of protein or carbohydrate sources, the type of fat and fatty acids in the food (i.e., inclusion of omega-3 fatty acids from fish oil), the inclusion of organically grown plant ingredients or humanely produced animal-source ingredients, and the inclusion of locally or regionally sourced ingredients (see below). Inclusion claims that are less helpful in differentiating among products are those that make claims about the food containing antioxidants (all processed dry foods must include antioxidants to prevent rancidity), essential vitamins and minerals (again, they all got 'em) or "contains fiber for gastrointestinal health." As we discussed previously, a balanced and complete diet should contain fiber—usually about 3 to 6 %—there is nothing that can help you to differentiate between good and not-so-good foods.

Exclusion claims

Claims of exclusion can be particularly difficult to interpret and decipher, given the rapidity with which new dietary theories, fads and health-promoting practices arrive on the market today and the fervor with which certain ingredients are denigrated. Unfortunately, pet food manufacturers exacerbate these trends expressly to boost sales. When enough dog owners begin to believe a common ingredient is harmful, manufacturers respond by making label claims that their food is free of the targeted ingredient, which via circular reasoning, appears to confirm to pet owners that the ingredient is harmful. As a rule of thumb, new feeding trends, most of which have little or no scientific evidence, arrive on the scene in the pet food market a few years after they show up in human foods. Recent examples include the Atkins Diet (high protein, low carbohydrate dog foods), gluten-free diets (gluten- and grain-free pet foods), probiotics in yogurt (as supplements and incorporated into dog foods) and one that is somewhat unique to pet foods, the "no fillers" claim, an essentially nonsensical term that we discussed in detail in Chapter 4.

Exclusion claims that may be helpful to some owners when selecting a food include claims of no genetically modified organisms (GMOs), no animal-products that were treated with antibiotics or growth hormones or no artificial antioxidants (BHA, BHT or ethoxyquin). Selection of products that purposely excluded these things generally comes from a life philosophy of reducing the consumption of highly processed or treated foods. These can be legitimate choices, provided the purported health benefit claims that one makes about these choices are limited to those that have actual evidence. Although there is no published evidence of health benefits associated with consuming less processed foods, there is legitimate evidence (which is beyond the scope of this book) for environmental benefits and animal welfare benefits associated with these choices. However, this differs fundamentally from making statements that feeding these items *cause* dietary insufficiencies or disease in dogs. There is simply no evidence for such claims and they should not be made in good conscious.

The bottom line with inclusion/exclusion claims is that they can provide a way for a dog owner to choose a food that contains something they are looking for or that excludes something that they wish to avoid feeding to their dog. Nothing wrong with that. There are many ways to feed a healthy diet and, just as with humans, many different ingredients and foods that can be fed to our dogs to keep them healthy and happy. Problems arise, however, when dog owners, not the pet food companies (notice that labels make no health claims about exclusion/inclusion items) take this a step further and make unsubstantiated claims about why the ingredients they seek are preventing disease or the ingredients that they are avoiding cause disease. Just as label claims may be misleading (and they have AAFCO and the FDA's CVM to reprimand them if they get out of line), so too can be the claims of dog owners (many of whom are quite vocal and have blogs). More about this later; now I would like to get back up on the soapbox and make an appeal for including quality claims that could be helpful, if pet food companies would just start including these on their labels or, at the very least, on their websites.

Digestibility claims (allowed, but rarely provided)

The term digestibility refers to the collective proportion of all nutrients in the food that is available for absorption from the gut (intestine) into the body. Because a highly digestible food provides a higher proportion of absorbed nutrients than a less digestible food, digestibility provides a direct measure of a dog food's nutritional value and quality. The reason that a food's digestibility is so vitally important to our dogs' well-being is precisely because the majority of commercial foods sold today are developed, tested and marketed as "complete and balanced." This means that the food must provide all of the essential nutrients that, in their correct quantity and balance, a dog needs on a daily basis. Since this is clearly a lot to ask of a single processed food, I think we are justified as dog owners to demand that the food's ingredients are available enough (i.e., are digested and absorbed) to nourish the dog. As a food property, digestibility is more important for dog foods than for human foods because as humans, we generally consume a wide variety of foods, all of which vary in degree of digestibility and nutrient availability. This mix of foods and the nutrients that they provide can be expected, in most cases, to nourish us and provide the essential nutrients that our bodies need. Conversely, most dog owners feed their dogs a single food over a period of months or years. In this situation, measures of that food's ingredient quality and digestibility become vitally important. And, pet food companies correctly teach us that one of the best measures of ingredient and diet quality is a food's digestibility.

The reason for this is that a food's overall digestibility (called "dry matter digestibility") is increased by the inclusion of high quality ingredients and decreased when poor quality ingredients are included. In addition to dry matter digestibility, which gives you a sense of the entire food's quality, we can also measure the digestibility of the protein in the diet, since this too varies dramatically among different protein sources, with high quality proteins being much more digestible than low quality proteins. In addition to the quality of ingredients in the food, several other factors that influence a food's digestibility include processing care and handling, cooking temperatures and storage procedures. When a finished product's digestibility is measured, *all* of these factors will influence the results. Obviously, this is a very important measure, and one that could provide valuable information to pet owners, if they were privy to it.

However, this is where things get weird. The vast majority of pet food companies do not report digestibility values on either their food labels or in their supporting materials. Some pet food industry folks will argue that these values are not reported on labels and supporting materials because AAFCO has not yet established a standard protocol for digestibility studies to produce these values. This is a convenient but untenable excuse, seeing that apparent digestibility is measured using standard protocols both in academic and industry studies and is regularly reported in published research papers. Moreover, many companies (not all, unfortunately) regularly conduct digestibility trials to compare the quality of their products to those of their competitors, although these data rarely make it into the public realm. There is simply no defensible reason that this information is not made readily available to dog owners, especially given the propensity of pet food manufacturers to make claims such as "highly digestible," "easily digested," and "high quality ingredients" on their labels and websites.

Here is the science: A food's digestibility (technically called apparent dry matter digestibility) is most effectively measured using a feeding trial. The selected food is fed to a group of dogs for a standard period of time during which intake (amount consumed) and excretion (the amount in the fecal matter) is carefully measured. Dry matter (the entire food) and nutrient (protein, fat, etc.) digestibility is determined by subtracting the amount excreted from the amount consumed and calculating this difference as a percentage. It is not a terribly complicated or involved test, although it does require access to dogs who are being fed the food (and only that food) and full collection of feces for a few days (no big deal to people who are used to picking up poop with their hands covered only by a thin plastic baggie). But here is the kicker—although many dog food manufacturers regularly conduct digestibility tests on their foods, they do not make this information available to the dog owners who purchase their foods. And yet, at the same time they tell consumers that products vary significantly in digestibility and ingredient quality, and that digestibility is a good measure of a food's quality (and, as we discussed previously, that *their* food has high, or superior digestibility and contains quality ingredients).

Although it is natural to assume that all of a food should be digested and so the very best food would have a dry matter digestibility of 100 %, this is not only impossible but also undesirable and unhealthy. Fecal bulk is provided by undigested food, in particular many of the food's fiber-containing ingredients. Components of food that are not digested by an animal's own digestive enzymes make it to the large intestine where intestinal microbes digest them to varying degrees. This process and the microbial populations that are supported by it are essential for a healthy gastrointestinal tract (in all animals, including humans). As a general rule of thumb, commercial dry dog foods with reported dry matter digestibility values of 75% or less are of very poor quality, those with values of 75 to 82 % are moderate in quality, while foods with a dry matter digestibility of greater than 82 % are high quality. In general, raw diets that contain little starch will have digestibility coefficients (percentages) that are slightly higher than those of a dry food made with comparable ingredients. However, if the raw food contains uncooked plant starches (potato, tapioca, corn, etc.), digestibility values will decrease because of the inability of dogs to digest uncooked starch. Of course, dog owners can only make purchasing decisions based upon a product's digestibility if they are provided this information in the first place (which we are not).

In fact, as I recently discovered, this information is denied even when a consumer requests it directly from the company. This also is a bit odd, seeing that companies promote their foods as high quality (and often as highly digestible). While writing this chapter, I contacted companies that produced over 30 different brands of dog food and politely requested that they send me protein and dry matter digestibility values for their adult maintenance dog foods. Of the 32 requests that I sent, I received no response at all in 27 cases, even though many of these stated on their "request for information" pages that a response would be sent within 48 hours. Of the five responses that I received, two brands (Blue Buffalo and Diamond's Taste of the Wild) sent responses saying that they do not measure the digestibility of their foods but that their foods are made from highly digestible ingredients and so are very digestible (huh?). In other words, "we do not measure it, but trust us when we tell you that our foods are really, really digestible." Amazingly, Diamond even provided a value for the food digestibility that they do not measure, telling me that their foods are 85 to 88 % digestible. (Note: Do not believe data that have not been measured.) A third company, Timberwolf Organic, assured me only that "our foods are extremely digestible." Only two companies provided actual data. Nature's Variety provided a range, saying that their foods fall within the "80th percentile" range. (I did not want to quibble with them about the rather important distinction between "percentage" and a "percentile," since after all they were one of the two companies that even provided information.) The second company, winning the grand prize for both transparency and quality, is Merrick's Organix. They sent a responding email within three days, telling me that their Organix dog foods are between 82 and 84 % digestible. Thank you, Organix! Too bad more companies are not choosing to walk their digestibility talk, even though they are more than happy to talk the digestibility talk in their claims. Bottom line: if high digestibility or quality ingredients are claimed, ask for digestibility data from the company. They should provide this information if they are making quality claims to consumers.

Ingredient source and manufacturer

I am mentioning ingredient source and manufacturers last because we covered these selection criteria in detail in Chapter 9. To recap here: Following the massive pet food recall of 2007, many American pet owners became more aware of the ways in which pet foods are manufactured (i.e., the use of co-packers) and of the fact that many pet food ingredients are sourced from outside of the United States. This became of momentous import when adulterated shipments of wheat gluten and rice gluten purchased from suppliers in China made their way into pet foods and sickened and killed several thousands of dogs and cats. Understandably, a significant proportion of dog owners are now concerned with where the ingredients of their dogs' food originate and who is making their foods. And, because pet food companies are aware of the importance of this to many consumers, foods that contain regionally or domestically (USA) sourced ingredients will make this claim on their labels. Additionally, the claim of "Made in the USA" is found on some products. Although this claim does not really suggest that it applies to ingredient source, the Federal Trade Commission (FTC) regulations that oversee this type of claim require that "all or virtually all" of the parts and processing of a product are of United States origin to include this claim on a product label. For pet foods, AAFCO interprets this FTC regulation to mean that a food with the "Made in the USA" claim can contain *no or negligible foreign-acquired content.* This means that the dog food must be both sourced and produced within the United States. If more than a "negligible" amount of the ingredients are imported, then the company cannot legally make this claim. Unfortunately, neither the FTC nor AAFCO specify exactly what percentage of a food is more than "negligible" which leaves this regulation open for at least some interpretation. Still, if you read a "Made in the USA" claim on a pet food package, you can also assume that most, if not all of the ingredients in that food were sourced within the US.

And, speaking of claims…

So, the message to be gleaned from all of this is to be savvy of the use of marketing ploys when reading label claims and to avoid using claims that fall under the categories of romance, general and even purported health benefits as selection criteria when choosing among dog foods. When considering claims that may have some substance, look for (and ask for, if you have to) the substantiating studies. Just like human food companies, pet food companies take liberties with their claims to sell pet food. Be aware of these liberties and biases, look for *evidence-based nutritional claims* and use a healthy skepticism when reading labels. Okay, got it. Good to go.

Not so fast, dear reader…we are not finished yet. Yes, companies make claims that may push the regulatory boundaries between food (no pre-market substantiation needed) and drug (pre-market substantiation required) claims. However, many companies also hire trained companion animal nutritionists, conduct research and possess an enormous collective volume of nutritional knowledge that allows them to formulate and sell foods that are complete and balanced in accordance with set standards and that comply with AAFCO, FDA and FTC regulations. Although I am the first to allow that we need stricter regulations governing pet food label claims (as we probably also need for human foods), it is also true that there are regulations in place and that both State Feed Control Officials and the CVM monitor pet foods and their labels and remove claims (and fine companies) that are not in compliance.

The same cannot be said to be true for dog owners, pet professionals and of course bloggers, who, well can claim just about any darn thing that they want. No regulatory oversight exists for an individual's "opinion" about what is healthful (or harmful) for dogs to eat, what ingredients are desirable and healthful and which are (often arbitrarily) targeted as being filler, allergy-inducing or even toxic. Here is an example. About a year ago, I was teaching a basic nutrition seminar to the staff at a small, family-owned and -operated pet food company located in Denmark. In addition to the production staff, also in attendance were retailers who sold the company's foods in pet supply stores and over the internet. One man and his wife operated an online pet supply store that sold this company's foods. Just like all businesses today, the owner had a very active presence on Facebook and other social media sites and conducted frequent social media promotion campaigns. He was quite creative and resourceful and organized numerous contests and photo sharing opportunities for his customers, resulting in a site that was generally received very positively. At one point in our discussions

189

about nutrition, he raised his hand and asked for some advice about how best to respond to emails that espoused highly inflammatory and negative views about the company's foods or about particular ingredients, products or feeding philosophies. He said that he always replied politely and provided literature, but more often than not the sender was not interested in a discussion about nutrition and feeding, but rather was looking for a new platform to broadcast his or her views about nutrition and pet food. Moreover, as can happen in social media, these "conversations" occasionally degenerated into a flame-fest during which other (often anonymous) writers piled on and escalated the accusations further. He was understandably very frustrated by these experiences and was sincerely looking for a better way to engage with people who had strong views about nutrition and specifically about commercial pet foods. His question led to a spirited discussion about how to present evidence-based science on social media sites. The statement that I remember most from the conversation is him saying in exasperation [I paraphrase]: "They can say anything that they want at all and make any outrageous claims about our foods that they like and people just pile on…we, on the other hand, have to adhere to [EU] regulations and laws, and at least try to stay within the science of nutrition, yet people listen and believe their claims, without any proof at all being presented to them."

So, is his frustration warranted? I think, in all fairness, he has a valid point. There are many examples of public opinion swaying public behavior without having any scientific evidence to back up the original claims. Because food is an emotional issue for owners (remember: Food is love with our dogs), opinions about ingredients and foods can quickly become polarized, even in the face of no supporting scientific evidence. People begin to consider some ingredients to be "bad" and others "good", based only upon something that they read in Jane Smith's blog or because Joe next door who happens to know a lot about dogs told them so. The current grain-free trend in dog foods is a great example of this polarization of views and opinions. Let's look at that issue as an example.

First, I think most would all agree that humans can and do feed themselves with a variety of different feeding philosophies. We can be meat-eaters, vegetarians, vegans, gluten-free and also can enjoy foods from a wide range of ethnic food choices and cooking/taste preferences, while still managing to support health and remain well-nourished. So too is it for our dogs. Dogs can be fed a grain-free food and be healthy, happy and well fed. They can also be fed balanced diets that are vegetarian, gluten-free, corn-free, by-product-free or GMO-free and can be fed foods that are formulated to contain organic ingredients, contain cooked starches such as potato, rice, tapioca and even (gasp!) wheat and corn, or are made only from raw ingredients or are fed on a rotation basis. All of these approaches, if formulated to provide the correct amounts of all of the essential nutrients and energy, can (and do) support health and well-being in our dogs.

That said, *if* you as an owner prefer to feed grain-free or raw or dehydrated or home-made or organic, *and* you select a balanced diet for your dog, this is all fine and good and we should have happy owners and dogs. However, and this is a BIG however, what you cannot and should not do is to make unsupported claims about your particular feeding preference if those claims have not been substantiated by *scientific* evidence. And the truth of the matter regarding grain-free or gluten-free dog foods is that to date there is no published scientific evidence demonstrating that healthy dogs (i.e., dogs who do not have diagnosed gluten-induced enteropathy or demonstrated allergies to wheat) are healthier when fed a gluten-free diet than when fed a food that contains wheat. Nor are they less likely to gain weight, have allergies, get cancer or fart less often than dogs fed other foods. (Likewise, as we discussed in Chapter 7, there is no evidence that feeding raw diets has health and wellness benefits such as improved immune status, more efficient digestion and healthier skin/coat.) If we as owners expect that the claims that pet food companies make about their foods, ingredients and nutrients be supported by actual scientific research (and really, we should demand it), then the standards for the claims made by bloggers, self-appointed nutrition experts and Joe next door who happens to know a lot about dogs should be the same. 'Nuff said. Bottom line: If you do not have the scientific (not anecdotal) evidence to support a claim about a food or feeding philosophy, you should not be making it.

Give me some of that magic dog food, please

The next time that you go to your local pet supply store to purchase food for your dog or dogs, take a few moments to read and compare the claims on a variety of different brands of dog food. I think that you will notice two things. The first is that many of the claims on different brands are identical, making it impossible to differentiate one from another in any meaningful way. The most popular and frequently seen claims of today are those that promote a food's natural properties (labels are overrun with these), the *inclusion* of antioxidant nutrients, vitamins or minerals (not helpful, they all should have these) and the *exclusion* of corn, wheat, grains, gluten or artificial preservatives. By now, you should know why these claims are either not helpful at all or of somewhat limited aid in your selection process. The second thing that you will notice is the proliferation of health-related claims on foods (just as you should notice these with many human foods). Commercially available dog foods not *only* make that hefty claim of providing complete and balanced nutrition for your dog's stage of life (or even for all of his stages of life), they also may purport to do the following: boost your dog's immune system, keep his joints healthy and mobile, slow the signs of aging, support his cognitive function, keep his waistline trim, make him smarter (if he is a puppy) and promote efficient digestion.

Do such claims lead dog owners to expect too much from their dog food? Has this explosion of label claims led to a problem that is analogous to what we witness with the proliferation of the "drug culture" of today? Rather than the "take a pill" solution to all of life's problems, this is the "feed this food" solution to all of a dog's current or potential health problems. Quick, easy, takes no extra work or study other than buying the food and feeding it. Although certainly some of these claims have (some) science behind them, does this explosion in claims and the apparent quest for the holy grail of nutritional health lead to unrealistic expectations of what a food can do for our dogs?

We saw that the regulatory decisions that separate a food claim from a drug claim can turn on a single word or phrase. And certainly, the claims that we are seeing on dog food labels do not make overt assertions to cure illness or prevent disease. However, might not dog owners interpret at least some of these claims in this way? And if they do, can this lead to actions and decisions that are not in the dog's best interest? For example, might the claim "supports your dog's immune system" be interpreted to mean that the food will help to prevent infectious disease and can take the place of an effective (and tested) vaccination program? End result: owner does not vaccinate. Similarly, could the claim that a food "promotes intestinal health" entice an owner of a dog who is showing signs of giardia or inflammatory bowel disease to try the food, rather than taking the dog to his veterinarian for needed care? Perhaps most likely is the belief that simply switching to a food that carries the *"less active"* claim will resolve a dog's weight problem, without the more labor intensive but important components of increasing daily exercise and carefully monitoring portion size.

Despite purported noble intentions, I propose that the excessive use of health-related claims on dog food labels may in fact mislead us into expecting too much from dog foods. As much as the love that I have for my dogs makes me wish to believe it, the truth is that the food that I feed to my dog will not cure a cancer, prevent infectious disease, eliminate hip dysplasia, make a dog young again or turn my dog into a more competitive agility dog. There are multiple factors that affect each individual dog's health, energy level and well-being. These include genetics, maternal care, early development, living situation, training experiences, exposure to infectious agents and toxins, exercise and diet. Of all of these factors, diet is the single one over which we as owners exert total and complete control and that is quite easy for us to modify. As a result, we are primed to accept dramatic health claims for diet that provide a simple and easy answer. Certainly feeding a healthful diet can reduce my dog's risk for some health disorders, and can (and should) help to keep him healthy and happy. But, really, much as I would like it to, I cannot expect the food that I select for him to be the solution to all that might befall him during his life. We must avoid the temptation to believe claims that are not supported by science. Sorry folks, there is no magic food. However, there are smart choices. And these you can definitely learn to make for your dog.

11

Who's Keeping Our Dog Food Safe?

It's simple. The food that we feed to our dogs should nourish them. Most of us understand this to mean that the food will supply all of the energy and essential nutrients that our dogs need each day in a volume of food that is both tasty (palatable) and filling (satiating). We also expect a nourishing food to support our dog's health, wellness and vitality. And, naturally, in order to nourish our dogs, the food that we choose to feed to our dogs must be *safe*, meaning that it will not cause nutrient deficiencies, toxicities or imbalances, that it is free of microbial or fungal contaminants, and that it has not been adulterated with non-food components (either deliberately or unintentionally). It is to this final set of criteria—safety—that we now turn.

When I started graduate school in companion animal nutrition, typical discussions of "food safety" centered on the nutritional attributes of commercially produced foods. Because most foods were being formulated to meet AAFCO protocols for the "complete and balanced" claim, nutritionists were concerned with ensuring that the foods that they formulated were nutritionally complete and did not lead to nutrient deficiencies or toxicities. While worries of microbial or fungal contamination were certainly present, such concerns were not predominant, as they often are today. Moreover, at that time, microbial contamination or intentional tampering with ingredients was not the first thing that pet owners thought about when they were trying to choose a healthful food for their dog.

Sadly, this is not the world that we live in today. If you discuss dog food with any dog professional or committed dog owner, expect the subject of food safety to be part of that conversation. The most widespread concerns are microbial contamination (for example, salmonella), intentional adulteration (for example, melamine) and less frequently, fungal infestation (aflatoxin). Moreover, and not without cause, dog owners have less confidence in the pet food industry as a whole than even as recently as six years ago, prior to the unprecedented pet food recalls of 2007.

The extent of this sea change is illustrated by the results of a recently published survey. During the spring of 2013, the pet health website petMD queried pet owners regarding pet food safety. They reported that 86% of respondents said that the quality control measures used by pet food manufactures were very important to them. This is certainly not surprising, given the frequency with which pet food recalls occur today.

However, this high degree of concern was accompanied by a glaring disconnect—only *15 %* (about one in nine owners) of the same pool of participants said they knew or were able to determine whether or not a pet food manufacturer was complying with any type of quality control measure or set of regulations. So, while the assurance of food safety is highly important to dog owners, there exists no clear or obvious way for consumers to determine whether or not a company is actually producing a safe food (other than to trust them, of course—an approach that did not work very well in 2007). Similar to the situation with food quality measures such as diet digestibility, the industry agrees that food safety is important, yet provides consumers with no way to judge that safety when selecting a pet food. Dog folks are aware of this disconnect. The same survey reported that 82 % of participants believed that pet food manu-facturers are "not doing all they can to keep pet food free of salmonella and other contaminants."

The perception that pet food manufacturers are not trustworthy and that they are not doing enough to ensure that foods are safe is understandable, but is not com-pletely accurate. Pet food manufacturers are required to adhere to a set of quality control measures (we will look at these later), and also have the option of apply-ing for additional voluntary certifications that assess quality control and food safety. However—and this is vitally important for consumers—as AAFCO regulations stand today, manufacturers are not allowed to include any type of quality claims on their packages, and this includes quality control claims or certifications. This means that there is currently no simple way for a consumer to evaluate a manufacturer's quality control measures when comparing foods by their labels. Manufacturers can, however, make food safety claims and provide information about voluntary certifications on their websites and supporting materials. This is helpful, but is it enough?

What are the risks (who's recalling and why)?

Let's begin by asking why we are concerned about food safety in the first place. What are the major risks that dog owners need to consider when choosing foods? Following the unprecedented number of pet deaths and the breadth of brands affected during the pet food recall of 2007, many dog owners and professionals have developed a heightened sensitivity to pet food safety. For many, food safety is now a chief concern when selecting a food for their dog. For others, the recalls and other quality control concerns have led them to forego commercial products altogether. These changes should come as no surprise given that there has been rarely a month during which one or more brands of dog food have *not* been recalled. During the calendar year of 2011, 26 US pet food companies recalled 131 pet food products; during 2012, 24 compa-nies recalled 67 pet foods. During 2011, on average, a different company recalled five pet food brands every two weeks. For the public, these recalls have become a universal approach to monitoring pet food safety, although certainly an approach of the "closing the barn door after the horse has escaped" variety. Regardless, a look at recalls does provide information regarding what the risks actually are and how frequently they are occurring, hopefully with the outcome of leading to better preventive controls.

By far the most frequent cause of pet food recalls today is microbial contamination with *Salmonella spp.* Salmonella is a fecal bacteria that can contaminate a wide variety of foods, including raw meat and poultry, eggs, unpasteurized dairy products and commercially produced dog foods (both extruded and raw foods). Pet food contamination creates a risk for the pets who are ingesting the food and to humans who are handling the food and who live with dogs who may be excreting the bacteria in their feces. Contrary to the belief of some, dogs can and do get sick from salmonella infection. Although very few of the salmonella-induced pet food recalls have been associated with illness in either dogs or humans, especially when compared with the total number of recalls issued within a given year, illness is a definite risk. For example, an outbreak of salmonellosis in the summer of 2012 caused by a strain of salmonella called *Salmonella infantis* sickened almost 50 people in 20 states and Canada and was eventually traced back to dry dog food produced by the Diamond Pet Food plant in Gaston, South Carolina. Both Diamond-owned brands and brands that the company co-packed (manufactured for other companies), such as Kirkland, Canidae and Chicken Soup for the Dog Lover's Soul, were affected. Additionally, although not confirmed as being connected to the infected foods, six dogs and two cats reportedly became ill and died after eating the tainted food. To date, this is the only confirmed case in which infection to humans or dogs could be traced directly back to contaminated pet food, although this route of infection has been suspected in several other recalls. This means that the vast majority of recalls for salmonella are based entirely upon detecting the presence of *salmonella* during quality control checks and not, as is commonly believed, as a result of illness. While dogs (and people) certainly could become ill in many of these cases, a direct cause-effect link is not commonly established. In the 2012 Diamond recall, subsequent investigations of the Diamond plant identified numerous health and sanitation violations that included production line infractions, inadequate ingredient screening, employee hygiene violations and the use of damaged and inadequately cleaned equipment.

In recent years (following the melamine recalls of 2007), we have seen a dramatic increase in the number of salmonella-induced pet food recalls. This has most likely occurred because of increased vigilance of both pet food manufacturers and the federal government (FDA), leading to increased surveillance and reporting. And, without question, the establishment of the early detection reporting system by the FDA, called the Reportable Food Registry, which requires immediate reporting of safety problems with human and pet foods has enhanced detection. (Prior to the use of this system, the detection of *salmonella* relied principally upon plant inspections to identify problems.) While the increase in recalls has further eroded public confidence in the pet food industry, they also provide a strong incentive for companies to correct problems and improve their quality control measures to avoid repeated problems and the enormous loss of profit and consumer trust that occurs with a recall.

It seems rather odd to many of us that extruded pet foods, which are cooked at a high temperature, should be so susceptible to microbial contamination. Although these foods typically include a variety of ingredients that may be contaminated prior to production, the cooking process is expected to kill any contaminating microbes. However, following extrusion, all dry dog foods are "enrobed" or coated with a palatant (taste enhancer) and this process is typically not conducted in a sterile environment. Post-production contamination of dry dog foods may also occur when proper pre- and post-production segregation of ingredients and the finished product are not followed, when there is inadequate staff training or when equipment is not properly maintained, as we saw with the Diamond recall. If contamination occurs during the enrobing, handling or packaging process, *salmonella* organisms will be present in the finished food, where they can survive for many months.

A second type of contamination that can affect processed foods, most specifically dry, extruded foods that contain plant ingredients, is aflatoxin. Aflatoxin is a toxin produced by the mold *Aflatoxin flavis* that has varying degrees of toxicity to mammals and birds. Dogs and cats are highly sensitive to aflatoxin. The consumption of a pet food that contains aflatoxin leads to liver failure within days, which is often irreversible and fatal. The mold that produces aflatoxin grows in a variety of plants, including peanut, cottonseed and corn. Crops are at increased risk for aflatoxin contamination following seasons in which plants are highly stressed by dry or excessively hot conditions or when grains are stored for long periods prior to shipment. For example, the very hot and dry summer of 2012 in the Midwest led to increased aflatoxin contamination in that summer's corn crop. Some of this corn found its way into pet foods, leading to a recall of several brands of Hy-Vee dog food in February of 2013. Luckily, no pet illnesses were reported in that recall. Once aflatoxin is present in an ingredient, it is not destroyed by processing or heat treatment and persists following pet food extrusion and packaging. Therefore, pre-production testing of all susceptible ingredients is essential to keep pet foods free of aflatoxin.

Although not as common as microbial contamination, nutrient imbalances can also be the underlying cause of a pet food recall. These are most often the result of a mistake in the food's formulation or a problem with one or more ingredients, which today usually means a problem with the ingredient supply chain or ingredient sourcing. Two recent examples with cat foods were Nutro's 2009 recall of several brands of cat food for excessively high levels of zinc, presumably caused by a formulation error, and in the spring of 2013, another Diamond recall, this time for low levels of the B-vitamin thiamine in several cat food brands. Generally speaking, nutrient imbalances are relatively rare in commercial foods today. However, they can be a safety risk in improperly formulated homemade diets or when a single food item is fed in excess.

A final important risk to pet food safety, and one that is perhaps most frightening of all, is intentional adulteration. This possibility first came to public attention during the 2007 pet food recalls, when a Chinese supplier sold wheat flour that was adulterated with two nitrogen-containing compounds (melamine and cyanuric acid) to make the product appear to be a more expensive ingredient, wheat gluten. The Chinese company sold the contaminated ingredient to an import/export company in Arizona called ChemNutra, which in turn resold it to the pet food manufacturer, Menu Foods. Menu Foods, as the largest co-packer of canned foods in the United States and Canada, included the ingredient in many of its contracted brands. The combination of melamine and cyanuric acid is highly toxic to cats and dogs, causing kidney disease that was fatal in many cases. Ultimately, more than 150 brands of pet food representing more than 5300 different products were involved and subsequently recalled, and it is estimated that several thousand dogs and cats died (accurate records of pet deaths are not recorded, as they are with human deaths, so estimates vary). This massive and unprecedented recall severely eroded public confidence in commercial pet foods (a loss of confidence that has not recovered to this day), and also exposed the degree to which pet food manufacturing and ingredient procurement were centralized, consolidated and inadequately regulated in the United States. Supply chains for many pet food ingredients were (and continue to be) expansive, complex and, in many cases, completely hidden from consumer scrutiny. Foreign suppliers, many in Asia, source and combine products from numerous small farms or manufacturers whose identities are lost as the ingredients are comingled, sold, consolidated and resold. Therefore, while it does not always come immediately to mind for consumers, the source of ingredients is important not only for reasons of ingredient quality but also for pet food safety.

The melamine recalls led to over 12,000 consumer complaints to the FDA about commercial pet foods during 2007. By comparison, the FDA typically received less than 200 pet food-related complaints per year (prior to 2007). As a direct result of the melamine-tainted food recalls, the Food and Drug Administration Amendments Act (FDAAA) was passed. This legislation required the establishment of a Pet Food Early Warning Surveillance System. Upon implementation, this system increased the FDA's ability to identify problems with contaminated foods quickly and has helped to enhance their degree of oversight of the pet food industry. Although not without its problems, this change has been a positive one for dogs and owners. Let's look at a few of the details of this act and the two primary agencies that currently regulate pet food safety in the United States.

FDA and AAFCO: their roles in pet food safety

In the US, pet food safety is regulated at two levels: federal and state. The two most important organizations involved are the Food and Drug Administration's Center for Veterinary Medicine (CVM) and the Association of American Feed Control Officials (AAFCO).

FDA's Center for Veterinary Medicine (CVM)

Federal regulations that impact dog foods are enforced by the Food and Drug Administration's (FDA) Center for Veterinary Medicine (CVM). These regulations include rules for the proper identification of foods, quantity statements and inclusion of the manufacturer's address and proper listing of ingredients on the label of all commercial pet foods. As we discussed in Chapter 10, the CVM is also intimately involved in determining (and acting upon) whether or not a pet food label claim is considered to be a drug claim, which is expressly prohibited. However, the FDA itself does *not* have authority over ingredient definitions or nutritional standards for pet foods and therefore typically defers to AAFCO in these areas. Most importantly for pet food safety, is that FDA that is directly responsible for pet food recalls and for tracking reported problems with or concerns about pet food safety.

Following the 2007 recalls, the passage of two federal laws helped to strengthen FDA oversight of pet foods. First, the FDAAA, as I mentioned earlier, required the FDA to establish a specific pet food section within their Reportable Food Registry, which was previously used only for human foods. This became active in 2009 and requires that pet food companies electronically report all incidences of contamination or adulteration when there is a reasonable possibility of adverse consequences to animal or human health. They are required by law to make these reports within 24 hours of discovery of the problem. This system receives reports only from the pet food industry (i.e., manufacturers) and from federal and state feed control officials and is not accessible to pet owners or veterinarians. However, in addition, the FDAAA also required the establishment of an early warning surveillance system that is specifically for pet owners (consumers) and veterinarians. Consumer complaints are (and always have been) the FDA's primary surveillance tools for food and drug safety. An owner or veterinarian may either call the FDA directly and speak with a consumer complaint coordinator or can report a problem electronically via the agency's online Safety Reporting Portal (SRP) (www.safetyreporting.hhs.gov.) According to the FDA, the website acts as a direct line of communication between consumers and the FDA, allowing the public to pass information and concerns directly to the agency. And, it appears to be working. Shortly after the portal's electronic door opened in May of 2010, two practicing veterinarians identified problems occurring with a client's cats who were all consuming a single brand of canned food. They reported the potential link between the cats' illness and the food using the Safety Reporting Portal, which led to the CVM contacting the manufacturer. The manufacturer identified the problem to be low thiamine levels in several food batches and promptly launched a product recall. An important strength of this system is its accessibility to the general public and to pet professionals such as veterinarians. Figure 11.1 provides instructions and an abbreviated list of needed information to have available when reporting suspected food safety problems to the FDA's SRP.

In addition, the passage of the Food Safety and Modernization Act (FSMA) in 2010 enhanced FDA (via CVM) authority over pet food safety matters. One of the most important provisions of this act, though yet to be implemented, is to allow the FDA more proactive (rather than reactive) oversight of pet food safety. Specifically, prior to FSMA, the FDA had no authority to force a pet food manufacturer to issue a product recall. Rather, they could "request" such an action, but had no regulatory power to compel the company to comply. A major (and needed) change established with the passage of the FSMA was to increase the FDA's recall authority. However, because this change has yet to be implemented its actual regulatory strength is yet to be demonstrated.

Contact	**FDA (Phone):** Call your state's FDA Consumer Complaint Coordinator
	FDA (Online): Report electronically via the FDA Safety Reporting Portal (www.safetyreporting.hhs.gov)
	Pet food company: Toll-free telephone number on product label or via company website
	State Feed Control Official: AAFCO directory (www.aafco.org)
Product information	Name of food and description (from label)
	Lot number, UPC Code, Net Weight
	Purchase Date, Location and Store
	Description of food storage, preparation and handling
	Description of problem with food (if applicable): Examples include foul odor, off-color, leaking container, presence of foreign objects
Pet information	Species (dog, cat, etc.), age, breed, weight, reproductive status
	Health status: previous history, current or pre-existing conditions
	Diet history: quantity of suspected food ingested, other foods consumed
	Clinical signs (vomiting, diarrhea, lethargy, etc.)
	Veterinarian's contact information
	Medical records and/or results of tests (attachments can be included)
	Reason for suspecting food as the cause of symptoms/illness

Figure 11.1 Reporting a pet food complaint to the FDA. *

* Modified from FDA's *"How to Report a Pet Food Complaint."* For full list see: www.fda.gov/AnimalVeterinary/SafetyHealth/ReportaProblem/ucm182403.htm

Association of American Feed Control Officials (AAFCO)

The AAFCO is a bit of an odd duck, as organizations go. Contrary to the belief of some dog bloggers, AAFCO is not an industry trade group, nor is it a lobby group for pet food manufacturers. It is also not a governmental agency and it has no official or sanctioned regulatory powers. One might then ask, well, what the heck is it? As I said, AAFCO is a bit of a strange bird. It is a private organization that establishes non-binding guidelines for the production of all animal feeds, which includes pet foods. And a bit more weirdness: although not a government agency, only government officials can be members of AAFCO. These include state feed control officials (the state employees who monitor pet food labeling compliance in foods sold in their state, among other things), and some federal officials, notably members of the CVM. Industry and private groups can attend AAFCO meetings and contribute advice or information to task forces or working groups, but they are not voting members. These groups typically include representatives from pet food companies, professional groups and animal/pet advocacy organizations. Although industry representatives are not voting members, they do have influence within AAFCO through participating in tasks forces and advisory groups, and some critics argue that this influence may be excessive. However, it is difficult to separate the necessary academic training and expertise that is needed for this work from the pet food industry since most companion animal nutritionists either work directly for a pet food company or are in academia where all or most of their research funding comes from the industry.

What exactly does the phrase "non-binding guidelines" mean for pet food regulations? Well, a primary function of AAFCO is to attempt to both standardize and regulate the ingredients and nutritional content of pet foods. Each year they publish a manual called the "Official Publication" that includes current ingredient definitions, a set of nutrient standards and feeding protocols for proving (substantiating) foods' nutritional adequacy, and a set of pet food labeling rules. The AAFCO model regulations (called "model" because AAFCO cannot officially enforce them) are adopted (i.e., put into law) by individual states in the US. However, and this bears repeating: nothing that AAFCO recommends has the power of law *unless* it is adopted by individual state legislatures. In other words, it is up to the states to make the AAFCO *model* pet food regulations into *actual* regulations. Currently, about half of the states in the US have legislated the complete AAFCO model regulations. States that have not done this rely upon other states to "carry the regulatory burden" if you will, since pet food companies all formulate their foods to the highest level of standards (i.e., complete adoption of AAFCO model pet food regulations) to allow sale of their products across all state lines. This inconsistency among states leads to variability in the type of oversight and the degree vigilance in enforcement by state feed control officials.

So, how exactly does AAFCO influence pet food safety? When we think in terms of safety, AAFCO is most concerned with making sure that dog foods are *nutritionally* safe. Foods are certified to provide dogs with "complete and balanced" nutrition if they either meet AAFCO nutrient standards (one set for growth/reproduction and a second set for adult maintenance) or if they pass a set of feeding trial protocols established by AAFCO. Feeding trials have historically been held up by the industry as the "Gold Standard" for substantiating nutrient content. However, these have been criticized because they are generally short in length (ten weeks to six months, depending on the claim), include a relatively small number of animals and require a rather short list of rudimentary measures of health. Still, such protocols do require feeding the food to dogs (which the analysis method does not), and do require that those dogs remain healthy. While there are shortcomings to these protocols, the AAFCO standards at least ensure a minimum level of nutritional adequacy, and are required for foods that carry the ubiquitous "complete and balanced" claim. In addition, AAFCO provides a set of model Good Manufacturing Practice (GMP) regulations that states are encouraged to adopt (but remember they are not required to adopt AAFCO model regulations). These GMPs include staff training, manufacturing equipment care and maintenance, appropriate handling and storing of ingredients, proper packaging and labeling practices, proper storage, inspection and testing of finished products and record keeping that are specifically designed for the pet food industry.

A few other agencies

While the FDA and AAFCO are the most important regulatory players, a few other governmental agencies also play a role in pet food regulation and safety. The United States Department of Agriculture (USDA) is responsible for ensuring that pet foods are clearly labeled as "pet food" and that slaughter house ingredients that are not intended for human consumption (oddly, called "inedible") do not end up in the human food supply. The USDA is also the agency that inspects and regulates all research facilities, issuing certification for proper animal housing, handling and care. The National Research Council (NRC) is a private, nonprofit organization that collects, evaluates and summaries research in a variety of fields, including animal nutrition. In the pet food industry, the NRC has no authorized regulatory power. However, its animal nutrition committee publishes recommendations for both dog and cat nutrient requirements. The most recent edition of this was published in 2006. Prior to the AAFCO nutrient profiles, the NRC recommendations were the standard that was used for pet food formulations. Today, these serve as a detailed resource for revisions of AAFCO guidelines and for nutritionists and pet food companies.

Pet food manufacturer's responsibility

The Federal Food, Drug and Cosmetic Act (FFDCA) is a federal law that requires pet food manufacturers, like human food manufacturers, to produce safe foods. These responsibilities include using effective and sanitary food processing methods, demonstrating reliable and proven preventive measures against contamination at all points during production, use of proper food handling and storage techniques, monitoring for pathogens and proper record keeping practices. Prior to 2007, the act encouraged (but did not require) pet food manufacturers to have a valid Hazard Analysis and Critical Control Points (HACCP) program in place and also recommended that pet owners only purchase foods from pet food manufacturers that had an HAACP program. However, once again, this recommendation to owners was mere tilting at windmills, seeing that it was not communicated to owners in any meaningful way and pet foods were not identified regarding this criterion.

Following the 2007 melamine recalls, several federal regulatory changes were added to existing requirements with the intent of strengthening oversight and closing loopholes. The US Congress passed the 2007 FDA Amendments Act (FDAAA) to improve governmental and manufacturing responsiveness to the contamination of pet foods and other products. As we have discussed, the FDAAA requires manufacturers to report incidents of possible contamination to the FDA within 24 hours and to investigate the cause and report their findings. Today, if contamination or adulteration of a pet food is confirmed, the food is recalled. This is a completely new regulation, and an important one, since prior to this change manufacturers were not compelled to report incidents nor to issue recalls. If the contamination is confirmed, the pet food must be recalled. Although recall initiation is usually voluntary by the manufacturer at the request of the FDA, the FDA can secure a court order to mandate a recall if the manufacturer is reluctant. However, this has rarely been needed because pet food companies are well aware of the bad press that such an order would cause. Still, it is important to emphasize that product recalls are always *reactive*, not *proactive* and by definition only occur after a product is on the shelves, being sold to owners and fed to pets. Clearly, this is not the best way to keep our dogs safe. and a sounder approach is to concentrate on ways to prevent recalls in the first place.

The 2011 Food Safety Modernization Act (FSMA) attempts to be proactive by requiring pet food manufacturers to have documented food safety protocols. Although many pet food producers already had food quality and safety programs in place that were based on standard Hazard Analysis and Critical Control Points (HACCP) programs, the new law makes this an enforceable *requirement*, rather than a voluntary practice. An HACCP protocol covers all aspects of the food manufacturing process, from the acquisition and handling of raw ingredients, through food processing, packaging and distribution. It also identifies specific points of risk in the manufacturing process and outlines exact plans for addressing risk management and monitoring for the presence of contamination or adulteration.

The FSMA also includes new regulations for the pet food ingredient supply chain and strengthens FDA oversight over foreign ingredients. This is extremely important given the increased dependency upon foreign sources of ingredients that was observed leading up to the 2007 melamine recall. Although not yet implemented (which is a bit worrisome), FSMA includes a requirement that ingredient and food importers verify that all foreign suppliers have produced their ingredients and foods to the same standards that are required of domestic producers. (Kind of shocking that this was not a requirement previously, don't you agree?) Essentially, importers must demonstrate that all imported food and ingredients were produced under the same or equivalent conditions mandated in the Food, Drug and Cosmetic Act, including the new provisions for preventive controls established by the FSMA. Additionally, third-party (independent) verification of these measures will be required. Not surprisingly, many companies are balking at these new requirements and lobbying to weaken them. We will see what actually transpires once guidelines are published and this requirement is implemented by the FDA. As it stands today, some of the more stringent FSMA requirements for foreign suppliers include third-party monitoring of shipment records and points of transfer, annual on-site inspections, verifying hazard analysis and risk-based preventive control plans and periodically sampling and testing shipments.

Third-party certifications
In addition to the new requirements for documented food safety protocols, some pet food companies are obtaining additional (and voluntary) third-party certifications for their business, manufacturing and food handling processes. Third-party certification is the Gold Standard for food safety, and these efforts should be commended (and can be used when you are making food selection decisions for your dog). One of the best known of these standards is ISO certification. ISO, the International Organization for Standardization (www.iso.org), is a global developer of voluntary standards that provide specifications for good business practice, safe and efficient manufacturing process, and reliable and repeatable record keeping for a wide range of industries, including human and pet foods. Two types of ISO certification are applicable to pet

food manufacturing. The ISO 9000 family of certifications is a quality management certification that provides guidance for companies to ensure that their products and services consistently meet governmental and professional standards for producing safe and reliable products. For pet foods, the ISO 9001:2000 certification also focuses on reducing potential risks for food contamination and poisoning. The ISO 22000 family of standards specifically addresses food safety management by identifying and controlling areas of food safety risk through all phases of production, including ingredient traceability and integrity. Therefore, pet food production at plants carrying ISO 9000 or ISO 22000 certifications will have additional safety layers that specifically address contamination with salmonella and other microbial contaminants. This of course does not mean that all risks for contamination are eliminated, but that additional safety nets are in effect at these factories. Last, another ISO certification that may be attained by pet food companies and that may be important to some dog folks is the ISO 14000, which addresses environmentally friendly and sustainable manufacturing practices. Several pet food manufacturers have attained one or more of these ISO certifications: examples include Natura (now owned by P&G), Royal Canin (owned by Mars) and Aller Petfood (a family-owned, Danish pet food manufacturer). Check company and brand websites, as companies that attain one or more ISO certifications will naturally be stating this when asked about their food safety measures.

The American Feed Industry Association (AFIA, www.afia.org) has also developed a voluntary third-party auditing program for manufacturers of pet foods and ingredients. These are called, respectively, the Pet Food Manufacturing Facility Certification Program and the Pet Food Ingredient Facility Certification Program. These two AFIA programs are part of AFIA's domestic Safe Feed/Safe Food Certification Program and are designed to meet or exceed the new pet food requirements of the Food Safety Modernization Act. While not a guarantee of pet food safety, the AFIA programs evaluate a manufacturer's product safety programs and include on-site audits. Several AFIA certifications have been issued already, with more companies applying (Figure 11.2).

Pet food facility	Locations
Hampshire Pet Products	Joplin, Missouri
International Protein Colloids, Inc.	Venus, Texas
The Nutro Company	Kansas City, Missouri
The Nutro Company	Victorville, California
The Nutro Company	Lebanon, Tennessee
Procter and Gamble	Aurora, Nebraska
3D Corporate Solutions, LLC	Joplin, Missouri

Figure 11.2 AFIA certified pet food facilities (summer 2013). *

* Visit AFIA's Safe Feed/Safe Food Program for updates: www.safefeedsafefood.org

Last, the American Institute of Baking (AIB) which is now known as AIB International (www.aibonline.org) also provides independent auditing and certification to food manufacturers. The extensive AIB Certificate of Achievement program includes annual audits of the facility's food safety program, HACCP protocols, management and operation methods, pest control programs, buildings and equipment maintenance, and cleaning practices. Each category is individually scored, ranked and tallied, resulting in an overall AIB score and rating for the company. Traditionally, AIB certification was provided only to producers of human foods, but in recent years several pet food and pet food ingredient companies have applied for and passed AIB certification. AIB certification also includes rigorous (and unscheduled) inspections of food production facilities. Examples of pet food manufacturers that have passed AIB certification (at time of publication) are listed in Figure 11.3. One issue to note with these listings is that co-packers of pet foods can (and do) apply for and acquire third-party food safety certifications. An example is C.J. Pet Foods, a co-packer that manufactures a wide variety of different brands of food. So, if your food is co-manufactured, it may be helpful to find out who the co-packer is and to inquire about their safety record and certifications.

Pet food manufacturer	Plant location
C.J. Pet Foods	Bern, Kansas & Pawnee City, Nebraska
Omega Fields	Newton, Wisconsin
Precise Pet Products	Nacogdoches, Texas
Natura (P&G)	Fremont, Nebraska
Trouw Nutrition (ingredients)	Highland, Illinois

Figure 11.3 American Institute of Baking Certified Pet Food Manufacturers.

The dog owner's role

Is there a role for dog owners in pet food safety, as the purchasers of these products? After all, is it not a reasonable expectation that commercially prepared dog foods are safe to feed to our dogs? Is it really the responsibility of dog owners to police the pet food industry? I think most would agree that it should not be our responsibility, but rather that it is the obligation of the industry to demonstrate both transparency and adequate regulation for ingredient sourcing, manufacturing practices (including the use of co-packing) and safety protocols. However, given the catastrophe of 2007 and subsequent (and continuing) repeated recalls for *salmonella* contamination in the succeeding years, it seems that trusting in current regulations and in the companies themselves is simply not enough. Just as we have a right to demand the production and sale of safe food for humans, so too should we demand this for our dogs. As critical consumers, when we consider dog food safety, there are several actions that we can take when selecting foods.

First, consider a company's track record. If a pet food manufacturer has recalled multiple brands of food on repeated occasions, it should immediately raise a red flag. But how does one find this information? Lucky for dog folks today, there are several reliable sources to obtain current and past pet food recall information. The first is the FDA Recall and Withdrawal website (www.fda.gov/animalveterinary/safetyhealth/recallswithdrawals). This website reports recalls (voluntary or under the directive of the FDA) of all animal feeds, not just pet food. It lists these in chronological order, with the most recent recorded first. Another online source that uses FDA-generated information to provide a recall list for pet foods and treats is dentist Mike Sagman's popular "Dog Food Advisor" site (www.dogfoodadvisor.com/). In addition to keeping an updated list of recalls, the site also provides automatic notifications to interested owners, which is very helpful. When you are comparing foods or considering a new brand, take a quick visit to either of these sites and peruse the list to find out if the brand, the company that owns the brand or the co-manufacturer (if there is one) of the brand has issued product recalls within the last year. If you see a recall, investigate a bit further to discover what type of problem occurred and if repeat or multiple violations are present. While a single recall that occurred over a span of several years does not necessarily signify that the company is not up to snuff, multiple recalls that involve more than one brand or that are caused by a variety of manufacturing violations should definitely send up a red flag.

A second action that all dog owners should take is to always report suspected problems with foods. As we discussed previously in this chapter, the FDA's Safety Reporting Portal includes a specific section that enables pet owners to report problems or concerns about pet foods (www.safetyreporting.hhs.gov). It goes without saying that if you suspect that a food is causing a problem for your dog, you should immediately stop feeding the food and seek veterinary care. Reporting the problem to the FDA's site is also important, as they cannot act upon problems that they do not know about.

Using the FDA recall list and reporting suspect problems are both *reactive* actions rather than *proactive*, and are helpful only in identifying potentially harmful brands of food rather than providing you with a way to identify brands that are more likely to be safe. A proactive measure that owners can use to select brands that are safe is to look for third-party food safety certifications. Remember, these will be listed and discussed on company websites because currently pet food packages are not allowed to carry such claims. If you do not find any information about food safety on the brand's website, or if the information is incomplete, send an email to the company and request this information. The more that pet food companies hear from consumers who are concerned about food safety, the more likely they are to consider the value of attaining voluntary and third-party quality control certifications.

Second, knowing where all of a product's ingredients were sourced (i.e., originated) and the location of the food's manufacturing plant are essential when considering pet food safety today. The two countries that supply the majority of foreign-sourced pet food ingredients and pet products are China and Thailand. Companies have turned to overseas markets for ingredients and even for finished products because both the cost of ingredients and the costs of production are significantly cheaper when produced overseas than when produced in the United States. This "bargain" comes at a very expensive price—namely, a loss of security due to lax or non-existent (or easily circumvented) safety regulations in foreign countries. Selecting pet foods that include only domestic ingredients or that exclude all ingredients that originated outside of the United States is not only a safety measure for your dog—it also sends a message to pet food manufacturers that owners are paying attention to where the ingredients in their dogs' foods are coming from. Again, if this information is not provided on the brand's website, be a critical consumer and send an email requesting this information. While the new FSMA standards should eventually require that these countries meet US safety standards, these requirements are not yet in place and the details of implementation are not yet known. As a result, many owners choose to actively avoid foods, treats and toys that are produced overseas.

Last but not least, in my opinion, it is time to demand a higher degree of transparency from the pet food industry, all around. As dog owners and consumers, we deserve to know where ingredients come from, what those ingredients are made from (and how they are handled, processed and regulated), and where and by what company the food is produced and kept safe. And, the most expedient way for pet food manufacturers to communicate this information to their consumers is via the pet food label (package). Some pet food companies do include ingredient source information, production location and some (rather vague) ingredient quality information on their packaging materials. However, this information is voluntary and is not required. Improved regulations that would include certificates of quality (food safety) control, ingredient source (and usable measures of quality) and identification of the food's manufacturer (by name, not just the location of the distributor) would go a long way towards enhancing consumer confidence in pet foods, improving food safety and providing dog owners with information that actually aids in the selection process.

Dog food logic—seek choices that are *really* choices

While shopping this past weekend, I decided to revisit my breakfast cereal choice. In our local (national chain) supermarket, an entire aisle is devoted to breakfast cereals. I attempted to count them. I lost count (and patience) when I approached *150 different brands*. There were more than 30 brands and varieties of oatmeal alone. I spent a few more minutes reading labels of brands that were similar (i.e., almost identical) to my own favored cereal. Again, I abandoned this effort, grabbed a new box of my favorite, tossed it into the cart and finished my shopping. When I returned home, I made a bowl of cereal (I still do like it a lot) and sat down at the computer to conduct a bit more research. I learned that American consumers may choose among more than 350 brands/varieties of breakfast cereal (should one choose to spend his or her time in this way). Moreover, three companies, Kellogg's, General Mills and Post, produce the vast majority of these brands, continually competing with each other (and with themselves) for additional shelf space, consumer loyalty and profit.

The parallels to the pet food industry are clear. We have a lot of options when it comes to choosing a food for our dogs—too much choice actually. And although we are exposed to a seemingly countless number of brands and varieties, the market is dominated by five big corporations: Mars, Nestle-Purina, P&G, Colgate-Palmolive (Hills) and Del Monte. However, there is one very important difference between my having too much choice with my breakfast cereal and the same dilemma with selecting food for my dogs. When selecting a dog food, I am choosing a food that is designed (and heavily promoted) as the sole provider of all of the essential nutrients and calories that my dog needs in a given day. Moreover, this food is meant to sustain him and maintain his health when fed over the long term, for months and years of his life. Not to put too fine a point on it, but that requirement lends a lot more responsibility to choosing a good dog food than it does when choosing a breakfast cereal, which is just one of many food items that I consume in a given day or week to sustain my own health and vitality.

This is why dog food selection is so difficult and so important for our dogs. We must train ourselves to pay close attention to what is proven and known via science, and to ignore marketing ploys, unsupported health claims, and downright misleading statements, all of which may be made by pet food companies, by Joe next door who happens to know a lot about dogs, and by bloggers, dog food "experts" and other dog gurus who insist that they have all of the answers that you may need for your dog's nutritional health. Feeding is nurturing. Feeding is love. Providing nutritious food to our dogs is associated with rituals (remember the "dinner time song"?) and caretaking, and is bound up with all of the good things in life that we share with our dogs. Nutrition, however, is also science. And science, when it works as it should, provides us with a testable method for determining what nutrients our dogs need during their lives and which foods are capable (or incapable) of providing them with a healthful diet. Science can provide information about the digestibility of ingredients, the usefulness of functional nutrients such as omega-3 fatty acids or glucosamine, the differences between a puppy's and an adult dog's nutrient needs, what may or may not be important when feeding my canine athlete, and how best to keep my dog healthy should I choose to feed him a homemade, raw, vegetarian or grain-free diet. Not only do we need science to choose a nutritionally sound food, we need it to sort the hype from the truth and to protect us from our own cognitive biases and decision-making errors. Unfortunately, as pet food regulations and labeling standards exist today, this is no easy task. Marketing, not science, prevails on pet food packaging, just as it does on my breakfast cereal or on your yogurt container. Similarly, emotion, not science, drives the sincere yet unsupported claims that individual pet owners, bloggers, and Joe next door who knows a lot about dogs make regarding feeding dogs a raw, grain-free, gluten-free, corn-free, wheat-free, whatever-new-comes-down-the-pike-free diet.

Follow the data and the evidence. Pay attention to information sources. Find and read the research studies. Avoid cognitive traps and logical fallacies. Make (and believe) only supportable claims. Read label claims (especially health claims) with a highly critical eye. Demand safe foods. Seek foods that include quality ingredients and be willing to pay for them. It's not necessarily going to be easy and may take some sleuthing, but this is about your dog's health, not about choosing a flavor of jam in a market that is overrun with jam brands and flavors. Take the time, choose well, sing your dinner time song, and nurture your dog.

Appendix 1

Evidence Pyramid Paper Abstracts

Paper 1: Faber TA, et al: "Galactoglucomannan oligosaccharide supplementation affects nutrient digestibility, fermentation end-product production and large bowel microbiota of the dog." *J Anim Sci,* 89:103-112, 2011.

Abstract: A galactoglucomannan oligosaccharide (GGMO) obtained from fiberboard production was evaluated as a dietary supplement for dogs. The GGMO substrate contained increased concentrations of oligosaccharides containing mannose, xylose and glucose, with the mannose component accounting for 35% of DM. Adult dogs assigned to a 6×6 Latin square design were fed 6 diets, each containing a different concentration of supplemental GGMO (0, 0.5, 1, 2, 4 and 8%) that replaced dietary cellulose. Total tract DM and OM apparent digestibilities increased ($P < 0.001$) linearly, whereas total tract CP apparent digestibility decreased ($P < 0.001$) linearly as dietary GGMO substrate concentration increased. Fecal concentrations of acetate, propionate and total short-chain fatty acids increased ($P \leq 0.001$) linearly, whereas butyrate concentration decreased ($P \leq 0.001$) linearly with increasing dietary concentrations of GGMO. Fecal pH decreased ($P \leq 0.001$) linearly as dietary GGMO substrate concentration increased, whereas fecal score increased quadratically ($P \leq 0.001$). Fecal phenol ($P \leq 0.05$) and indole ($P \leq 0.01$) concentrations decreased linearly with GGMO supplementation. Fecal biogenic amine concentrations were not different among treatments except for phenylethylamine, which decreased ($P < 0.001$) linearly as dietary GGMO substrate concentration increased. Fecal microbial concentrations of *Escherichia coli, Lactobacillus spp.* and *Clostridium perfringens* were not different among treatments. A quadratic increase ($P \leq 0.01$) was noted for *Bifidobacterium spp.* as dietary GGMO substrate concentration increased. The data suggest positive nutritional properties of supplemental GGMO when incorporated in a good-quality dog food.

Paper 2: Barry KA, et al: "Low-level fructan supplementation of dogs enhances nutrient digestion and modifies stool metabolite concentrations, but does not alter fecal microbiota populations." *J Anim Sci,* 87:3244-3252, 2009.

Abstract: Five adult dogs were utilized in a 5 × 5 Latin square design to determine the effects of fructan type and concentration on nutrient digestibility, stool metabolite concentrations and fecal microbiota. Five diets were evaluated that contained cellulose alone or with inulin or short-chain fructooligosaccharides (scFOS) each at 0.2 or 0.4% of the diet. Dogs were fed 175 g of their assigned diet twice daily. Chromic oxide served as a digestibility marker. Nutrient digestibility; ileal and fecal pH and ammonia concentrations; ileal IgA concentrations; and fecal short- and branched-chain fatty acid concentrations, microbiota and concentrations of phenol, indole and biogenic amines were measured. No differences were observed in ileal pH or ammonia or fecal concentrations of indole or valerate. Ileal DM, OM and CP digestibility coefficients; total tract DM and OM digestibility coefficients; and fecal concentrations of phenylethylamine increased linearly ($P < 0.05$), and fecal concentrations of phenol decreased linearly ($P < 0.05$) with inulin supplementation. Fecal concentrations of acetate, propionate and total short-chain fatty acids decreased quadratically ($P < 0.05$) with inulin supplementation. Ileal DM, OM and CP digestibility coefficients increased linearly ($P < 0.05$), and fecal phenol concentration decreased linearly ($P < 0.05$) with scFOS supplementation. Total tract DM and OM digestibility coefficients as well as fecal butyrate and isobutyrate concentrations increased quadratically ($P < 0.05$) with scFOS supplementation. Although a greater level of inclusion is needed to modify gut microbiota populations, low-level inclusion of inulin or scFOS is effective in modifying key nutritional outcomes in the dog.

Paper 3: Middlebos IS, et al: "Evaluation of fermentable oligosaccharides in diets fed to dogs in comparison to fiber standards." *J Anim Sci,* 85:3033-3044, 2007.

Abstract: Blends of fermentable oligosaccharides in combination with nonfermentable fiber, cellulose, were evaluated for their ability to serve as dietary fibers in dog foods. Using a 6 × 6 Latin square design, 6 diets were evaluated that contained either no supplemental fiber, beet pulp, cellulose, or blends of cellulose, fructooligosaccharides and yeast cell wall added at 2.5% of the diet. Six dogs were fed 175 g of their assigned diet twice daily. Chromic oxide served as a digestibility marker. Nutrient digestibility, fecal microbial populations, fermentative end products and immunological indices were measured. Total tract DM and OM digestibilities were lowest ($P < 0.05$) for the cellulose treatment. Crude protein digestibility was lower ($P < 0.05$) for the treatments containing carbohydrate blends. The cellulose treatment had the lowest ($P < 0.05$) concentration of bacteria, and all diets containing fermentable fiber had greater ($P < 0.05$) fecal bifidobacteria concentrations compared with the diets without supplemental fermentable fiber. *Lactobacilli* concentrations tended to be greater ($P < 0.08$) in treatments containing fermentable fiber compared with the cellulose treatment. Bifidobacteria and lactobacilli concentrations were similar for the beet pulp treatment compared with the fermentable oligosaccharide blends. Total fecal short-chain fatty acid concentration was greater for the beet pulp treatment (P < 0.05) compared with the control and cellulose treatments. The treatments containing fermentable fiber had greater (P < 0.05) fecal butyrate concentrations compared with cellulose and control treatments. Immune indices were not affected by treatment. Our results suggest that dog foods containing blends of fermentable and nonfermentable carbohydrates produce similar physiological results as dog food containing beet pulp as a fiber source. Therefore, blends of these carbohydrates could be useful substitutes for beet pulp in dog foods.

Paper 4: Flickinger E, et al: "Nutrient digestibilities, microbial populations and protein catabolites as affected by fructan supplementation of dog diets." *J Anim Sci,* 81:2008-2018, 2003.

Abstract: Fructans are fermentable carbohydrates and include short-chain fructooligosaccharides (scFOS), inulin and hydrolyzed inulin (oligofructose, OF). Two studies with dogs were designed to examine the effects of low concentrations of fructans on nutrient digestibilities, fecal microbial populations and endproducts of protein fermentation and fecal characteristics. In Exp. 1, 11 adult male beagles were fed corn-based, kibbled diets supplemented with or without OF to provide 1.9 ± 0.6 g/d. Dietary inclusion of OF decreased (P < 0.05) nutrient digestibilities, but did not affect fecal characteristics. Increasing OF concentration tended (P < 0.06) to linearly decrease fecal ammonia concentrations, but not those of branched-chain fatty acids (BCFA), amines, indole or phenols. Fecal concentrations of total short-chain fatty acids (SCFA) and butyrate tended to be higher in OF-supplemented dogs (P < 0.10), as was the ratio of bifidobacteria to total anaerobes (P = 0.15). In Exp. 2, adult female hounds were fed a meat-based kibbled diet and were assigned to four scFOS treatments (0, 1, 2 or 3 g/d) in a 4 × 4 Latin square design. Ileal nutrient digestibilities tended to increase (P < 0.15) with increasing concentrations of scFOS. On a DMI basis, fecal output tended to decrease linearly (P < 0.10) in response to increasing scFOS supplementation, whereas fecal score tended to exhibit a quadratic response (P = 0.12). In general, fecal concentrations of SCFA, BCFA, ammonia, phenols and indoles were not altered by supplemental scFOS. Supplementation of scFOS increased fecal concentrations of total aerobes (P < 0.05) and decreased concentrations of *Clostridium perfringens* (P < 0.05). From these data, it seems that low levels of supplemental fructans have divergent effects on nutrient digestibility and fermentative endproducts, but do not adversely affect nutrient digestibility or fecal characteristics and may improve colonic microbial ecology in dogs.

Paper 5: Sunvold G, et al: "In vitro fermentation of selected fiber sources by dog fecal inoculum and in vivo digestion and metabolism of fiber-supplemented diets." *J Anim Sci,* 73:1099-109, 1995.

Abstract: Two experiments were conducted to evaluate single sources and blends of dietary fiber in dog food. In Exp. 1, 14 fibrous substrates were fermented in vitro using dog feces as the source of inoculum. Organic matter disappearance was lowest (P < .05; < 10%) for Solka Floc and oat fiber and greatest (P < .05; > 80%) for fructooligosaccharides (FOS) and lactulose.

Solka Floc, oat fiber, gum karaya and xanthan gum produced the least (P < .05; < 1 mmol/g of substrate OM) total short-chain fatty acids (SCFA). Lactulose, citrus pectin and guar gum produced the greatest (P < .05; > 6.8 mmol/g of substrate OM) total SCFA. In Exp. 2, six diets were formulated based on results obtained in Exp. 1. Treatments included 1) beet pulp (BP), 2) Solka Floc (SF), 3) citrus pulp (CP), 4) stool blend (SB), 5) SCFA blend (SC) and 6) combination blend (CB). Digestibility of DM and total dietary fiber (TDF) was greatest (P < .05; 87.3 and 60.8%, respectively) for dogs consuming the SC diet. Feces from dogs fed SC were scored as more unformed and liquid in consistency than feces from dogs fed the other diets. Dogs consuming the SF and SB diets had the lowest (P < .05; 11.0 and 4.1%, respectively) TDF digestibilities. Organic matter disappearance values derived from substrates fermented in vitro reasonably predicted the fiber digestibility of diets fed to dogs. Moderately fermentable dietary fiber sources, such as BP, promote excellent stool characteristics without compromising nutrient digestibility, and may promote gastrointestinal tract health by optimizing SCFA production.

Paper 6: Sunvold G, et al: "In vitro fermentation of selected fibrous substrates by dog and cat fecal inoculum: influence of diet composition on substrate organic matter disappearance and short-chain fatty acid production." *J Anim Sci,* 73:1110-22, 1995.

Abstract: Two in vitro fermentation experiments were conducted to evaluate the influence of source of dietary fiber fed to dogs and cats on fermentative activity of their fecal microflora. In Exp. 1, six English Pointer dogs were fed a diet containing either a non-fermentable fiber (Solka Floc) or a fermentable fiber (citrus pulp). A fecal sample from each dog was used as the inoculum source to determine in vitro OM disappearance (OMD) and short-chain fatty acid (SCFA) production from selected fibrous substrates. When data were pooled across substrates and fermentation times, a lower (P = .02) OMD (24.8 vs 29.4%) and a higher (P = .01; 3.8 vs 2.2) acetate to propionate ratio (A:P) occurred for the Solka Floc than for the citrus pulp diet. In Exp. 2, six short-hair cats were fed a diet containing no supplemental fiber (NF) or a diet containing beet pulp (BP). When data were pooled across substrates and fermentation times, NF resulted in a greater (P < .01) A:P than the BP diet (3.4 vs 1.5). The BP treatment resulted in a slightly higher (P = .07) OMD (42.0 vs 39.3%) and a higher (P = .07) propionate production (.74 vs .47 mmol/g of OM) than the NF diet. In summary, in vitro substrate OMD increased and A:P decreased when fecal inoculum from dogs and cats fed diets containing a supplemental source of fermentable fiber was used. In vitro fermentation of fibrous substrates by fecal microflora from dogs and cats increased with inclusion of fermentable fiber in the diet.

Appendix 2

Essential Amino Acids, Vitamins and
Minerals

Essential and Nonessential Amino Acids for Dogs	
Essential Amino Acids	**Nonessential Amino Acids**
Arginine	Alanine
Histidine	Asparagine
Isoleucine	Aspartate
Leucine	Cysteine
Lysine	Glutamate
Methionine	Glutamine
Phenylalanine	Glycine
Taurine (conditional)	Hydroxylysine
Tryptophan	Hydroxyproline
Threonine	Proline
Valine	Serine
	Tyrosine

Fat Soluble Vitamins	
Vitamin A (retinol)	Necessary for vision, skeletal growth and maintenance of healthy skin and hair coat
Vitamin D	Regulates calcium absorption and metabolism; promotes normal bone calcification
Vitamin E (alpha-tocopherol)	Acts as a biological antioxi¬dant that protects cells and tissues from oxidative damage
Vitamin K	Involved in normal blood clotting; also provided by bacteria of the large intestine

Water Soluble Vitamins	
Thiamine (B_1)	Required for nervous system function and energy utilization
Riboflavin (B_2)	Required for oxidative reactions and cellular use of nutrients
Niacin	Required for normal nutrient metabolism and energy utilization
Pyridoxine (B_6)	Involved in protein and amino acid metabolism
Pantothenic Acid	Needed for carbohydrate, fat and amino acid metabolism
Biotin	Metabolism of fats and amino acids; needed for healthy skin and hair coat
Vitamin B_{12} and Folic Acid	Together are essential for red blood cell formation
Choline	Precursor of neurotransmitter acetylcholine; found in cell membranes
Vitamin C (ascorbic acid)	Needed for formation of collagen; is a water soluble antioxidant

Essential Minerals	
Calcium and phosphorus	Necessary for skeletal growth and maintenance, blood clotting and nerve and muscle function. A dietary ratio of calcium to phosphorus of 1.0 to 1.5 parts calcium to 1.0 part phosphorus is optimal
Magnesium	Component of the skeleton; necessary for muscle contractions and nerve impulse transmission
Sulfur	Needed for maintenance of healthy cartilage; necessary for synthesis of the hormone insulin and the blood clotting agent heparin
Electrolytes—sodium, potassium, chloride	Regulate body fluids and acid-base balance; necessary for nerve transmission, muscle function and energy metabolism
Iron	Component of the oxygen-carrying proteins, hemoglobin and myoglobin; component of enzymes involved in cellular use of energy
Copper	Needed for formation and activity of red blood cells, required for normal pigmentation of hair and skin
Zinc	Acts a co-factor in many enzymes and is necessary for normal nutrient metabolism; needed for healthy skin and hair growth
Trace minerals	**Cobalt** is a component of vitamin B12 **Iodine** is an essential component of thyroid hormones **Manganese** is needed for nutrient metabolism and cartilage formation **Selenium** is necessary to protect cells from damage due to oxidation

Appendix 3

Calculating Your Dog's Daily
Energy (Calorie) Needs

There are several different equations that may be used to estimate the daily energy (calorie) needs of dogs, also known as metabolic energy requirement or ME. The two equations provided here are those recommended by the current NRC *Nutrient Requirements of Dogs and Cats* (2006). Other (equally accurate) equations are also available. (Note: Weight in pounds can be converted to kilograms by dividing the number of pounds by 2.2. For example, a 50-pound dog weights 22.7 kilograms.)

Inactive Adult Dogs:

ME (metabolizable energy) requirement (kcal/day) = 95 x $(Wkg)^{0.75}$

Active Adult Dogs:

ME requirement (kcal/day) = 130 x $(Wkg)^{0.75}$

Energy equations are developed for adult animals at maintenance (i.e., they are not gaining or losing weight, are not elderly or growing and, if female, are not pregnant or lactating). Adjustments for growth and for stages of reproduction (when energy needs are higher) can be made by multiplying the estimate provided using the dog's current weight by the adjustment factor below. (Note: In all cases, the use of an energy equation and adjustment factors for life stages will provide an *estimate* of a dog's daily requirement, not an exact number. This estimate should be used as a general guideline, which can then be adjusted up or down in accordance with the dog's response to feeding.)

Stage of Life or Activity	Adjusted Energy Requirement
Post-weaning (8 weeks to ~ 4 months)	2 x adult maintenance ME*
40% adult body weight	1.6 x adult maintenance ME
80% adult body weight	1.2 x adult maintenance ME
Late gestation	1.25 to 1.5 x adult maintenance ME
Lactation**	3 x adult maintenance ME
Prolonged physical work	2 to 4 x adult maintenance ME

* Use an energy estimate calculated for an adult dog of the same weight
** Estimate for peak lactation when puppies are 3 to 4 weeks of age

The table below provides calculated energy estimates (kcal/day) for inactive and active dogs of varying weights. Use the provided age adjustments to calculate estimates for a growing dog.

Estimated Metabolizable Energy Requirements of Adult Dogs

Weight (lbs)	Weight (kg)	Inactive (kcal/day)	Active (kcal/day)
4	1.82	148.61	203.37
8	3.63	249.94	342.02
12	5.45	338.77	463.58
16	7.26	420.34	575.21
20	9.08	496.2	680.00
25	11.35	587.45	803.88
30	13.62	673.53	921.67
35	15.89	756.08	1034.63
40	18.16	835.72	1143.62
45	20.43	912.90	1249.24
50	22.70	987.97	1351.96
55	24.97	1061.18	1452.14
60	27.24	1132.74	1550.06
65	29.51	1202.82	1645.96
70	31.78	1271.57	1740.04
75	34.05	1339.10	1832.45
80	36.32	1405.57	1923.33
85	38.59	1470.89	2012.79
90	40.86	1535.31	2100.96
95	43.13	1598.85	2187.90
100	45.40	1661.56	2273.71
105	49.94	1784.68	2442.19
110	54.48	1905.03	2606.88
115	59.02	2022.89	2768.17

Appendix 4

Common Ingredients in Commercial Dog Foods

and their Primary Nutrient Contributions

Animal Digest: Material that results from chemical and/or enzymatic hydrolysis of clean and un-decomposed animal tissue. The animal tissues used shall be exclusive of hair, horns, teeth, hooves and feathers, except in such trace amounts as might occur unavoidably in good factory practice and shall be suitable for animal feed. (Note: Used as flavor-enhancer, palatant.)

Animal Fat: Obtained from the tissues of mammals and/or poultry in the commercial processes of rendering or extracting. It consists predominantly of glyceride esters of fatty acids and contains no additions of free fatty acids. If an antioxidant is used, the common name or names must be indicated, followed by the words "used as a preservative."

Ascorbic Acid: A white, crystalline, water-soluble vitamin, occurring naturally in citrus fruits, green vegetables, etc. Ascorbic acid is a form of vitamin C, which is an antioxidant good for normal metabolism

Barley Flour: Soft, finely ground and bolted barley meal obtained from the milling of barley. It consists essentially of the starch and gluten of the endosperm.

Beef (meat): The clean flesh derived from slaughtered cattle, and is limited to that part of the striated muscle that is skeletal, or that which is found in the tongue, in the diaphragm, in the heart or in the esophagus; with or without the accompanying and overlying fat and the portions of the skin, sinew, nerve and blood vessels that normally accompany the flesh.

Beet Pulp: Also "beet pulp, dried molasses" and "beet pulp, dried, plain." The dried residue from sugar beets. (Note: included as a source of moderately fermentable fiber.)

BHA/BHT: Butylated hydroxyanisole (BHA) and butylated hydroxytoluene (BHT), both of which are chemical preservatives that act as antioxidants in processed foods.

Bone Meal: The dried, ground and sterilized product from un-decomposed bones.

Brewer's Rice: The dried extracted residue of rice resulting from the manufacture of wort (the liquid portion of malted grain) or beer; it may contain pulverized dried spent hops in an amount not to exceed 3 percent.

Chicken By-Product Meal: Consists of the ground, rendered, clean parts of the carcass of slaughtered chicken, such as necks, feet, undeveloped eggs and intestines, exclusive of feathers, except in such amounts as might occur unavoidably in good processing practice.

Chicken Meal: Consists of the ground, rendered, clean parts of the carcass of slaughtered chicken, excluding necks, feet, undeveloped eggs, intestines and feathers, except in such amounts as might occur unavoidably in good processing practice.

Chicken: The clean combination of flesh and skin with or without accompanying bone, derived from the parts or whole carcasses of chicken or a combination thereof, exclusive of feathers, heads, feet and entrails.

Corn Gluten Meal: The dried residue from corn after the removal of the larger part of the starch and germ and the separation of the bran.

Dehydrated Eggs: Dried whole poultry eggs freed of moisture by thermal means.

Fish Meal: Clean, dried, ground tissue of un-decomposed whole fish or fish cuttings, either or both, with or without the extraction of part of the oil.

Ground Corn: The entire ear of corn ground, without husks, with no greater portion of cob than occurs in the ear corn in its natural state.

Ground Brown Rice: The entire product obtained by grinding the rice kernels after the hulls have been removed.

Lamb Meal: Rendered product from lamb tissues, exclusive of blood, hair, hoof, horn, hide trimmings, manure, stomach and rumen contents except in such amounts as may occur unavoidably in good processing practices.

Meat and Bone Meal: Rendered product from mammal tissues, including bone, exclusive of blood, hair, hoof, horn, hide trimmings, manure, stomach and rumen contents, except in such amounts as may occur unavoidably in good processing practices.

Meat By-Product Meal: Non-rendered, clean parts, other than meat, derived from slaughtered mammals. It includes, but is not limited to, lungs, spleen, kidneys, brain, livers, blood, bone, partially defatted low-temperature fatty tissue and stomachs and intestines freed of their contents. It does not include hair, horns, teeth and hooves.

Meat Meal: The rendered product from mammal tissues exclusive of blood, hair, hoof, horn, hide trimmings, manure, stomach and rumen contents, except in such amounts as may occur unavoidably in good processing practices.

Pearled Barley: Dehulled barley grain.

Poultry By-Product Meal: Ground, rendered, clean parts of the carcasses of slaughtered poultry such as necks, feet, undeveloped eggs and intestines, exclusive of feathers except in such amounts as might occur unavoidably in good processing practices.

Poultry Fat: Obtained from the tissue of poultry in the commercial process of rendering or extracting. It shall contain only the fatty matter natural to the product produced under good manufacturing practices and shall contain no added free fatty acids or other materials obtained from fat.

Poultry Meal: The dry rendered product from a combination of clean flesh and skin, with or without the accompanying bone, derived from the parts of whole carcasses of poultry exclusive of feathers, heads, feet and entrails. (Also includes chicken meal if the origin is strictly chicken.)

Rice Bran: Pericarp or bran layer and germ of the rice, with only such quantity of hull fragments, chipped, broken or brewer's rice and calcium carbonate as is unavoidable in the regular milling of edible rice.

Soybean Hulls: Consist primarily of the outer covering of the soybean.

Soybean Meal (De-Hulled): Obtained by grinding the flakes remaining after removal of most of the oil from de-hulled soybeans by either a mechanical or a solvent extraction process.

Soybean Mill Run: Composed of soybean hulls and such bean meats that adhere to the hulls and such bean meats that adhere to the hulls which results from normal milling operations in the production of de-hulled soybean meal.

Turkey Meal: The ground clean combination of flesh and skin with or without accompanying bone, derived from the parts or whole carcasses of turkey or a combination thereof, exclusive of feathers, heads, feet and entrails.

Wheat Bran: The coarse outer covering of the wheat kernel as separated from cleaned and scoured wheat in the usual process of commercial milling.

Wheat Flour: Wheat flour together with fine particles of wheat bran, wheat germ and the offal from the "tail of the mill." This product must be obtained in the usual process of commercial milling and must not contain more than 1.5 percent crude fiber.

Whey: The product obtained as a fluid by separating the coagulum from milk, cream or skimmed milk and from which a portion of the milk fat may have been removed.

Primary Nutrient Contribution of Common Ingredients

Protein	Carbohydrate	Fat	Dietary Fiber
Beef	Alfalfa meal	Animal fat	Apple pomace
Brewer's dried yeast	Barley	Chicken fat	Barley
Chicken meal	Brewer's rice	Corn oil	Beet pulp
Chicken liver meal	Brown rice	Fish oil	Cellulose
Chicken by-product meal	Carrots	Flax seed (full fat)	Citrus pulp
Chicken	Dried kelp	Poultry fat	Oat bran
Chicken by-products	Dried whey	Safflower oil	Peanut hulls
Corn gluten meal	Flax seed	Soybean oil	Pearled barley
Dried egg product	Flax seed meal	Sunflower oil	Peas
Duck	Grain sorghum	Potatoes	Rice bran
Fish	Ground corn		Soybean hulls
Fish meal	Ground rice		Soybean mill run
Flax seed meal	Ground wheat		Tomato pomace
Lamb	Molasses		
Lamb meal	Oat meal		
Meat by-products	Pearled barley		
Meat meal	Peas		
Meat and bone meal	Potatoes		
Poultry by-product meal	Rice flour		
Rabbit	Wheat (ground)		
Salmon	Wheat flour		
Soy flour or grits			
Soybean meal			
Turkey			

Appendix 5

Choosing Smart

A Dog Food Choice Flow Chart

The Dog Food Choice Flow Chart is designed to help you to identify the set of selection criteria that are most important to you and your dog as you consider the many (too many, perhaps) options that you have when choosing a food. The chart is *not* intended to provide you with a definitive answer for a particular type, brand or product line of dog food. Rather, it is intended to identify the primary factors to consider and to provide a concise guide for your personal "Dog Food Logic," making decisions based upon evidence and avoiding cognitive errors and other pitfalls. The criteria and questions within the flow chart are condensed versions of book material, so many refer you to pages of the book that will provide more detailed information. They are divided into three major categories: attributes about your dog, food characteristics and information that you know about the manufacturer. Good luck—I hope that the flow chart is helpful to you as you train yourself to make smart choices for your dog!

Your Dog: There are several important dog demographics to consider. Let's begin with your dog's life stage:

-Life Stage

- **Growing puppy or adult?** If your dog is a youngster, and especially if he is a large or giant breed, consider his rate of growth and how to feed him to support a moderate (not high) rate of development.

- **Reproductive status?** Although the effects are not strong, neutered dogs *do* generally require slightly fewer calories per day than do intact dogs of the same age/size.

- **Young adult versus mature adult?** Just like people, as dogs mature, they require fewer calories per unit of body weight to maintain an optimal body condition.

- **Senior?** Determine when your dog should be classified as a senior based upon her breed/size, health, activity level and actual age. Dogs differ tremendously in how they age. Remember, aging is *not* an illness; there are plenty of healthy and happy seniors!

-Activity Level

- **What activities?** Consider the activities that you enjoy with your dog. For each consider:
  - Frequency: Is the activity daily, several times a week, a few times a month?
  - Intensity: How hard does your dog exercise during this activity?
  - Duration: How long does your dog exercise during this activity?
- **Body condition:** Does your dog tend to lose weight or body condition when she is engaging in these activities or do they not appear to impact her weight or condition?
- **Seasonal changes?** Do you have periods of the year when your dog is highly active versus periods of the year when he is more of a couch potato? If his active periods are intense, consider feeding two different foods, depending upon the time of year, competition season, etc.

-Health

- **Health effects that are most commonly targeted by health claims on pet food labels and by manufacturers:**
  - Skin and coat (supporting good skin/coat condition, manage allergic/inflammatory conditions)
  - Gastrointestinal health (stool quality, food intolerances/allergies, diarrhea)
  - Mobility (joint health, support activity, manage stiffness and signs associated with osteoarthritis)
  - Cognitive function (promoting learning in growing puppies, preventing cognitive decline in senior dogs)
- **General health claims:** If you are attracted to a food that includes a general health claim (improves coat, supports healthy skin, aids mobility, improves puppy learning), ask for evidence. Consider: Are these published studies or are you seeing an advertisement piece?
- **Health problems?** Does your dog have health problems for which you are considering a dietary approach? Is so, consider that:
  - Dog foods that carry health-related claims include both over-the-counter (OTC) products and veterinary prescription products.
  - *Neither* OTC claims nor veterinary foods require pre-market substantiation (i.e. not required to be evidence-based), although most, if not all veterinary prescription products do have some supporting research.
- **Suggested sequence of steps:**
  - When a health problem is present, visit your veterinarian for a complete examination and diagnosis.
  - If there is a confirmed diagnosis, is there a diet that is formulated to manage the disorder?

    ◦ If yes, what evidence exists to support the use of the diet? What type of evidence is it? How strong and reliable is the evidence? Are there published clinical trials with dogs that demonstrate effectiveness?

The Food:

-Homemade or Commercially Prepared?

- If choosing homemade, select a food recipe (or recipes) that has been well-formulated and tested.

- If you are a trainer or other dog professional and advising clients, always direct clients to reputable sources for recipes and feeding advice.

-Cooked or Raw?

- Dogs can be fed well using either a cooked (extruded, canned or home-prepared) food or a raw diet (home-prepared or commercial).

- If feeding raw, always consider food handling hygiene, effects on ingredients (e.g., uncooked starches are not highly digestible) and nutrient balance.

- If health claims are made for feeding raw versus cooked foods, seek scientific evidence that supports these claims.

-Are you interested in the inclusion or exclusion of particular ingredients?

- What ingredients are you seeking and why? What is the evidence supporting the use of these ingredients?

- What ingredients are you avoiding and why? What is the evidence that supports the exclusion of these ingredients?

-How important is food and ingredient quality to you?

- What quality information are you seeking (digestibility, ingredient type, etc.)?

- What evidence is available to you regarding these quality criteria?

-Is cost an important criterion for you?

- What do you think is a reasonable amount to pay per day to feed your dog?

- Which foods fall within this range?

The Manufacturer:

-Who are they and what do you know about them?

- What do you know that is admirable? What do you know that is not admirable or concerning?

- Is the size or type of ownership (multi-national corporation versus smaller company or family-owned) important to you?

-Manufacturing location and ingredient sourcing

- Is it important to you that the company produces their foods in the United States?

- Is it important to you that the company produces their own food versus having one or more of their brands co-packed?

- Is ingredient sourcing (domestic versus foreign suppliers, growing or housing conditions) important to you?

-What are the company's (brand's) typical marketing/advertising practices?

-What is the manufacturer's safety record?

-Does the company demonstrate both transparency and responsiveness?

- If you request information about manufacturing practices, ingredients or safety processes, is the company prompt and helpful in replies?

- Are replies responsive, providing you with the information that you requested?

Putting it all together

-Identify the criteria that are important to you.

-Rank these in order of most important to least important.

-Consider the *degree of confidence* that you have in the information that is available to you (i.e., is it science-based evidence versus testimony versus marketing versus Joe next door who knows a lot about dogs?).

-Select a food based upon the (solid, science-based) evidence and the criteria.

-Sing your dinner time song; nurture your dog.

Interest in Learning More?

Selected References and Bibliography

Cited and Relevant Papers

Ahlstrom O, et al: "Fatty acid composition in commercial dog foods." *J Nutr,* 134:2145S-2147S, 2004.

Aldrich G: "Rosemary extract acts as a natural antioxidant." *Petfood Industry,* September 2010.

Aldrich G: "The formulator's dilemma: how processing affects pet nutrition." *Petfood Industry,* February 2012.

Aldrich CG, Daristotle L. "Petfood and the economic impact." *Proc. California Animal Nutrition Conference*, Fresno, CA. pp. 1140-148, 1998.

Altom EK, Davenport GM, Myers LJ and Cummins KA: "Effect of dietary fat source and exercise on odorant-detecting ability of canine athletes." *Res Vet Sci,* 75:149-155, 2003.

Axelsson E, Ratnakumar A, Arendt M-L, et al: "The genomic signature of dog domestication reveals adaptation to a starch-rich diet." *Nature,* 495:360-364, 2013.

Baskin CR, Hinchcliff KW, DiSilvesttro RA, et al: "Effects of dietary antioxidant supplementation on oxidative damage and resistance to oxidative damage during prolonged exercise in sled dogs." *Amer J Vet Res,* 61:886-891, 2000.

Buchanan RL, Baker RC, Charlton AJ, et al: "Pet Food Safety: A shared concern." *Brit J Nutr,* 106:S78-S84, 2011.

Burkhard PR, Burkhardt K, Haenggeli C A, Landis T: "Plant-induced seizures: reappearance of an old problem." *J Neurology*, 246:667-670, 1999.

Butterwick RF, Erdman JW, Hill RC, et al: "Challenges in developing nutrient guidelines for companion animals." *Brit J Nutr,* 106:S24-S31, 2011.

Case LP, Czarnecki GL: "Protein requirements of growing pups fed practical dry-type diets containing mixed-protein sources." *Am J Vet Res,* 51:808–812, 1990.

Chen A, Hung K, Peng N: "A cluster analysis examination of pet owners' consumption values and behavior—segmenting owners strategically." *J Targeting Measure Anal Market,* 20:117-132, 2012.

Courcier EA, Mellor DJ, Thomson DM and Yam PS: "A cross sectional study of the prevalence and risk factors for owner misperception of canine body shape in first opinion practice in Glasgow." *Prevent Vet Med,* 102:66-74, 2011.

Courcier EA, Thomson RM, Mellor DJ and Yam PS: "An epidemiological study of environmental factors associated with canine obesity." *J Small Anim Practice,* 51: 362–367, 2010.

Darley JM and Gross PH: "A hypothesis-confirming bias in labeling effects." *J Personality Social Psychol,* 44:20-33, 1983.

Diego MA, et al: "Aromatherapy positively affects mood, EEG patterns of alertness and math computations." *Int J Neurosci,* 96:217-224, 1998.

Dörrie J, et al: "Carnosol-induced apoptosis and downregulation of Bcl-2 in B-lineage leukemia cells." *Cancer Letters,* 170:33-39, 2001.

Dunlap KL, Reynolds AJ and Duffy LK: "Total antioxidant power in sled dogs supplemented with blueberries and the comparison of blood parameters associated with exercise." *Compar Biochem Physiol,* 143:429-434, 2006.

Dzanis DA: "Regulation of pet foods in the United States." *Compend Contin Ed Vet,* July 2009; 324-328, 2009.

Eirmann L, Cowell C: "Pet food safety: The roles of government, manufacturers and veterinarians." *Compend Contin Ed Vet,* January 2012; E1E3, 2012.

Fiske ST: "Attention and Weight in Person Perception: The impact of negative and extreme information." *J Personality Social Psychol,* 38:889–906, 1980.

Frankel EN, et al: "Antioxidant activity of a rosemary extract and its constituents, carnosic acid, carnosol and rosmarinic acid, in bulk oil and oil-in-water emulsion." *Journal of Agricultural and Food Chemistry,* 44:131-135, 1996.

Freeman LM, Michel KE: "Evaluation of raw food diets for dogs." *J Amer Vet Med, Assoc* 218:705-709, 2001.

Freeman LM, Schreiner KE and Geronimo Terkla D: "Survey of opinions about nutrient requirements of senior dogs and analysis of nutrient profiles of commercially available diets for senior dogs." *Intern J Appl Res Vet,* Med 9:68-79, 2011.

Frei C. *Pet Industry Statistics Show the Power of Pet Humanization; Packaged Facts* (blog); http://blog.marketresearch.com/blog-home-page/bid/209521/Pet-Industry-Statistics-Show-the-Power-of-Pet-Humanization#sthash.OfYn9pgl.dpuf

German AJ, Holden SL, Mather NJ, et al: "Low-maintenance energy requirements of obese dogs after weight loss." *Brit J Nutr,* 106:S93-S96, 2011.

Greer KA, Canterberry SC, Murphy KE: "Statistical analysis regarding the effects of height and weight on life span of the domestic dog." *Res Vet Sci,* 82:208-214, 2007.

Gross KL, Burchett S, Harmon DL, et al: "Effect of altering starch cook and resistant starch content of extruded food products on nutrient digestibility in the dog." *J Vet Intern Med,* 12: 241-245, 1998.

Hammel EP, Kronfeld DS, Ganjam VK, et al: "Metabolic responses to exhaustive exercise in racing sledge dogs fed diets containing medium, low and zero carbohydrate." *Am J Clin Nutr,* 30:409-418, 1976.

Heuberger, R and Wakshlag J: "The relationship of feeding patterns and obesity in dogs." *J Animal Physiol Anim Nutr,* 95: 98–105, 2011.

Huston L: *Concerns About Pet Food Recalls and Safety Paramount to Owners*, petMD Survey Finds, petMD http://goo.gl/jY5Zus

Jenkins CC, Allen TA, and Roudebush P: "Application of evidence-based medicine to veterinary clinical nutrition." *Proc Hills Symp Lower Urinary Tract Disease*, pp. 5-12, 2011.

Joffe DJ and Schlesinger DP: "Preliminary assessment of the risk of Salmonella infection in dogs fed raw chicken diets." *Can Vet J,* 43:441-442, 2002.

Kerr RK, Vester-Boler BM, Morris CL, et al: "Apparent total tract energy and macronutrient digestibility and fecal fermentative end-product concentrations of domestic cats fed extruded, raw beef-based and cooked beef-based diets." *J Anim Sci,* 90:515-522, 2012.

Kerr KR, Beloshapka AN, Morris CL, et al: "Evaluation of four raw meat diets using domestic cats, captive exotic felids and cecectomized roosters." *J Anim Sci,* 91:225-237, 2013.

Kronfeld DS: "Diet and the performance of racing sledge dogs." *J Am Vet Med Assoc,* 162:470-473, 1973.

KuKanich KS: "Update on Salmonella spp. contamination of pet foods, treats and nutritional products and safe feeding recommendations." *J Amer Vet Med Assoc,* 238:1430-1434, 2011.

Langer EJ: "The illusion of control." *Journal of Personality and Social Psychology,* 32:311-328, 1975.

Lefebvre SL, Reid-Smith R, Boerlin P, Weese JS: "Evaluation of the risks of shedding Salmonella and other potential pathogens by therapy dogs fed raw diets in Ontario and Alberta." *Zoonoses Public Health,* 55:470-480, 2008.

LeJeune JT, Hancock DD: "Public health concerns associated with feeding raw meat diets to dogs." *J Amer Vet Med Assoc,* 219:1222-1225, 2001.

Leonard EK, Pearl DL, Finley RL, et al: "Evaluation of pet-related management factors and the risk of Salmonella spp. carriage in pet dogs from volunteer households in Ontario (2005–2006)." *Zoonoses Public Health,* 58:140–149, 2011.

Locatelli ML, Howhler D. "Poultry byproduct meal: Consider protein quality and variability." *Feed Manage,* 2003;54:6-10.

Lord C, Ross L, Lepper M: "Biased Assimilation and Attitude Polarization: The effects of prior theories on subsequently considered evidence." *J Personality Social Psychol,* 37: 2098-2109, 1979.

McCaffrey R, Thomas DJ, Kinzelman AO: "The effects of lavender and rosemary essential oils on test-taking anxiety among graduate nursing students." *Holist Nurs Pract,* 23:88-93, 2009.

Morley PS, Strohmeyer RA, Tankson JD, et al: "Evaluation of the association between feeding raw meat and Salmonella enterica infections at a Greyhound breeding facility." *J Am Vet Med Assoc,* 228:1524-1532, 2006.

Murray SM, Patil AR, Fahey GC Jr, et al: "Raw and rendered animal by-products as ingredients in dog diets." *J Anim Sci,* 75:2497-2505, 1997.

Nestle M, Ludwig DS. "Front-of-package food labels: Public health or propaganda?" *J Amer Med Assoc,* 303:771-772, 2010.

Petfood Industry Magazine: "Top 25 global Pet food companies profiled in database." *Petfood Ind Mag,* pp. 22-26, January 2013.

Pomeranz JL: "Front-of-package food and beverage labeling." *Am J Prev Med,* 2011;40:382-385.

Pomeranz JL. "Front-of-package food and beverage labeling: New directions for research and regulation." *American Journal of Preventive Medicine.* 2011 Mar; 40(3):382-385.

Reynolds AJ, Fuhrer L, Dunlap HL, et al: "Effect of diet and training on muscle glycogen storage and utilization in sled dogs." *J Appl Physiol,* 79:1601-1607, 1997.

Roberto CA, Shivaram M, Martinez O, Boles C, Harris JL, Brownell KD. "The Smart Choices front-of-package nutrition label. Influence on perceptions and intake of cereal." *Appetite,* 58:651-657, 2012.

Roberts WA. "Claiming a function." *Prepared Foods,* Sept 2006; 11-20, 2006.

Schlesinger DP, Joffe DJ. "Raw food diets in companion animals: A critical review." *Can Vet J,* 52:50-54, 2011.

Schunemann C, Muhlum A, Junker S, et al: "Prececal and postileal digestibility of various starches in the dog and pH values and concentration of organic acids in colonic chyme and feces." *Adv Anim Physiol Nutr,* 19: 44-57, 1989.

Schwartz, B: "The tyranny of choice." *Sci America,* pp. 71-75, April, 2004.

Sebranek JB, et al: "Comparison of a natural rosemary extract and BHA/BHT for relative antioxidant effectiveness in pork sausage." *Meat Science,* 69:289-296, 2005.

Stiver SL, Frazier KS, Mauel MJ, Styer EL: "Septicemic salmonellosis in two cats fed a raw-meat diet." *J Am Anim Hosp Assoc,* 39:538-542, 2003.

Stockman J, Fascetti AJ, Kass PH, Larsen JA: "Evaluation of recipes of home-prepared maintenance diets for dogs." *J Amer Vet Med Assoc,* 242:1500-1510, 2013.

Stone GG, Chengappa MM and Oberst RD: "Application of polymerase chain reaction for the correlation of Salmonella serovars recovered from Greyhound feces with their diet." *J Vet Diagn Invest,* 5:378-385, 1993.

Strohmeyer RA, Morley PS, Hyatt DR, Dargatz DA, Scorza AV and Lappin MR: "Evaluation of bacterial and protozoal contamination of commercially available raw meat diets for dogs." *J Amer Vet Med Assoc,* 228:537-542, 2006.

Suarez L, Peña C, Carretón E, et al: "Preferences of owners of overweight dogs when buying commercial pet food." *J Anim Physiol Anim Nutr,* 96: 655–65, 2012.

Taylor J: "Bright future for refrigerated, frozen and raw pet food." *Petfood Ind,* December 2011.

Weese JS, Rousseau J and Arroyo L: "Bacteriological evaluation of commercial canine and feline raw diets." *Can Vet J,* 46:513-516, 2005.

Weeth LP: "Home-prepared diets for dogs and cats." *Compend Contin Ed Vet,* March 2013; E1-E3, 2013.

Books

American Veterinary Medical Association. *U.S. Pet Ownership & Demographics Sourcebook.* AVMA, Schaumburg, IL, 244 pp., 2012.

Ariely, Dan. *Predictably Irrational: The Hidden Forces that Shape Our Decisions.* Harper Collins Books, New York, NY, 280 pp., 2008.

Ariely, Dan. *The Upside of Irrationality: The Unexpected Benefits of Defying Logic at Work and at Home.* Harper Collins Books, New York, NY, 334 pp., 2010.

Association of American Feed Control Officials. *AAFCO Official Publication.* AAFCO, Atlanta, GA, 2013.

Billinghurst, I. *Give Your Dog a Bone.* Bridge Printery, Alexandria, Australia, 265-280 pp., 1993.

Case, LP. *Canine and Feline Behavior and Training: A Complete Guide to Understanding Our Two Best Friend.* Delmar Cengage, Clifton Park, NY, 332 pp., 2010.

Case, LP. *The Dog: Its Behavior, Nutrition and Health (2nd edition).* Blackwell Publishing, Ames, IA, 479 pp., 2005.

Case, LP and others. *Canine and Feline Nutrition: A Resource for Companion Animal Professionals (3rd edition).* Mosby-Elsevier, St. Louis, MO, 562 pp., 2010.

Chabris, Christopher and Simons, Daniel. *The Invisible Gorilla.* Crown Books, New York, NY, 306 pp., 2010.

Coppinger R, and Coppinger, L. *Dogs: A Startling New Understanding of Canine Origin, Behavior and Evolution.* Scribner Publishing, New York, NY, 352 pp., 2001.

Damasio, A. *Descartes' Error: Emotion, Reason and the Human Brain.* Penguin Putnam, New York, NY, 336 pp., 1994.

Damasio, A. *The Feeling of What Happens.* Harcourt, Orlando, FL, 386 pp., 1999.

Dobelli, Rolf. *The Art of Thinking Clearly*. Harper Collins, New York, NY, 358 pp., 2013.

Duhigg, C. *The Power of Habit: Why We Do What We Do in Life and Business*. Random House, New York, NY, 286 pp., 2012.

Eagleman, David. *Incognito: The Secret Lives of the Brain*. Random House, New York, NY, 290 pp., 2011.

Fine,C. *A Mind of Its Own; How Your Brain Distorts and Deceives*. W.W. Norton & Company, Ltd, London, UK, 243 pp., 2006.

Gilovich, Thomas. *How We Know What Isn't So: The Fallibility of Human Reason in Everyday Life*. The Free Press, New York, NY, 216 pp., 1991.

Greenfield, Kent. *The Myth of Choice: Personal Responsibility in a World of Limits*. Yale University Press, New Haven, CT, 244 pp., 2011.

Grier, Katherine. *Pets in America: A History*. Harcourt Inc, New York, NY, 496 pp., 2006.

Groopman, Jerome. *How Doctors Think*. Mariner Books, New York, NY, 336 pp., 2008.

Groopman, Jerome and Hartzband, Pamela. *Your Medical Mind: How to Decide What is Right for You*. Penguin Books, New York, NY, 308 pp., 2011.

Hallinan, Joseph T. *Why We Make Mistakes*. Broadway Books, New York, NY, 283 pp., 2009.

Hand, Michael S and others. *Small Animal Clinical Nutrition (5th Edition)*. Mark Morris Institute, Topeka, KS, 1314 pp., 2010.

Heath, Chip and Heath, Dan. Decisive: How to Make Better Choices in Life and Work. Crown/Random House, New York, NY, 316 pp., 2013.

Ipsos-Reid. *Paws and Claws: A Syndicated Study of Canadian Pet Ownership*, 125 pp., 2001.

Kahneman, Daniel. *Thinking Fast and Slow*. Farrar, Straus and Giroux, New York, NY, 512 pp., 2011.

Kvamme JL and Phillis, TD. *Petfood Technology*. Watt Publishing, Mt. Morris, IL, 576 pp., 2003.

Kuhn, Thomas. *The Structure of Scientific Revolutions*. University of Chicago Press, Chicago, IL, Third Edition, 229 pp., 1996.

Lehrer, Jonah. *How We Decide*. Houghton Mifflin Harcourt, New York, NY, 302 pp., 2009.

Lilienfeld, Scott and others. *Fifty Great Myths of Popular Psychology: Shattering Widespread Misconceptions about Human Behavior*. Wiley-Blackwell, New York, NY, 332 pp., 2010.

McRaney, David. *You Are Not So Smart*. Dutton Books (Penguin), New York, NY, 302 pp., 2011.

Mlodinow, Leonard. *Subliminal: How Your Unconscious Mind Rules Your Behavior*. Pantheon Books, New York, NY, 260 pp., 2012.

National Research Council: *Nutrient Requirements of Dogs and Cats*. National Academy Press, Washington, DC, 398 pp., 2006.

Nestle, Marion. *Pet Food Politics: The Chihuahua in the Coal Mine*. University of California Press, Berkeley, CA, 219 pp., 2008.

Nestle, Marion and Nesheim, Malden C. *Feed Your Pet Right*. Free Press Publishing, New York, NY, 376 pp., 2010.

Shermer, Michael. *The Believing Brain: How We Construct Beliefs and Reinforce Them as Truths*. Times Books, New York, NY, 386 pp., 2011.

Shermer, Michael. *Why People Believe Weird Things*. Owl Books, New York, NY, 349 pp., 2002.

Schwartz, Barry. *The Paradox of Choice: Why More is Less*. Harper Collins Books, New York, NY, 265 pp., 2004.

Serpell, J. *In the Company of Animals. 2nd Edition*. Cambridge University Press, Cambridge, UK, 48-66 pp., 1996.

Travis, Carol and Aronson, Elliot. *Mistakes Were Made, (But Not by Me)*. Harcourt Inc., New York, NY, 292 pp., 2007.

Wilson CC, Turner DC (editors). *Companion Animals in Human Health*. Sage Publications, Thousand Oaks, CA., 1998

Wiseman, Richard. *Paranormality: Why We See What Isn't There*. Macmillan, New York, NY, 341 pp., 2011.

Websites and Blogs

Association Pet Obesity Prevention (APOP): http://www.petobesityprevention.com/

Fallacy Files: http://www.fallacyfiles.org/adnature.html

Feed Right for Pets: http://feedright4pets.com/

Pet Industry News: http://petindustrynews.blogspot.com/

Pet Industry Weekly: http://weeklypets.blogspot.com/

Petfood Connection: http://www.petfood-connection.com/

The SkeptVet Blog: http://skeptvet.com/Blog/

The Skeptic's Field Guide to Fallacies in Thinking: http://www.skepticsfieldguide.net/

What's The Harm (website and blog about critical thinking): http://whatstheharm.net/whatisthis.html

ABOUT THE AUTHOR

Linda Case is a canine nutritionist, dog trainer and science writer. She earned her B.S. in Animal Science at Cornell University and her M.S. in Canine/Feline Nutrition at the University of Illinois. Following graduate school, Linda was a lecturer in companion animal science in the Animal Sciences Department at the University of Illinois for 15 years and also taught companion animal behavior and training at

Photo by Kathy Steepleton, At a Glance Photography

the College of Veterinary Medicine. Linda currently owns AutumnGold Consulting and Dog Training Center in Mahomet, IL (http://www.autumngoldconsulting.com), a company that provides scientific writing, training programs and research support to dog owners, pet food companies and animal advocacy organizations. Linda is the author of numerous publications and four other books, including *Canine and Feline Nutrition: A Resource for Companion Animal Professionals* and *Canine and Feline Behavior and Training: A Complete Guide to Understanding Our Two Best Friends* and the popular blog "The Science Dog" (http://thesciencedog.wordpress.com/). She and her husband Mike currently share their lives with four dogs; Cadie, Vinny, Chip and Cooper, and Pete the cat. In addition to dog training, Linda enjoys running, hiking, swimming and gardening—most of which she happily shares with her dogs.

Index

Also available from Dogwise Publishing

Go to www.dogwise.com for more books and ebooks.

The Healthy Way to Stretch Your Dog
A Physical Therapy Approach
Sasha Foster

Research on human athletes is changing what we know about stretching. For example, it is now recognized that aggressive stretching should only take place after muscles are warmed up and shortened from exertion. Authors Sasha and Ashley Foster have applied this latest research to dogs—many of whom compete in vigorous canine sporting events—so that you can learn how to safely and effectively stretch your dog to prevent injuries, maintain joint integrity, and improve you dog's fitness whether he is an elite canine athlete or a lap dog.

Get the Ball Rolling
A Step by Step Guide to Training for Treibball
Dianna Stearns

The best dog sports are those that are fun for both you and your dog while offering the opportunity to build your skills as a trainer and strengthening your relationship with your dog. Treibball meets all of these criteria which is why it is growing in popularity among dog people worldwide. Treibball includes elements of herding trials, canine "soccer" and obedience. The author presents the training protocols step-by-step and uses non-force methods including clicker training and shaping to get the desired behaviors.

Canine Cross Training
Building Balance, Strength and Enurance in Your Dog
Sasha Foster

What are the four conditioning components of top athletes? Most physical therapists agree that they include balance, strength, endurance and flexibility. The same characteristics apply to canine athletes as well and form the basis of this new book by Sasha Foster, co-author of the award winning The Healthy Way to Stretch Your Dog. When the four conditioning components are executed in a systematic approach using the key exercise principles of frequency, intensity and duration, you can train your dog to reach his fullest potential in whatever canine sport or activity you choose to participate in—and help keep him fitter and more injury-free over a longer period of time.

From the Ground Up
Agility Foundation Training for Puppies and Beginner Dogs
Kim Collins

You might have a dog who you think will be a super-star on the agility course, but unless you work with him "from the ground up," you may end up being disappointed. Author Kim Collins takes the position that there is a lot of training and relationship building that needs to go on before you ever begin to train the specific skills needed for agility. So this is the perfect book for you if you have a puppy or a young dog and are planning a career in agility in the future as it provides a complete training plan for both his pre-agility work and when he is ready to head out on the course.

Dogwise.com is your source for quality books, ebooks, DVDs, training tools and treats.

We've been selling to the dog fancier for more than 25 years and we carefully screen our products for quality information, safety, durability and FUN! You'll find something for every level of dog enthusiast on our website www.dogwise.com or drop by our store in Wenatchee, Washington.